Date Due

DEC 5 2000			
DEC 03 2010			

BRODART, CO.   Cat. No. 23-233-003   Printed in U.S.A.

CHILDREN & DISASTERS

CHILDREN
&
DISASTERS

Norma S. Gordon
Norman L. Farberow
Carl A. Maida

BRUNNER/MAZEL
Taylor & Francis Group

USA Publishing Office: BRUNNER/MAZEL
A member of the Taylor & Francis Group
325 Chestnut Street
Philadelphia, PA 19106
Tel: (215) 625-8900
Fax: (215) 625-2940

Distribution Center: BRUNNER/MAZEL
A member of the Taylor & Francis Group
47 Runway Road, Suite G
Levittown, PA 19057-4700
Tel: (215) 269-0400
Fax: (215) 269-0363

UK BRUNNER/MAZEL
A member of the Taylor & Francis Group
1 Gunpowder Square
London EC4A 3DE
Tel: 171 583 0490
Fax: 171 583 0581

CHILDREN & DISASTERS

1 2 3 4 5 6 7 8 9 0

Edited by Edward A. Cilurso and Diane Foose. Typeset by Cheryl Hufnagle. Cover design by Claire C. O'Neill. Printed by Edwards Brothers, Lillington, NC.

A CIP catalog record for this book is available from the British Library.
∞ The paper in this publication meets the requirements of the ANSI Standard Z39.48-1984 (Permanence of Paper).

Library of Congress Cataloging-in-Publication Data

Available from the publisher.

ISBN 0-87630-932-5 (case)

CONTENTS

PREFACE

Children & Disasters concerns itself with the impact of major disasters on the mental health and emotional functioning of children. A disaster imposes severe strain on everyone in the community, but children comprise a particularly vulnerable group that requires special attention. Reactions of children to disasters have both short-term and long-term effects. Children and their families who are victims of a disaster are primarily normal people, but their functioning may be disrupted temporarily because of the severe stress. It is probable that the passage of time alone can help reestablish equilibrium and functioning for many of these children, without outside help. However, informed intervention often will speed recovery and, in many instances, will prevent serious problems later. Depending on the disaster, the local circumstances, and the special needs of the community, each intervention program will have its own characteristics that illustrate creative application of current knowledge to meet situational needs.

The book uses the model of short-term crisis counseling to provide a practical "hands-on" approach to program design. It is targeted to those concerned with the design and management of treatment services for the emotional needs of children affected by major disasters. The background, training, and experience of the people who have this responsibility will vary. Besides experienced mental health professionals, such as those who specialize in working with children who are emotionally disturbed and their families, there also may be health care professionals, such as physicians, nurses, and rehabilitation specialists who are experienced in working with children; trained paraprofessionals and volunteer counselors, suicide intervention workers, and emergency mental health counselors who are experienced in working with crises; school personnel, including teachers, counselors, and administrators; and federal and state emergency planners and coordinators.

The programs described in this book are designed to provide early intervention to populations undergoing stress reactions to a catastrophic event. The interventions suggested are aimed at enhancing the skills of mental health professionals, educators, and peer counselors in responding to the intensified demands of disasters. The crisis intervention model can be applied to programs for individual children and families; multifamily groups; and groups of children in mental health, educational, and community settings. The intervention approaches provide information about the event itself; reinforce the legitimacy of the anxieties and fears that children and their families are experiencing; encourage the expression of feelings in group and individual settings (for younger children through drawing and play); build on the coping capacity of individuals and their families; and provide concrete coping skills and techniques to alleviate stress reactions.

Chapter 1 begins with a discussion of the history of disaster research from the World War II years, where the focus primarily was on the community and collective behavior, to the present developments of crisis theory and community mental health. Significant landmarks in the course of this history are the conceptualization of the post-traumatic stress syndrome and attachment theory. Developmental theory and stress models have increased understanding of the reactions to the destruction of a community by a severe disaster.

Chapter 2 emphasizes the legal requirement in the Disaster Relief Act of 1974 that mandates the incorporation of mental health services in the preparation of emergency plans for predisaster and postdisaster response. Steps in the construction of such a framework are outlined, including the development of procedures for mobilization and utilization of resources, the provision of staff training in debriefing, the initiation of crisis counseling and services for children and families, and the planning of how to work with schools and existing children's services at local agencies.

Chapter 3 delineates the wide variety of tasks that the mental health professional may be called on to provide to children and their families in the ensuing chaos and confusion of a severe disaster. These tasks may range from fieldwork on the scene; in the home, school, or playground; or in Red Cross shelters, disaster assistance centers, and emergency tents to providing follow-up care and referral for children identified as being emotionally disturbed, and educating parents and emergency personnel about emotional reactions that they might encounter both in children and themselves. The work may include helping teachers and medical and emergency services personnel through the provision of debriefing and defusing and the identification and prevention of burnout.

Chapter 4 describes predisaster training aimed at providing mental health professionals, child care program staff, and school personnel with reviews of age-typical behaviors, reactions often encountered within developmental age groups, community networking, diagnostic techniques, and specialized materials. Suggestions are made for designing programs to meet the needs of ethnic groups and to overcome the difficulties in arranging counseling for children when there is culturally based resistance. Techniques found useful for assessment and treatment of children in different age groups are described.

Chapter 5 presents some theories found useful in understanding child and family behaviors in a world that suddenly has become confusing and unfamiliar, with alteration of familiar relationships, destruction of community property, and sometimes even loss or injury of loved ones. Mental health professionals need to be familiar with the usual phases of recovery and to be able to anticipate reactions that are both regressive and distressing. The concepts of vulnerability, resilience, and competence, which are helpful in understanding the reactions of the child and family in a disaster situation, are introduced. Attention is paid to the involvement of parents in their children's treatment; especially, ways to help parents resolve their own emotional distress so that they can better respond to their children's needs.

Chapter 6 delves into the details of working with children and families in a disaster through the employment of crisis intervention procedures and techniques. It discusses how case-finding and referrals for care may develop from the mental health professional's own early contacts and from emergency services personnel who have come into contact with children and their families. Descriptions of outreach, educational, and therapeutic approaches in varying formats follow, such as individual and group sessions, debriefings, defusings, and school-based interventions. Assessment tools for both diagnosis and research are described.

Chapter 7 outlines a community-based planning process in which mental health professionals participate, along with established emergency services organizations and nonprofit agencies, community-based organizations, Neighborhood Watch, and homeowners associations. A discussion follows on how the role of mental health in predisaster planning has increased in recent years and what remains to be done in the areas of needs assessment, approaches to multicultural communities, training for professional associations, coordination with existing counseling resources in schools and workplaces, and establishment of community advisory boards.

The examples of natural disasters described in this book have occurred mainly in the western United States, most commonly in California, because these are the disasters with which the authors have had most experience and personal involvement. Information about disasters in other parts of the United States has been included when available. The authors are confident that the experience gained, the lessons learned, and the recommendations made are relevant to communities in other areas of the United States.

ACKNOWLEDGMENTS

We want to thank William Clark, Brian Flynn, Beth Nelson, and Portland Ridley, of the US Department of Health and Human Services for providing us with information and direction. We are grateful to Ralph Swisher and Holly Harrington of the US Federal Emergency Management Agency for their time, patience, guidance, and for sharing valuable materials. We are most grateful to the staff of the Natural Hazards Research and Applications Information Center in Boulder, especially Mary Fran Myers, who encouraged and supported our research efforts over the years, and Dave Morton, the Center's Librarian, who assisted us in locating reference and source materials.

Linda Fain of the State of California Department of Mental Health shared the innovative prevention materials developed by her program, and final reports of crisis counseling programs throughout the state over the past decade. Joe Leviness of the State of New York Department of Mental Health, Bonnie Seltzer of the State of North Dakota Division of Mental Health and Substance Abuse, and Maureen Underwood of the University of Medicine and Dentistry of New Jersey, shared materials on the programs developed in their states.

We would like to thank Herbert Blaufarb of the San Fernando Valley Child Guidance Clinic, Marcia R. Harris of the Didi Hirsch Community Mental Health Center, and Julieanne Pogue of the Valley Community Clinic, for the valuable case materials they shared with us. We wish to acknowledge Pat Sable for her contributions to the section on attachment theory, and Helen Warren Ross for her suggestions and resources on child development theory. Robert Pynoos and Alan Steinberg of the University of California, Los Angeles, generously shared their own research in child trauma. We would like to extend our thanks to both William Arroyo, of the Los Angeles County Department of Mental Health, and Stephen J. Howard, a pioneer in the field of disaster and child mental health, for their encouragement and assistance.

We would like to acknowledge the editor of this series, Charles R. Figley, for his valuable role in spearheading the development and growth of the International Society for Traumatic Stress Studies from its modest beginnings with a handful of disaster mental health pioneers into a major professional society, and for his encouragement and support during the entire process of putting this book together.

Norma Gordon expresses her deep appreciation to her husband, Edwin, for his caring and patience. Norman Farberow would like to thank his wife, Pearl, for her constant encouragement and support. Carl Maida would like to thank his wife, Barbara, for her creative support during the writing of this book.

Perspectives on Disaster

The disruptive effects of disasters on societies and individuals have been described in written history, diaries, and autobiographical and legendary fictional accounts. The roots of disaster research can be found in the pioneering studies by A. Freud and Burlingham (1944) at the Hampstead war nurseries that brought attention to the problems experienced by young children who were forced to separate from their families during wartime. Their studies influenced subsequent research and clinical efforts to help children who were undergoing overwhelming stress, and provided the basis for Bowlby's landmark developmental theories of attachment, separation, and loss (1973). The pathbreaking work of Lindemann (1944); Bloch, Silber, and Perry (1956); and Wallace (1957) established the field of disaster research in the American social and behavioral sciences. Efforts to investigate disasters evolved out of community studies in the social sciences, including social psychology, sociology, and cultural anthropology. Because early disaster research stemmed from these community studies, it focused more on understanding the collective behavior of groups following a disaster. The study of the psychological effects of a disaster on individuals came later.

Research on the psychological impact of disasters and the development of intervention models to help individuals cope with stress reactions emerged from crisis theory in psychology and from the community mental health movement (Blaufarb & Levine, 1972; Caplan, 1964; Howard, 1980; Richard, 1974). Legislation allocating funds for crisis counseling programs provided the impetus for the development of crisis mental health interventions at the federal level. The Disaster Assistance and Emergency Mental Health Section of the National Institute of Mental Health, with the funding from the Disaster Relief Act of 1974, Section 413, mandated funds for crisis counseling and training in disaster. This legislation marked the first time that the federal government acknowledged the need for mental health interventions following a disaster, and created the incentive for local communities to initiate crisis counseling programs (Farberow & Frederick, 1978; Lystad, 1985). Regrettably, these federal funds are earmarked for crisis counseling and training and do not include support for research activities. As a result, early systematic research on the social and psychological reactions associated with disasters often was not done.

Despite the common knowledge that children are adversely affected by disasters, no conceptual research framework was available for understanding the effects of disaster on children. The field of emergency mental health was just beginning to develop from the fields of both emergency medicine and mental health. During the past two decades, a significant body of social and behavioral science literature has been written on the psychological effects of disaster. The study of the psychological effects of disasters on children came out of the actual experiences of practitioners who observed children's reactions after a disaster. Research was begun on the types of reactions and emergent disorders, duration of symptoms, individual vulnerability, and differential impact (Bolin, 1982; Bromet, Hough, & Connell, 1984; Burke, Borus, Burns, Millstein, & Beasley, 1982; Newman, 1976; Saylor, 1993). Mental health intervention programs designed specifically for children resulted from these clinical observations (Farberow & Gordon, 1981).

Another significant contribution to the field resulted from the Vietnam War with the development of post-traumatic stress disorder as a diagnostic category used to classify the reactions of Vietnam veterans. This has provided a conceptual framework for further understanding the effects of other disasters on individuals. The framework has yielded an increasing body of clinical research in this area, and has encouraged researchers to study the applicability of post-traumatic stress disorder on children. Children exhibit a limited range of post-traumatic stress behaviors compared to adults (Handford et al., 1986; McFarlane, Policansky, & Irwin, 1987; Yule & Williams, 1990). However, the relevance of this diagnostic category to children has been explored in a number of research activities (Frederick, 1985; Terr, 1981; Pynoos et al., 1987; Pynoos, Nader, & March, 1991) .

☐ Disaster as a Community Crisis

Natural disasters are prototypical community-scale crises. Fires, floods, earthquakes, hurricanes, and tornadoes all are natural events that are unpreventable and often unpredictable. Disasters have an effect on all populations, whether living in urban, suburban, or rural areas and regardless of economic status, cultural assimilation, or recent immigration. Disasters are psychologically and physically disruptive to the lives of individuals and they affect family life, friendships, and interactions between households and other institutions in the wider community (Bolin, 1982; Drabek & Kay, 1976).

The loss of residence, with its attendant displacement and many other ramifications, is a common hazard for survivors of a disaster, even when there has been no loss of life (K. T. Erikson, 1976b; Ordway, 1984). Being displaced from a home often results in a loss of rootedness that is marked by depression, despair, and longing for a secure base (Gordon et al., 1986). Even when there has been only a relatively small amount of residential damage, a disaster can have a serious impact. Transportation and utilities often are affected. Because schools and work sites often are damaged, schoolchildren and employed adults may be forced to remain at home or to be relocated to temporary school and work settings.

Disaster victims have described how their prior perception of the world as secure and reliable has changed after a disaster has rendered their surroundings uninhabitable and even unidentifiable (Antonovsky, 1979, 1987). The victim's previous perception of the community as a "safe place" is eroded in direct relationship to the extent of destruction—the world is no longer safe and secure (K. T. Erikson, 1994). The impact of the event is increased when death and injury occurs to loved ones, and further heightened when there is loss of pets and familiar objects in the home and landmarks in the environment. Children are especially place-oriented; locales convey a concrete sense of security and familiarity to their lives (Bowlby, 1973; Richards, 1974; Winnicott, 1971). A disaster affects children's sense of identity which, to a large extent, is mediated by their family, but also is conveyed significantly by their home, neighborhood, and community.

Social phenomenology, ecological systems theory, attachment theory, and traumatic stress studies can foster understanding about how crises in the physical and social environments influence both individual and community life. Social phenomenology, grounded in perceptual experience, bodily expression, and institutional life, views the body as a community of senses that organizes an individual's experience and gives meaning to the world (O'Neill, 1989; Seamon & Mugerauer, 1989; Tuan, 1977; Turner, 1984). A sense of community, or the social life world, develops when the individuals in a community share sets of commonly shaped experiences and a coherent worldview. A person becomes conscious of his or her own identity and social world, and gains a sense of functional personal-social coherence, by learning sets of skilled actions in the family, in the school, at play, and at work. This constantly changing and developing network of relationships situates an individual in a social field of institutional and community life and of culture.

Renowned for his field theories of human behavior, Lewin (1935, 1951) viewed behavior as a function of the interplay between the person and the environment. For Lewin, the crucial factor in understanding an individual's psychological field is the person's own interpretation of it. This phenomenological conception of the environment focuses on the way that an individual perceives his "life space." Lewin established a topological psychology of how the regions, boundaries, pathways, and barriers in this space direct human action. A person's behavior is not merely steered from within, but is motivated by the environment. For Lewin, objects, activities, and other people in the psychological field also direct a person's behavior.

Drawing on Lewin's topological psychology, Bronfenbrenner's (1979, 1989) ecological systems theory frames human development as a dynamic, mutually reciprocal, process. The child not only influences the variety of settings he or she encounters, such as the home, day care center, school, or playground, but he or she is simultaneously influenced by these environments. Bronfenbrenner conceived the ecological environment as a nested arrangement of four concentric structures, each contained within the next: the microsystem, mesosystem, exosystem, and macrosystem. The microsystem includes the activities, roles, and interactions of the child in a specific setting where people engage in face-to-face behavior. The mesosystem is the interrelations between two or more settings in which the developing person actively participates: The child's development is affected by the interconnections between home, school, and neighborhood. The exosystem refers to those settings beyond the child's immediate experience that nevertheless affect him or her, such as the parent's place of work or the activities of the local school board. The macrosystem does not refer to a specific setting, but to the consistencies across the microsystem, mesosystem, and exosystem, and to the values and beliefs of the culture or society in which the child lives. Head Start is a prime example of the influence of the macrosystem on child development in the United States (Craig & Kermis, 1995, p. 18).

Attachment theory states that personal identity and self-concept develop through bonding with significant persons within the social field: at home, at work, and in the community (Bowlby, 1988; Marris, 1974; Parkes & Stevenson-Hinde, 1982; Young & Willmott, 1957). This constellation of attachments provides a "secure base," anchoring a person in his or her social world (Harwood, Miller, & Irizarry, 1995; Waters, Vaughn, Posada, & Kondo-Ikemura, 1995). That sense of security frequently is severely affected after a community-scale crisis. The frightening circumstances that accompany a major disaster generally are unfamiliar to most people. These include the physical sensations and feelings of helplessness when experiencing the movement of the earth caused by earthquakes; (Gordon et al., 1995) the terrifying forces of strong winds, floodwaters, and fire; the ruthlessness of wide-scale damage to property; the frustrating disruption of transportation and communication systems; the numbing witnessing of death and injuries, and, in some instances, looting and violence (Erikson, 1976b). The resulting "mazeway disintegration" stems from feeling displaced and insignificant in a once familiar environment that seems to have disintegrated (Wallace, 1957).

Confusion results when people are traumatized by extreme conditions and perceive the immediate environment in a disconnected way: The familiar appears less familiar and the sense of personal security is challenged. As the environmental mazeway disintegrates, a person's spatial perception becomes distorted, threatening further loss of the security provided by familiar settings. Many people experience a social void, accompanied by feelings of intense loss of their environmental anchors. Fried (1963) observed this in the relocation experiences of families forced to abandon Boston's West End as a result of urban renewal:

> The crisis of loss of a residential area brings to the fore the importance of the local spatial region and alerts us to the greater generality of spatial conceptions as determinants of behavior. In fact, we might say that a *sense of spatial identity* is fundamental to human functioning. It represents a phenomenal or ideational integration of important experiences concerning environmental arrangements and contacts in relation to the individual's conception of his own body in space. It is based on spatial memories, spatial imagery, the spatial framework of current activity, and the implicitly spatial components of ideals and aspirations. (p. 156).

Survivors of a natural disaster, civil disorder, war, forced resettlement, and other forms of involuntary displacement also experience traumatic stress (Fritz, 1957; Tyhurst, 1957; van der Kolk, 1988). The most common indicators of traumatic stress for children and adults include manifest, persistent symptoms of heightened emotional arousal, sleep disturbances, irritability, difficulty concentrating, and heightened physiological reactivity. Generalized anxiety reactions, such as fatigue, feeling on edge, excessive worry, increased recurrent headaches, appetite change, heart palpitations, and insomnia, also frequently are experienced.

Pynoos, Steinberg, and Wraith (1995) hypothesized a tripartite developmental model of childhood traumatic stress, which is derived from the nature of the traumatic experience, the subsequent traumatic reminders, and secondary stress. They stated that resistance and vulnerability directly mediate the distress and should be differentiated from resilience, which refers to early effective efforts at adjustment and recovery. Their theory takes into consideration the developmental cycle of the family, which includes the current phase of the domestic group as a whole.

The Conservation of Resources (COR) stress model addresses the postcrisis impact of resource loss on individual functioning and coping behavior (Freedy, Shaw, Jarrell, & Masters, 1992; Hobfell, 1989). The COR model postulates that individuals use social and personal resources as tools to maximize their well-being. The model contains four resource categories: object resources or possessions having functional or status value; condition resources or social roles; personal characteristic resources, namely self-image and worldviews; and energy resources, like time, money, and information. Major disasters may affect, reduce, or even eliminate one or more of these resources, producing stress in direct relationship to the extent of the stress that occurs from personal or community loss.

A phenomenon that is common to children and adults who are victims of natural disasters and to those who are involuntarily resettled is the reaction of denial that the event may recur, such as an aftershock of a devastating earthquake or the prospect of further displacement. Anxiety resulting from coping with the effects of disaster produces a form of cognitive dissonance (Festinger, 1957). Those who have experienced repeated crises or losses appear to be less able to become attached to a "place" or locale, such as a home, workplace, or community. These people also tend to be less able to develop cohesive personal relationships and to formulate a clear, purposive view of the future.

☐ The Varieties of Disaster Experience

The Emergency Response System

The emergency response system becomes activated when a large-scale disaster occurs (Kreps, 1989). This system includes established organizations, such as law enforcement, fire departments, health care, and expanding relief organizations, like the Red Cross and the Salvation Army (Dynes, 1970). Loosely structured communities in a metropolis more often will deal with catastrophes through nongovernmental organizations rather than governmental agencies (Brown, 1980). These organizations work with, and often are integrated into, the functioning state and local governmental agencies that form the emergency response system. Federal and state governmental agencies only become active after a major disaster declaration. The Red Cross, a nongovernmental agency, provides emergency services in both larger scale and smaller scale events.

A major natural disaster often results in an overburdened emergency response system. When service demands exceed the capacity of local resources, assistance also will become available through state resources and prearranged local mutual aid. Federal assistance is made available only after a formal declaration of a disaster has been made by the president. The following case study illustrates how the organizational resources of an urban community, which included public and nonprofit agencies, responded to both the material and the emotional needs of residents in the wake of the 1991 East Bay Hills firestorm in the San Francisco Bay Area.

The 1991 East Bay Hills Firestorm

On October 20, 1991, a firestorm destroyed more than 3,000 homes and killed 25 people in the hillside residential neighborhoods of Oakland and Berkeley, California. The residents predominantly were long-term homeowners and renters. Many of the homes were built before fire codes existed and had highly flammable wood shake siding and roofing. In addition, the overhanging branches of eucalyptus trees and brush had accumulated on many properties. With winds gusting up to 65 miles per hour, the firestorm spread through the affluent hillside communities, causing almost total residential loss by destroying 2,800 single family residences and 400 apartments in the 1,800 acre fire zone. The estimated cost of property damage was between $1.5 billion and $2.0 billion. Red Cross officials reported that over 4,500 people were left homeless and 150 were injured as a result of this disaster, which was recognized as the worst residential fire in California history. However, despite the scale of the fire, there were relatively few fatalities or injuries that required hospitalization. Nevertheless, many residents were severely traumatized emotionally, both as a direct result of life-threatening danger from the fire's onset and rapid spread, which forced them to evacuate their homes and neighborhoods, and their later return to find scenes of massive destruction, which included for many the loss of their homes and possessions.

The Alameda County Mental Health Services and the City of Berkeley Mental Health mobilized immediately to offer crisis services to the disaster victims (Alameda County Mental Health Services, 1993; City of Berkeley Mental Health, 1993; Gordon, Maida, & Farberow, 1992). They dispatched staff to the scene of the fires, offering assistance to emergency services personnel and to victims of the fire. Fortunately, both mental health agencies had an experienced and disaster trained staff. Two years earlier, Alameda County Mental Health Services had dealt with a major natural disaster: the Loma Prieta earthquake. City of Berkeley Mental Health had worked with several smaller scale crisis events, including a hostage crisis situation and a fraternity house fire in the university area.

Although the public mental health response was timely, problems occurred with coordination between the agencies in the allocation of resources and utilization of professional volunteers. These problems resulted from the absence of predisaster coordination and planning between mental health providers and the local emergency preparedness agencies. Administrators of the public mental health systems also experienced difficulty with jurisdictional vagaries. This affected adequate service delivery in the early phases of the disaster response. The Alameda County Mental Health Services was identified by the state of California as the lead agency at the time of the fire. It was assigned the responsibility of staffing the Disaster Assistance Center (DAC) and Red Cross shelters, and served as the official liaison and gateway to the emergency services network.

The fire also destroyed some homes within the city of Berkeley, prompting the city mental health administrators to mobilize a disaster response based on their responsibilities to the needs of their community. The city agency had been overlooked initially by the state mental health officials who routinely assist municipal agencies in obtaining federal funds to carry out emergency services. Part of the reason for this oversight was that the City of Berkeley Mental Health had only recently become an administrative unit separate from the Alameda County Mental Health Services. The oversight created problems in service delivery as well as unfortunate turf issues. Ultimately, the situation was clarified and the city agency was included in the state of California/National Institute of Mental Health (NIMH) loop. Funding for mental health services then became available to both the Alameda County and Berkeley mental health systems through the Federal Emergency Management Agency (FEMA) and NIMH.

Mental health and counseling services also were offered by the nonprofit sector. United Way agencies customarily operate independently of government mental health agencies in providing counseling services. During the first week or two, when the disaster victims primarily were concerned with their basic needs, the United Way agencies focused on providing this kind of assistance. However, the disaster, with its unique set of circumstances, caused problems in the subsequent efforts of the agencies to deliver counseling services. These problems eventually led to the formation of a mental health committee within the United Way planning structure that was given the specific purpose of addressing the issues of need and resource allocation of both public and private mental health services to residents of greater Alameda County.

Mental health professionals worked closely with fire and law enforcement personnel, escorting victims in and out of the disaster zone and offering counseling services at the DAC. However, as has been the experience in other disasters, counseling services per se initially were poorly utilized. Debriefing services offered by mental health professionals to the Red Cross volunteers also were poorly utilized, possibly because they were scheduled after shifts when the volunteers, many of whom were not local residents, were fatigued and eager to return home.

As in other recent disasters, there was an outpouring of volunteers from the mental health community to assist in the recovery efforts. Many of these were professionals who had been trained by the Red Cross, by NIMH-funded training programs in the Bay Area, or by local professional associations. However, the two public mental health agencies and the United Way agencies all reported difficulties in making effective use of the many volunteers because they lacked staff to screen the volunteers and to organize and administer the volunteer effort. Although there was a clear need for counseling services, agencies experienced difficulties with integrating the volunteers into their activities.

Illustrative of the problems in effective coordination of formal and volunteer resources were the difficulties experienced by the Red Cross, during the early phases of the disaster, in convincing the Alameda County Mental Health Services to accept the mental health professional volunteers that it had trained. The latter would allow the Red Cross mental health cadre to provide services to only the Red Cross volunteer emergency services personnel and not to the community. Other trained mental health professionals also reported frustrations with the county agency's lack of receptivity of their offers of help. This particularly was true during the early days of the disaster, when many professionals who had received training after previous disasters had come forth to offer assistance. These problems illustrate the need for communities to take steps, before a disaster occurs, to anticipate and mitigate the difficulties of volunteer coordination.

Because the fire was located in an affluent area contiguous to a major university and because it affected residents who had lived there for many years, offers of assistance from community resources, such as community homeowners associations, were even greater than in most disaster locales. The Phoenix Coordinating Council was established as an umbrella organization to coordinate a network of 50 new and preexisting neighborhood organizations in the devastated hillside communities. The council initiated a newsletter, *The Phoenix Journal,* to disseminate critical information to area residents and also began to serve as a voice in influencing governmental agencies and insurers. The Phoenix organizations, for example, exerted their influence in revising the building codes and architectural policies of local government development and planning councils. The North Hills Phoenix Association, representing a hillside area of about 1,500 homes, has continued to advocate on behalf of common concerns, such as fire safety, to city, state, and federal officials and to disseminate information about governmental decisions and services which affect the community. Recent efforts include repaving of area streets with underground utilities, and exploring ways to maintain vegetation management services in the hills. The new activism of volunteers has continued in Oakland in the years following the firestorm, with hundreds of residents receiving training as volunteer firefighters. A cadre of emergency services volunteers is now ready to assist Oakland Fire Department personnel in future disasters. Similar cadres have been developed in the Los Angeles as a result of the disastrous fires that have swept through its hills in recent years.

Communities-in-Crisis

Stable communities are characterized by a high-quality infrastructure, an array of municipal services, and strong social networks that link individuals who share common concerns. These qualities attract people to a community and contribute to their ongoing sense of residential attachment. Residents in these types of communities often form ad hoc networks and coalitions to address reconstruction efforts. Such "emergent" structures are significant sources of anchorage when the disorganization of a disaster occurs (Drabek, 1987). As new forms of collective behavior, these structures provide a facilitating social context for reestablishing normalcy (Quarantelli, 1984). Emergent accommodation groups often carry out postdisaster tasks that are not routinely handled by already established groups and organizations within a highly bureaucratized emergency services system (Quarantelli, 1970).

Less stable and less affluent communities, by contrast, frequently are less politically organized and often lack the advocates, or spokespersons, to identify service needs, set priorities, or request funding after a disaster (Iscoe, 1974, 1982). As a result, they are deprived of the extra services obtained by the higher income communities. Economically disadvantaged residents also generally have to spend more time attending to their immediate needs than those in affluent areas. And, because their frequently substandard housing is more likely to sustain greater damage, they are more likely to be displaced from their homes and neighborhoods for longer periods of time and to need shelters and other Red Cross services.

Some disaster-related tasks are carried out by "extending" organizations (Stallings, 1978). These are organizations already in service to the community that have initiated emergency activities. For example, the homeowners association in Topanga, California, developed a volunteer arson watch program to monitor fire hazards after a series of fires swept through the coastal canyon community in 1982. The fire watch program, which was modeled on the Neighborhood Watch effort against crime, has now been active for many years. Other voluntary efforts coevolve from those of already established organizations. In Santa Cruz, on California's central coast, many local mental health professionals volunteered their services to the mental health department after the earthquake of 1989. Because Santa Cruz residents had become aware of the need for a coordinated local response after severe flooding in 1982 immobilized municipal resources, the city's mental health authority spearheaded a response following heavy flooding and an earthquake that included volunteerism by local professionals, with active outreach efforts to shelters, schools, and trailer parks. The well-organized grassroots political organization in the relatively small-sized Santa Cruz community had made the mental health center staff familiar to community residents and the schools. Acceptance of their intervention efforts was immediate because the agency was well integrated with the community at large.

A major disaster will alter both the landscape and the status of its victims. Therefore, the ensuing loss of resources can limit an individual's potential, materially and psychologically. Centrifugal disasters, like a major airline crash, generally scatter their survivors away from the locus of the event. Thus, they create multiple disaster communities widespread across time and space (Lindy, Grace, & Green, 1981; Michael, Lurie, Russell, & Unger, 1985). By comparison, centripetal disasters, like a flood, hurricane, fire, or earthquake, impact a community by disrupting families and social networks that continue to share the same physical environment after the event. The community of survivors that experiences this type of disaster most often will stay in place and continue on as part of the recovery environment. Disaster victims frequently will become involved in collective endeavors out of a sense of communal loss and of a common need that typifies the shared experience of catastrophe (Wright, Ursano, Bartone, & Ingraham, 1990). The disaster community can crosscut boundaries of social class and ethnicity. The following brief cases illustrate the diverse ways that emergency organizations have responded to natural disasters over the past two decades in southern California's disaster-prone environments.

The 1971 Sylmar Earthquake

In the early morning of February 9, 1971, an earthquake measuring 6.4 on the Richter scale rumbled through the San Fernando Valley. The city of San Fernando, at the epicenter of the earthquake, suffered considerable property damage. Outreach services to children and families in the community were provided within days by a local mental health center and a local child guidance clinic. The city had a large Latino population that was wary of accepting counseling services. A local storefront legal clinic run by trusted community leaders was the central resource for this community. The Los Angeles County–Olive View Medical Center, the public health center and hospital, suffered major structural damage and was closed. Mental health outreach teams assisted troubled families who were referred by community leaders in the local ethnic communities. The teams participated in school-based interventions that provided consultation to classroom and support personnel. The local child guidance clinic, adopted a crisis intervention model. Using this model, the clinic was able to deliver services on a no-charge basis and also eliminate the usual intake or screening procedures. The clinic services were well publicized by the local news media, and hundreds of families utilized the services for their children.

Staff from the child guidance clinic also encouraged families to seek help and referred them to multifamily crisis counseling groups at the local schools, as well as to the clinic itself where parents could bring children who were exhibiting stress symptoms. Most of the parents who attended the multifamily groups sought advice about and reassurance that the skills and methods they were using were appropriate. The parenting techniques that had worked for them in the past had suddenly lost their effectiveness in helping their children with earthquake-related fears. The staff found that the parents were extremely anxious, which was making it difficult for them to cope with their children's fears. The crisis groups focused on providing the parents with skills to relieve their children's symptoms, along with information to help them understand the source of their own distress. The sequence in which the group facilitators proceeded to help the families was important, because it was necessary to help the parents learn how to handle their own fears before they could begin to understand how their fears were affecting their children. Both the parents and the children benefited from the support and advice provided to the parents by the clinic's staff. The children also benefited from the clinical interventions that they received in the art therapy and the group discussions.

The threat that a major dam might collapse in the aftermath of the earthquake further disrupted the community. Officials evacuated 80,000 people from their homes, and major roads were closed off. The resulting displacement that lasted 3 days heightened the fears of families and caused them to seek shelter with relatives and friends or in Red Cross shelters. It became extremely important to disseminate accurate information to an already traumatized population. The local child guidance clinic organized neighborhood meetings at schools to inform the community about the status of the earthquake. A team of geologists from a local university provided information about the earthquake, and a team of mental health professionals counseled worried parents and provided information about how to cope with the crisis. Interpreters were present at these meetings, particularly at those held in the city of San Fernando where many of the residents spoke only Spanish.

After damage assessments were completed and the dam was deemed safe, residents returned to their homes. The ongoing meetings, however, accomplished a number of key tasks in the recovery process. First, accurate information was provided in both English and Spanish by earth scientists knowledgeable in strategies of risk communication (Lave & Lave, 1991; National Research Council, 1989). This was especially important because residents who spoke only Spanish were unable to understand pertinent information provided by the English-language media, which resulted in rampant rumors and myths about earthquakes among this population. The community meetings provided residents with an opportunity to share their fears and experiences and to reassure each other. These efforts became an impetus for subsequent neighborhood self-help activities. The local child guidance clinic also became more fully integrated within the community through its outreach efforts to residents. The common experience of the disaster and its aftermath provided a sense of cohesion in a community to which many of the residents had recently migrated from other parts of the region or from abroad.

The Lake Elsinore Flood

After a disaster, organizations often will "expand" to include as clients members of an affected community who would not typically use their services. This happened in the case of the Lake Elsinore flood. The flood in the small southern California town of Lake Elsinore, which at that time was a rural area, displaced many residents from their substandard trailer courts in lowland areas surrounding the lake. Flood victims mainly were retirees who lost most of their personal possessions. Although many residents relocated by FEMA to a trailer camp, other residents, who displayed a distrust of outsiders typical of this kind of community, were hesitant to request assistance. Their sense of extreme caution has been described by Lindy (1985) as part of a "trauma membrane" that was developed by those who had survived the flood to protect themselves from further external psychic stress in the recovery environment.

Mental health professionals and Red Cross volunteers, who were residents of the community, created outreach teams. The Riverside County Department of Mental Health received federal funding from FEMA for a crisis counseling program. The agency assigned its staff to assist the local community in Lake Elsinore. The volunteer grassroots community organization, Lake Elsinore Aid, staffed offices on the main street of the small town and provided food and other materials to needy residents. The mayor and city council rallied to the support of this emergent group. The professional staff of the FEMA-funded program deferred to the community volunteers, who thus were able to offer assistance.

By using individuals familiar to community residents, the volunteer teams were able to negotiate entry into the homes where residents previously had been hesitant to admit strangers. The teams conducted a needs assessment survey of the victims who had been relocated to the trailer camps, as well as those who still lived in their damaged homes. The modest center that arose from Lake Elsinore Aid remained operational for a number of months after the flood and provided counseling to residents and assistance with material needs.

The Topanga-Malibu Floods

Another example of how organizations will "extend" beyond their routine missions to provide special services to survivors in a community that has been hit hard by a disaster occurred after the Topanga-Malibu floods in the 1980s and 1990s. Major flooding, resulting from a severe winter storm pattern, displaced many residents of Malibu and Topanga, two southern California hillside and canyon communities that had suffered extensive losses from floods and wildfires several years earlier. Each of these communities is self-contained and geographically separated from the major urban center of Los Angeles. Both have a community center, an elementary school, small markets, and a strong sense of community identity and pride.

Topanga is a canyon community traversed by one major north-south road. Because of its relative isolation, this community attracts residents who seek a high degree of privacy and who tend to be individualistic in their lifestyle and worldview. Homes range from expensive ranches to substandard shacks. At the time of the floods, the community included affluent celebrities, as well as numerous people who were homeless and had been living under bridges or in their automobiles. In one of the storms, damaged roads dictated that the only way to evacuate Topanga residents and to provide emergency medical assistance was by means of a helicopter. A team from the local mental health center offered crisis intervention counseling to children and families at the local community center, the Red Cross shelter, and the school. In the aftermath of the floods, Topanga residents provided a great deal of aid to each other, including efforts that were particularly supportive of the needs of children. A volunteer counseling program was developed by the staff of the Topanga Community Center. The local school, which also served as the Red Cross shelter, provided counseling to parents to help them understand the psychological needs of their children. Children were reported to be restless, fearful, and clinging. A community volunteer child care program provided supervised play activities for the children while their parents were tending to cleanup and rebuilding activities.

The Topanga Coalition for Emergency Preparedness (T-CEP) was formed following the 1993 Topanga-Malibu firestorm. Originally composed of representatives from major community-based organizations and advisory members from emergency services agencies, T-CEP has become an established part of the community and recently has applied for nonprofit status. The coalition sponsored a disaster preparedness fair at the Topanga elementary school, which brought together emergency services agencies and disaster safety vendors to educate the community and to sell a variety of safety items and survival kits. T-CEP staffs emergency preparedness booths at the annual Topanga Days fair and sponsors "HOTLINE," the emergency preparedness column published biweekly in the community newspaper. T-CEP also meets regularly with the Red Cross to identify and supply evacuation shelters in the canyon, and has developed a simple neighborhood emergency prepared- ness plan modeled after a FEMA-Office of Emergency Services plan for com- munity disaster response, recovery, and preparedness. T-CEP members have taken classes in first aid and cardiopulmonary resuscitation, damage assess- ment, crisis counseling, shelter management, and disaster response. They also have met with experts in medical care, animal assistance, wilderness first aid, and disaster communications (including ham radio operations and telephone rumor control). The coalition is establishing a disaster prepared- ness and emergency command center in a trailer donated by the Topanga Christian Science Church, with support from the Los Angeles County Board of Supervisors and the county fire and sheriff's departments.

Situated several miles north of Topanga is Malibu, a beach community that is economically and topographically similar to Topanga. Malibu was incorporated as a city in 1991 and has an annual budget of $7.5 million. Damage to Malibu often is highly publicized because of its many celebrity residents from the film industry. Malibu's 11,400 residents have experienced major floods, mud slides, and wildfires, in addition to earthquakes. Because of their magnitude and extent of damage, six have been federally declared disasters. These disasters have resulted in more than $95 million in damage. In fact, Malibu has spent nearly one third of its budget in recent years on disaster relief. In 1994, Malibu hired a full-time disaster coordinator to monitor the expenses incurred by the city in coping with this cycle of catastrophes. The coordinator has spent considerable time in preparing disaster relief claims for submission to FEMA that request reimbursement to the city for its part in reconstruction.

Malibu residents traditionally have mobilized existing community-based resources in an emergency. Students from Pepperdine University, which is situated adjacent to Malibu, have assisted with sandbagging and other flood control efforts. University buildings have served as shelters for local residents during the autumn wildfires. In a recent disaster, the campus itself had to be evacuated. The Tree People, a local environmental organization, also has recruited, mobilized, and supervised teenage volunteers as part of its disaster response efforts. Here again, a neighborhood alert program linked to the mayor's office is well organized. A telephone "tree" alerts neighbors to impending dangers and road conditions.

The 1987 Whittier Narrows Earthquake

After a major disaster, new organizations frequently will "emerge" to aid survivors in coping or with reconstruction. This was the case with the 1987 Whittier Narrows earthquake. An earthquake, measuring 6.1 on the Richter scale, occurred at 7:42 a.m. on October 1, 1987, in the Whittier Narrows area, about 7 miles south of Pasadena, California. The earthquake was severe enough to be felt in diverse residential areas in greater Los Angeles. The initial tremor was followed by more than 15 aftershocks in excess of 3 on the Richter scale. The disaster caused $65 million in estimated damage and killed at least three people. The Red Cross set up eight emergency centers in five small cities to provide food, shelter, and temporary quarters for the people left homeless by the earthquake. At least 400 people sought refuge at these shelters after their homes were damaged or destroyed. The president declared a state of emergency in Whittier, a city of 70,000. At least 800 homes and 30 businesses were damaged and 200 were judged to be unsafe, with total damage exceeding $12 million.

The earthquake was a frightening event to parents and children (Gordon & Maida, 1989). The media, particularly television, became the primary sources of information following the event. A study of 30 families revealed that almost all of the children did not recognize the event to be an earthquake, but rather just a loud noise. This response is particularly interesting since earthquake preparedness drills had been taking place at the schools prior to the quake, and television specials on earthquakes had recently been presented. Two thirds of the children reported that they sought emotional support from their parents and told their parents about their fears. Parents took charge and instructed their children what they should do. The children said that expressing their feelings and talking about the event with their parents alleviated some of their fears. However, 3 to 5 months later, almost half of the adult respondents still were feeling frightened and most of the children continued to have intrusive thoughts about the earthquake. Other parents reported post-traumatic effects on their children in the form of sleep problems and specific fears. Although these reactions appeared to diminish over time, they persisted in over half the respondents and undoubtedly were reinforced by several aftershocks that occurred during this period. In Whittier, the subsequent long reconstruction period was a continuing reminder of the damage caused by the earthquake.

The study also reported that two thirds of the adults experienced a high level of stress which affected the adult's parental capacity to deal with his or her children's fears and thus was a prime contributing factor to children's vulnerability. Parental control often is interrupted by the destruction of physical surroundings and following displacement of family members to a shelter environment. Many parents also reported that they were so occupied with the paperwork necessary for insurance claims and federal entitlements that the opportunity for parental control was considerably diminished.

Local agencies carried out the official emergency mental health response in Whittier after the earthquake. Over half of the 30 families interviewed in this study sought crisis counseling for postearthquake reactions. The clinical services that they received were primarily group intervention and some individual counseling. Ten of the families attended a one-time "earthquake crisis group" led by trained mental health professionals. The group focused on the children's fears, management of the children's behavior, and recommendations with respect to effective parenting. All of these services were reported by parents as being helpful in dealing with their children's reactions, and most indicated that they would seek similar help in the future.

The Whittier child guidance clinic provided immediate crisis intervention services, including outreach to the community and interface with the school district. The Whittier Child Guidance Clinic offered a program similar to the pioneering effort of the San Fernando Valley Child Guidance Clinic, but was able to achieve a more effective integration with the community because of the greater sophistication of the public at large with respect to mental health interventions during the intervening 15 years. The chief difference between the two operations was that the clinical services offered in Whittier extended over a longer period of time. The Whittier clinic was located in a neighborhood that had considerable damage to residences, public buildings, and nearby shopping districts. It is likely that this created a longer period of stress because of the constant physical reminders of the earthquake, which resulted in a longer period of seeking help.

Many local residents were active in helping their neighbors through the immediate crisis. A group of community leaders, some of whom had received training in counseling skills, organized a crisis counseling team on the day of the earthquake. Adult volunteers supervised teenagers who answered crisis calls on the telephone hotline. The team also helped Red Cross personnel respond to people who were permanently homeless who were a disruptive presence in the shelter (Bolin, 1993). Some people who were homeless and had mental illness reportedly came into the shelter and frightened the children because of their physical appearance and bizarre behavior. The shelter managers were torn between their concern about these people and the need to calm the fears of the families in the shelter. Members of the volunteer team were able to provide supportive services and counseling to the parents and children in the shelter. Perhaps as a result of the disruptive behavior, the shelter managers decided to close the shelter earlier than they had planned. This early volunteer effort lasted only 3 to 4 days and disbanded when the official disaster response agencies took over.

These examples illustrate how collective action emerges in communities-in-crisis. The literature suggests that such actions appear when there is a breakdown of authority, a lack of emergency planning and coordination, and the "organizational atomization of the community." (Drabek, 1987). These explanations, originating in crisis theory, are consistent with the resource mobilization approach to social movements. This approach describes how people, material, and ideas contribute to the efficacy of social movement organizations (Eyerman & Jamison, 1991). Social movements succeed or fail based on how well they respond to loss or threatened loss of material or organizational resources, such as that which occurs in major disasters. Quarantelli (1984), cites the primacy of interpersonal ties in any social movement. Such ties or social bonds are examples of how collective action can lead to social interaction. This relational perspective moves crisis theory toward the central premises of attachment theory and social phenomenology. However, it appears that these efforts emerge out of the perceived needs of residents and increase when the residents already have a strong sense of community identification.

☐ Summary

Large-scale disasters activate the community response system, such as law enforcement and fire departments and transportation and communication repair activities. Local governmental and nongovernmental relief agencies, like the Red Cross and the Salvation Army, provide initial emergency relief on a local scale but, for more severe disasters, state and federal resources also are needed. The importance of the impact of a disaster on the mental health of the individual and the community was not officially recognized until the federal Disaster Relief Act of 1974, when funds for crisis counseling and training for mental health services were mandated. Earlier studies had established the field of disaster research, but had focused more on the community and the collective behavior of groups following a disaster than on the psychological effects on individuals.

Only in the past two decades has a significant conceptual research framework for understanding the effects of disaster on the emotional lives of its victims emerged from crisis theory and the community mental health movement. A landmark in this development was the conceptualization of post-traumatic stress disorder as a diagnostic category. In addition, social phenomenology, ecological systems theory, and attachment theory have increased understanding about how crises in the physical and social environments influence both individual and community life. Severe natural disasters disrupt the sense of security and familiar world, confusion results when the familiar world disintegrates, and displacement occurs when the individual's sense of spatial identity is undermined. Traumatic stress brings persistent symptoms of heightened emotional arousal and physiological reactivity, along with generalized anxiety reactions. A tripartite developmental model of childhood traumatic stress hypothesizes that resistance and vulnerability mediate the distress, with resilience determining the early efforts at adjustment and recovery. The Conservation of Resources model focuses on how individuals use social and personal resources as tools to reach optimal functioning. Disasters produce stress in direct relationship to the extent of personal or community loss of resources. The degree of disruption of communities struck by disasters often seems to depend on the degree of "organizational atomization" of the local services and the level of affluence of the community. But, the degree of disruption actually is more dependent on the amount of predisaster planning and preparation of disaster response by the community, and the sense of community identification among its members.

CHAPTER

Helping Communities-in-Crisis

Emergency mental health services were a required component of the federally funded Community Mental Health Centers Act of 1963 (Price, Ketterer, Bader, & Monahan, 1980). Subsequent federal legislation, the Disaster Relief Act of 1974, included crisis counseling and training as mandated services and thereby established a collaboration between the Federal Emergency Management Agency (FEMA) and the National Institute of Mental Health (NIMH). The act provided for the funding of these services when a federally declared disaster has occurred in a community. The community-wide planning process mandated by this legislation requires local mental health authorities to participate in coordination with the agencies primarily responsible for emergency response, such as police and firefighters. Local mental health authorities are charged with responsibility for counseling individuals who are in distress and for training crisis counselors.

☐ The Community Crisis Response

Designing Disaster Response Programs

In the past 20 years, there have been numerous disaster mental health response programs throughout the country. A manual provided by NIMH makes general recommendations for program design based on the experience of successful models. Each community, however, will have its own special needs following a disaster. The design of public disaster mental health programs, as determined by NIMH and FEMA guidelines, provides funds specifically for crisis counseling and training. The Disaster Research Center at the University of Delaware has been the major source of information about research activities in the United States and abroad. Major funding sources for disaster research programs are the NIMH and the National Science Foundation. The Natural Hazards Research and Applications Information Center in Boulder, Colorado, with funds from NIMH and FEMA, has small grant funds for pilot research projects and also serves as a clearinghouse for disaster research information.

FEMA provides federal funds to NIMH to support local disaster mental health programs. The state mental health authority is the official applicant for these disaster funds, and it processes and approves the requests for funding and reimbursement from any of its localities. A disaster-stricken county is required to prepare its own application, including a needs assessment and plans for implementation, and submit it to the state for approval and submission to NIMH. However, a local or state mental health authority may initiate services as part of the emergency response, even before the proposal supporting the need for these services has been submitted, with assurance of reimbursement from federal funds. Public mental health services for children and families initially are provided at such locations as disaster assistance centers, Red Cross shelters, and schools. These services frequently are supplemented by private sector activities in other locations.

The actual format for these services is determined by the local community and its mental health authority. When additional personnel are necessary to deliver these services, program managers can recruit staff from among local mental health professionals, as well as from other public mental health jurisdictions. NIMH and FEMA funds for services also include funds for training staff in disaster intervention skills. The provision of training has served to develop a cadre of skilled disaster mental health specialists in areas where there have been prior disasters. The public mental health system has its own disaster plan for mobilizing its staff, along with additional personnel from the private sector in the community if needed. Even if the agency already has implemented its disaster plan, it is required to carry out an assessment of current needs in order to determine how it can meet the needs of the community and to obtain supplemental funds for staff to carry out its disaster program.

In communities where a major disaster has not occurred in the recent past, training assistance is available from the state mental health department, as well as from NIMH. The local mental health authority arranges the training and may recruit disaster mental health experts, including those recommended by NIMH, to serve as faculty. State and federal agencies also send out technical advisers to local communities to assist in the preparation of a disaster proposal. The following case study illustrates the importance of providing timely consultation.

The Mount Saint Helens Eruption

The Mount Saint Helens disaster in the state of Washington was unique in that the stress was ongoing because of the unknown nature of the eruption and the continuing potential danger of the ash to both individuals and the agricultural economy. The Mount Saint Helens eruption raised a subsequent threat to the city of Longview, situated northwest of the volcano. Residents of this small lumber industry community in southwest Washington faced the danger that further volcanic activity would result in major flooding. The need for collaboration was crucial in light of concern about the potential danger of continuing eruptions and the effect of those eruptions and potential flooding on a nuclear power plant in the area. A request for consultation was submitted to NIMH to provide technical assistance to the local mental health system. The state's Department of Mental Health and Social Services was the recipient of NIMH funding for training and crisis counseling. Mental health administrators and representatives of emergency services in the region met with two consultants in Longview. The goal of the consultation was to provide advice about coordination of community resources, inasmuch as the local mental health system had not been integrated with the emergency response system.

Ritzville, a rural community in the eastern agricultural portion of the state also was damaged by the eruption. Like many other communities in the path of the prevailing westerly winds, Ritzville had experienced serious problems from the volcanic ashfall. Transportation to work and to school was affected by road closings and the malfunctioning of car, truck, and tractor engines because of the ashfall. Residents suffered from respiratory problems caused by the air pollution, especially very young and older people. Children had to be watched carefully because they tended to equate the ashfall with snowfall, and they had to be cautioned against playing in the "sand." The physical scientists could not reliably predict when the disaster would end, so parents remained anxious and children were unable to settle back into a normal routine. Children were fearful, experienced sleeping difficulties, and, because they were restricted from much of their outdoor play activities, presented increasing problems inside the home to already stressed parents. The schools were forced to revise children's play schedules because the playgrounds could not be used.

Consultation began with a debriefing of the participants, all of whom had experienced the disaster. Participants talked about the problems in delivering outreach services to residents who were reluctant to use their services.

Consultants proposed several outreach strategies to overcome this hurdle, such as recruiting indigenous volunteers and arranging school meetings for teachers and parents. The consultation gave the administrators a better sense of how to implement outreach services, particularly with the schools, and how to interact with the emergency services network.

Consultations with public and private mental health providers focused on the reactions to the stress of daily life in a community in which basic activities, such as employment, school programs, and farming, continued to be disrupted. Physical and emotional recovery efforts of the community were being impeded by repeated, albeit minor, eruptions of ashes. The consultants recommended group interventions as an effective way to reduce stress. In both communities, consultants recommended school-based interventions to assist teachers and children to cope with the disruption caused by the volcano. Consultants normalized the stress reactions observed in the disaster victims and pointed out that they were appropriate in the light of the continuing impact of the ashfall. They also recommended that each community be informed about further emotional reactions that might be expected and they emphasized the usefulness of group meetings in reducing stress by sharing common concerns.

Program Consultation

Since the mid-1970s, communities have been required by law to have a disaster plan that includes emergency mental health services. To assist the local authorities in developing their integrated disaster plans, NIMH has assigned mental health consultants to various states. When a community lacks adequate local mental health resources, state and federal personnel are available to assist it in designing an appropriate program. The following example of a consultation to a county mental health authority in Texas illustrates the spirit of cooperation that is necessary to bring about an integrated community disaster plan.

Cities and towns in southern Texas are prone to hurricanes and other violent semitropical storms. At the onset of the hurricane season, NIMH assigned teams of consultants to the mental health authority in Texas to help administrators formulate an emergency services plan for the numerous branches of its system. The consultants recommended a planning process to assess the mental health needs of disaster-prone communities by convening a series of focus groups in each region. The groups identified the vulnerable populations in their region, and discussed how mental health agencies could mobilize to meet the needs of these people should a disaster occur. The Red Cross also participated in these planning sessions by providing information about its services.

Two weeks after the consultation and training session was held, a severe tropical storm struck the Houston area, requiring the evacuation of some parts of the city. After the storm, several mental health department staff members, who had previously participated in Red Cross shelter management training, volunteered to manage the shelters designated by the Red Cross for older people or people with mental illness. The mental health personnel from the local centers also were able to work with the children in the schools. The training and the experience of the storm strengthened the ties between the local mental health system and the Red Cross. The training also served to bring representatives from United Way agencies into the community disaster response. Similar consultations were carried out throughout the state.

The Harris County Plan

A rash of teen suicides in suburban schools in the greater Houston area provided the impetus for Harris County, Texas, to develop a comprehensive community-based plan for crisis intervention. The breakout of suicides brought forth an outpouring of offers of help from mental health professionals. Community leaders felt that an even more comprehensive response needed to be developed. United Way was enlisted to spearhead a needs assessment and to identify community resources, including available trainers for a crisis counseling training program. United Way brought in a consultant and a planning committee was formed to coordinate the planning of future interventions among the local mental health agencies, school districts, universities, Red Cross, and community-based organizations. The resultant plan was a response system that involved multiagency cooperation during a community-scale crisis. The plan called for developing phone trees, resource lists, and training sessions to prepare individuals and organizations in the event of subsequent community crises, including disasters. The unique aspect of this program was that the initiative came from the nonprofit sector and was expanded to include public and private agencies in the community.

The Planning Process

The first step in constructing a community plan is to understand the structure and capability of the existing mental health system. Every mental health authority has its own distinct system. Some are regionalized and are operated directly by a county authority; others contract mental health services with private organizations, including local universities. The second step is to design a plan that will reflect the community's existing organizational structures and capabilities so that, in the event of a disaster, the central organization can mobilize its resources and dispatch its staff in a timely manner. The third step is to incorporate staff training that will include services for children and families, crisis counseling, debriefing, and outreach strategies. In the case of services for children, disaster consultants must be prepared to work closely with school districts and with staffs of the children's services at local health care and social service agencies.

The local mental health authority will likely need additional staff in the event of a major disaster, and will need to coordinate with local agencies and with mental health professionals in the community to recruit, screen, train, and provide supervision. The difficulties in implementing disaster mental health services most often lie in developing methods for adequate assignment of staff and in setting up accountability and responsible use of funds for contracted services. When an agency receiving the funds is inexperienced in providing disaster services, with their specific documentation requirements, the control and monitoring of funds often can to be a problem. Experience has shown that there needs to be some flexibility with the funding provided for disaster services in order to allow for unanticipated needs following an emergency, an eventuality that must be negotiated with the funding source.

The Los Angeles County Department of Mental Health Disaster Plan

The Los Angeles County Department of Mental Health (LACDMH) disaster plan follows a centralized agency-based planning model. The county government is organized regionally, with a strong centralized administrative unit. The mental health department plan calls for mobilization on a regional model. The regional administrators become the responsible agents in an emergency, and their disaster coordinators activate the disaster mental health response. In a major disaster, new personnel can be assigned to prepare the documents required by the federal government.

LACDMH only recently has emerged as a full participant in the countywide emergency services planning process. For the purposes of disaster response, LACDMH originally was incorporated into the overall authority of the Department of Health Services. In recent years, when mental health services came to be administered autonomously, there was significant concern in defining its role in the overall plan. The following reports show how Los Angeles County activated its disaster mental health plan in two mass emergencies. The first report illustrates the more limited role of LACDMH in the county disaster plan after the 1987 Whittier Narrows earthquake. The second report demonstrates how the county disaster plan, with fully incorporated mental health services, was activated after the 1994 Northridge earthquake.

The 1987 Whittier Narrows Earthquake. Following the Whittier Narrows earthquake, LACDMH activated its disaster response plan that included outreach services and school-based interventions. Mental health agencies offered drop-in services targeted to the non–English-speaking populations. The disaster strongly impacted the recent immigrants who had survived prior earthquakes in Central America. Many of the newcomers were reluctant to leave their apartments, but also feared that aftershocks would cause their homes to collapse. They slept in their cars and in public parks, rejecting offers of shelter provided by the Red Cross. A major hurdle in providing services arose because many of the people were undocumented immigrants and were fearful of being identified as illegal aliens and being deported if they sought help. This was a serious obstacle to service delivery, despite concerted efforts to develop community awareness of the availability of services and to encourage utilization. Some of the new immigrants did seek medical help for their children at the pediatric unit of the Los Angeles County–University of Southern California Medical Center, which provided an opportunity to offer concomitant mental health outreach services. Mental health education materials have been developed in many languages, including Mandarin, Cambodian, Vietnamese, and Spanish, following the Whittier Narrows earthquake and have been put to use in subsequent disasters.

Two of the LACDMH contract mental health agencies rapidly mobilized disaster services on behalf of their constituencies. Pacific Clinics, located in nearby Pasadena, sought out the afterschool language and cultural programs attended by Chinese and Japanese children and thereby were able to provide mental health information to Asian families. The Whittier Child Guidance Clinic also had well-established services for children and prior experience in providing disaster mental health services. Following the earthquake, it mobilized outreach teams and provided counseling in the schools, with consultation to teachers, and debriefing groups for parents. The clinic administrator assertively sought FEMA funding when it appeared that these funds were going to be allocated only to agencies outside the Whittier area.

The 1994 Northridge Earthquake. On January 17, 1994, at 4:31 a.m. a major earthquake measuring 6.8 on the Richter scale shook Los Angeles. The temblor, centered in the community of Northridge in the San Fernando Valley, was the largest and most violent to hit an urban area in the United States since the 1906 San Francisco earthquake. It left 25,000 people homeless, 1.2 million without electricity, 150,000 without water, and 40,000 without natural gas. The initial earthquake was followed by over 3,000 aftershocks. The Northridge earthquake, perhaps the nation's most destructive disaster, caused at least $20 billion in estimated damages. Communities hardest hit were located in the San Fernando and Santa Clarita Valleys, and in Santa Monica and West Los Angeles. Over 55,000 structures were deemed uninhabitable. There were 61 earthquake-related deaths, 18,480 people were treated for injuries at local hospitals, and 1,533 were admitted to hospitals for care.

Thousands of residents were evacuated and remained homeless for extended periods of time. Over 13,000 people were housed at 47 emergency shelters. Many survivors lived in their automobiles or camped outdoors in makeshift shelters and tents. Almost 2,000 people were housed in army tents at five San Fernando Valley parks. Two area hospitals were closed because of extensive structural damage, and 35 other medical facilities were damaged. Residents of nursing homes and convalescent homes and patients from damaged hospitals also needed to be evacuated and relocated.

After the earthquake, tens of thousands of low-income residents fled in panic as the walls of their homes collapsed. They sought refuge in local parks and open areas of the San Fernando Valley. Despite the fact that Red Cross shelters in local schools and recreation centers were made available almost immediately, many residents rejected the use of still-standing buildings because of their continuing fears of further collapses that were heightened by frequent aftershocks. Many of the victims in these temporary encampments were immigrants from Central American countries, such as El Salvador, Guatemala, and Nicaragua. Their prior experiences with earthquakes in their homelands, where buildings continued to collapse after an initial quake, were the basis for their rejection of offers of enclosed shelter. Instead, they set up pup tents or their own makeshift shelters of cloth and cardboard under the trees. They gathered with their families and neighbors to cook meals on the public grills of city parks.

Once they set up camp, these quake victims sought drinking water, which was in short supply because the municipal water district was not functioning. During the first 2 days, adults spent a considerable amount of time seeking basic necessities. They usually were able to obtain supplies in less severely affected neighborhoods. However, there were some reports of price-gouging by local merchants. Certain areas of the camp were designated as communal, where food, water, clothes, diapers, blankets, and medical supplies were distributed from Red Cross and Salvation Army trucks. By the end of the first week, many of the families had moved into canvas army tents set up by the National Guard. They were issued cots, blankets, and a Red Cross comfort kit containing personal items, such as toothpaste and shampoo. The tent cities served as disaster communities for residents waiting to return to their damaged homes and neighborhoods. In the words of a National Guard lieutenant assigned to one of the many encampments erected in the wake of the earthquake: "It's like a community campground you see along the freeway. . . . They don't need us here as policemen. These people are taking care of themselves. I've seen it happen before. When a crisis occurs, instead of causing problems, people pitch in and help. People do."

LACDMH and the Red Cross initiated mental health activities as soon as emergency services became available. Mental health services were mobilized rapidly, in part because there had been a major staff recruitment effort after the Altadena and Malibu fires 3 months prior to the earthquake. The initial efforts were focused on the many families whose children were seriously traumatized by the earthquake. The early interventions provided debriefing; advice and information; reassurance; and opportunities for catharsis, ventilation, and sharing of common experiences.

LACDMH allocated funds to its contract agencies for postearthquake counseling activities for children and families. One agency was the San Fernando Valley Child Guidance Clinic (SFVCGC), which had prior experience in providing disaster services when it initiated group interventions for families and children who were victims of the 1971 Sylmar earthquake (Howard & Gordon, 1972). At that time, no federal funds were available for counseling services after a disaster. For the 1994 earthquake, the clinic once again offered counseling to multifamily groups and individuals, this time with FEMA funding. According to Herbert Blaufarb, director of Treatment Services, SFVCGC began providing earthquake counseling in clinics at Northridge and Panorama City a week after the quake occurred. The clinic conducted groups for families in both English and Spanish. The groups consisted of 10 to 15 families who brought their children to the clinic. The focus of these groups was educational—teaching parents how to tend to children's psychological needs and how to cope with their earthquake fears.

SFVCGC staff also participated in outreach activities by providing counseling for both children and adults at the Red Cross shelters and disaster assistance centers. Some of the shelters were in neighborhood churches and some were in tents. Staff members offered advice and reassurance to parents, and provided consultation to Red Cross and FEMA personnel. The importance of having clinic staff at these locations was indicated by the apathy and depression observed among shelter residents in the week following the quake. During the day, when the women were caring for the children and the men were out seeking work, the shelters were relatively quiet.

As a result of the many, relatively-high intensity, aftershocks in the weeks following the quake, the anxiety level remained very high. Many of the residents who had moved into the shelters had no homes to go to or were reluctant to return to their damaged houses. They were fearful of returning to buildings that they perceived to be hazardous. The shelter population primarily was composed of Latino families with relatively low incomes and who recently had immigrated to this country. At first, the residents were hesitant to talk about problems other than those having to do with housing, food, and shelter. As they became more familiar with the counselors, they began to talk about their fears, separation issues, and sleeplessness in adults and children.

Blaufarb observed that the very young children were doing better than the school-age children. (Personal communication.) The preschool children were playful and active; in contrast, the school-age children were fearful and clinging to their parents, reflecting the adults' fears. He also found that preexisting marital and family conflicts were exacerbated by the disaster and that they worsened as the days passed. It thus frequently became necessary for counselors not only to assist the families in working through their earthquake-related stress, but also to help them address preexisting problems. The counselors helped mediate family disputes. One example was that of a family with three school-age children whose home was severely damaged, but still inhabitable. The father was fearful of returning to the residence, despite reassurances that the home was safe. The mother asked for help from the counselor in working out these conflicts because she was eager to return home with her children, but the children reflected the father's fears. The counselor helped the family resolve their differences through group discussions and to return to their home as a first step in restoring a sense of normalcy to their lives.

☐ The Crisis Response in Schools

Mental health services have been provided in schools for many years. In the past, when school-based consultations have been requested, it most often has been for a child with problems or because of acts of violence that have occurred on the school grounds. School systems generally have preferred to use their own personnel to provide crisis services for their students. While school administrators have encouraged community participation when a crisis has occurred, they have been uneasy about outside professionals "invading" the school grounds. Although administrators recognize the value of mental health interventions, they are more comfortable in utilizing their own trained crisis teams to provide the needed services. In part, this is both because of the administrator's concern with insurance and security aspects and because of the desire to provide "total services" to their staff and students. Most schools now consider crisis response services to be their own responsibility and have developed crisis plans as part of their crisis team development and training activities, including critical incident stress debriefing. Planning has focused on the roles of their various professionals, the circumstances under which outside crisis teams would be mobilized, the linkages to be made with local emergency personnel, and when involvement with other agencies in the community should be sought.

As a result, schools are no longer isolated from the services of the community at large. The incidence of shootings and other acts of violence has increased on school campuses. These events frequently require the intervention of school crisis teams on behalf of both the children and the teaching staff. Over the past several years, urban school districts, such as the Los Angeles Unified School District (LAUSD), have developed and trained their own crisis teams, comprised of school counselors, nurses, psychologists, teachers, and administrative personnel. An example of the effectiveness of LAUSD school crisis teams is the way in which they were mobilized following the 1994 Northridge earthquake. Crisis team members helped organize groups of parents and children in the weeks following the earthquake. These teams facilitated discussions in schools that were damaged but still could be used for meeting with parents and children. Crisis teams also conducted debriefing sessions for school administrators prior to the reopening of schools.

The Cerritos Plane Crash

School crisis teams are on call in the event of any school-based crisis, which may vary as widely as a school yard shooting, plane crash, or fire. Very often, children witness these disasters when they occur in residential areas. A collision of aircraft occurred in Cerritos, California, resulting in the planes falling into a residential area adjacent to a schoolyard. Crisis teams immediately were mobilized to intervene in this disaster where many children witnessed the horror of the event and the subsequent rescue operations. Crisis teams from the local university also immediately responded to this tragedy.

Aeromexico's commercial airliner was filled with passengers when it collided with a small private plane above Cerritos and crashed on the streets adjacent to a school playground. The crash occurred during school hours and was witnessed by the teachers and children who were in the schoolyard during a recess. Parents rushed to the school, fearing for the safety of their children. The children were in a heightened state of anxiety because of what they had witnessed. For many months afterward, they remained fearful when they heard airplanes overhead or sudden unexpected, loud noises. This was a major local news event and members of the press aggressively sought interviews with residents near the crash site and from school personnel. Since there were no survivors of the crash, the traumatic effect on the children and other witnesses, including the press, emergency services personnel, and the community at large, was overwhelming.

The local school district and the county mental health department dispatched crisis teams to the scene to assess the effect of the crash on the teachers and students. They met with school administrators to formulate a plan of action. Crisis team members held debriefings with teachers to assist them in ventilating their own reactions to the crash, and to assess their ability to cope with the experience and to return to the classrooms.

Those teachers who were too upset were excused from their duties the next day. Crisis teams and teachers who returned to school conducted class-room interventions to defuse the intensity of the emotional reactions of the children. Many children were absent from school during the days that followed because their parents still were fearful. School personnel initiated crisis groups for the parents to assist them in coping with their own fears, as well as those of their children. The local child guidance clinic offered addi-tional individual and group services to the children and families, within days of the crash. Mental health professionals in the community volunteered to provide crisis intervention specifically for the schoolchildren and their families.

Many families complained about the intrusiveness of representatives of the press, who aggressively sought interviews from the children who wit-nessed the crash. The press later apologized and explained that this height-ened degree of aggressiveness had been because their state of trauma af-fected their good judgment. Members of the press later initiated their own debriefing sessions as a result of their experiences in witnessing the grue-some scenes of the crash and their subsequent distress.

☐ The Role of Schools in Disaster Response

Schools are an essential part of the community's disaster response because they are used for shelters, disaster assistance centers, and as community meeting places. Since schools are essential to the functioning of the com-munity, municipalities make a conscious effort to restore them to their nor-mal activities. A school also operates as a smaller community that includes administrators, teachers, health care personnel, support staff, parents, and children (Pynoos, Goenjian, & Steinberg, 1995), so it is desirable to reestab-lish this functional community as soon as possible after a catastrophe. Hence, school districts have been required to develop an emergency plan that in-cludes activities in response to community-scale disasters and to more lo-calized occurrences, such as school yard shootings, construction accidents, and transportation accidents. School crisis teams play a significant role in major disaster planning efforts. Many schools now include debriefings and counseling services as part of their immediate disaster response plan. Teach-ers and administrative and nonteaching personnel also receive training in postdisaster counseling interventions to supplement the often limited men-tal health services. The planning process is ongoing and requires periodic review of the emergency plan, training sessions for school personnel, and updating of resources. For school districts that need technical assistance in designing their postdisaster psychological response system, assistance is available from NIMH, the Red Cross, and local professional associations. The

Psychological Trauma Center affiliated with Cedars-Sinai Medical Center in Los Angeles has developed a school-based group consultation program for use after a community-wide trauma (Eth, 1992).

Incidents of school violence have increased throughout the United States in recent years, often resulting in community-wide trauma with impacts similar to those following a natural disaster. The Centers for Disease Control and Prevention, the U.S. Departments of Education and Justice, and the National School Safety Center (NSSC) collaborated on the first nationwide investigation of violent deaths associated with schools (Kachur et al., 1996). The study identified common features of 105 school-related violent deaths (of which 85 were murders) of children, age 5 to 19 years, in communities of all sizes in 25 states during the 2-year period, July 1, 1992 through June 30, 1994. The results indicated that a majority of the deaths occurred in urban communities or were associated with secondary schools. Analysis of the data also revealed that 65% of school-associated violent deaths were students, 11% were teachers or other staff members, and 23% were community members who were killed on school property. Both victims and offenders tended to be young and male; firearms were responsible for a majority of the deaths.

From continuing surveillance of school-based violence, NSSC has reported that instances of multiple killings have increased from 2 instances in 1992 and 4 in 1993 to a total of 10 deaths in the 1995–1996 school year, and 19 in the 1997–1998 school year to date. Further, a nationwide survey by NSSC in 1996–1997 of the principals of 1,234 public schools (U.S. Department of Education, 1997) indicated that the most frequently reported problems were physical fights or attacks without a weapon (44%), followed by theft or larceny (27%), vandalism (23%), physical attack or a fight with weapons (3%), robbery (2%), and rape or sexual battery (1%).

A major criminal act in 1995 that directly affected children and their families has further enhanced understanding of community-based crisis response activities. Information is gradually appearing in preliminary published reports about the bombing on April 19, 1995, of the Murrah Federal Building in Oklahoma City. The catastrophe killed 167 persons and injured over 700. The Red Cross immediately established a compassion center that was staffed by over 1,800 volunteers, many of whom were licensed mental health professionals who provided crisis intervention and support for families and friends who were affected by the tragedy. The Oklahoma Department of Mental Health and Substance Abuse Services was designated as the agency to succeed the compassion center's short-term crisis services with a short- to medium-term mental health response where indicated, and Project Heartland was opened about a month after the bombing. Subcontracts were extended to community agencies to attend to specific populations, such as children and youth, ethnic minorities, persons with preexisting emotional disorders, and older people. In addition, all licensed mental health professionals in the area were invited to assist in providing clinical services. Clients thus were able to choose from among 400 clinicians who agreed to participate. Referral of clients to this latter resource occurred when it became evident that long-term, intensive services were necessary, such as for clients with suicidal or homicidal ideation, thought disorder, violent behavior, or substance abuse.

Inasmuch as criminal activity, gang membership, and alcohol or other drug use are widely regarded as precursors for violent injury and death among young people, the Centers for Disease Control and Prevention has recommended that the full involvement of the community is critical to developing a sense of ownership for the problem of school violence and its solutions. The most effective strategies include school-based curricula that emphasize the development of problem-solving skills, social skills, and anger management. The NSSC, affililated with Pepperdine University in Malibu, California, works with local school districts and communities to develop safe school training and program planning based on the premise that eliminating violence from children's lives can point to solutions for eliminating violence from schools. The NSSC advocates active participation in parent-teacher-student association (PTSA) meetings and other school events, the presence of responsible adults as volunteers working in and for schools, community-wide information sharing, and training in both monitoring and reporting of threats of violence to individual and groups.

Many of the recommendations for proactive community engagement in reducing school violence apply to predisaster planning. Community involvement in the school disaster plan and a school-community preparedness committee can encourage families to play an active role in emergency planning. This committee usually is made up of parents, administrators, and teachers who participate in predisaster planning activities and disseminate information about the school's preparedness plan to the wider school community. The committee also can develop a list of resources available in the community that would be useful for children identified as needing therapy and continuing care. Additional activities that could emerge from this form of planning are presentations about the school emergency plan at PTSA meetings and at school assemblies, as well as at annual disaster preparedness drills.

The 1994 Northridge Earthquake

The LAUSD disaster response after the 1994 Northridge earthquake can be regarded as a model intervention because of its timeliness and sensitivity. LAUSD, the nation's second largest school district, was severely impacted by the earthquake. All 800 campuses, with an enrollment of more than 100,000, were closed from January 17 through 24. Approximately 300 LAUSD schools suffered structural damage. An estimated 1,000 classrooms were lost to quake destruction and, upon returning to school 8 days later, thousands of children found themselves in makeshift classrooms, such as offices and auditoriums. Approximately, 400 portable classrooms were deployed, with only 200 in place by early February. About 44 teachers assigned to San Fernando Valley campuses themselves were left homeless and some faculty members exhibited emotional responses serious enough to warrant crisis counseling (California State Department of Mental Health, 1995).

School district administrators understood that the psychological impact of the disaster would affect school functioning and recognized that early intervention was necessary before returning to classroom routines after the earthquake. The LAUSD and other school districts in the quake zone began their interventions with critical incident stress debriefings within 3 weeks after the initial earthquake. These early debriefings were reported to be helpful in restoring schools to their usual routines. The FEMA-funded LACDMH Project Rebound, which originally was created after the civil disturbances in Los Angeles in 1992 and continued during the 1993 wildfires in the area hillsides and canyons, had trained a cadre of disaster mental health specialists who were available to provide interventions for school personnel. Because of those recent disasters, there also were school staff who had participated in Red Cross crisis training and also were trained in debriefing techniques.

The initial debriefing activities were targeted to administrators and key personnel to provide them with an opportunity to talk about their own experiences and to express their own reactions to the disaster. Robert Pynoos, a renowned disaster expert from the Neuropsychiatric Institute's Trauma Psychiatry Service at the University of California, Los Angeles, conducted training sessions for LAUSD staff, including small group sessions for teachers, counselors, and other school personnel. Each session included a psycho-educational component to discuss the stress response and the grief process as normal ways of coping with disaster. The goal of these debriefings was to assist school personnel in understanding and learning to cope with their own psychological reactions so that they could better understand the children's grief and fears. Many of the teachers were residents of the community and themselves were disaster victims. The interventions helped them work through their own reactions so that they could to return to the classroom and more effectively carry out their teaching roles. The debriefing also served as training so that they could provide this kind of debriefing and its emotional support to their own students and to other personnel in their school.

FEMA funds allocated to LACDMH were used to provide funds for services to school district personnel and to students and their families. The

LACDMH coordinator reported that the demand for services from the department was great, requiring over 300 trained clinicians to provide on-site services. Within a month after the initial quake, parents were reporting that their children were experiencing sleep disturbances. Bed-wetting was reported among some sixth-grade students. Mental health services were offered at the LAUSD regional mental health clinic in the San Fernando Valley. The clinic administrators also coordinated outreach services and, with FEMA funds, were able to hire additional mental health professionals to supplement district personnel. They were assigned to local schools to provide counseling and to conduct parent outreach groups. Students, teachers, staff, and administrators availed themselves of crisis counseling, and all the groups were well attended.

The LAUSD response is noteworthy for recognizing the mental health needs of teachers and their role in addressing the disaster-related problems of their students. The earthquake resulted in a great deal of news coverage that included many announcements regarding public services, psychological counseling, and specific advice about coping with the disaster. A classroom intervention where the teacher debriefed students during their first week back to school was shown on the local public television station. This program not only showed the procedure used in the debriefing, but also illustrated the school's awareness of the presence of children's emotional distress as a result of the earthquake and the value of providing this type of classroom intervention.

Some principals resisted mental health interventions because they wanted to get back to the school routines as quickly as possible. In many other schools, teachers enthusiastically used debriefing techniques on the first day back in the classroom. In one high school that had extensive structural damage, school reopening was delayed for 5 weeks after the earthquake and school counselors were on hand to provide debriefings to teachers prior to the reopening. The campus was bustling the morning of the first day back to school, with television news crews present to report on the arriving students. Mental health consultants were hired by the district to observe the proceedings. The students were assigned to temporary structures because many of their classrooms still were being repaired, and both counselors and teachers were on hand with maps to guide them to the makeshift facilities.

Teachers had been trained to conduct debriefings in their homerooms. However, in one observation of a classroom debriefing, the students were found to be reluctant to discuss their personal experiences. This classroom debriefing was felt to be seriously impeded by the presence of many outside observers. That same day, informal rap sessions took place in the teachers lounge for both teachers and students. This type of interaction in less formal settings was found to be a more productive way to help both teachers and students work through the crisis. The rap sessions were continued as long as the need and demand remained.

The Valley Community Clinic, a privately funded, nonprofit agency in the San Fernando Valley, received funding from Project Rebound and developed teams of therapists to provide crisis counseling in the San Fernando Valley public schools. Many team members were interns who were supervised by the school psychologists and licensed clinical social workers. Students were referred to therapy when acting-out behaviors interfered with classroom performance. Prior to the disaster, only a few of these therapists had any experience or training in disaster mental health, although all had been trained in crisis intervention techniques. One of the interns attended specialized training provided by the Red Cross and shared the information that she had obtained, as well as the materials distributed at the training. While the interns did not receive prior training in disaster mental health, the supervision enabled them to apply and adapt their skills to meet the needs of children who were traumatized. The intern therapists also led classroom discussions to address the fears and anxieties of the children. Because the schools to which they were assigned allowed as much contact as needed, it was possible to carry out in-depth therapies in some cases where symptoms of depression and post-traumatic stress disorder persisted. The schools were especially cooperative in providing space for these outside counseling services. Because of the limitations created by school hours and other demands on the interns' time, arrangements were made for these services to be provided at the clinic.

The pressure to meet the needs of the children in the immediate aftermath of the earthquake presented a challenge to these new therapists, and the support that they received from the Valley Community Clinic enabled them to put in long hours at the schools. Initially, the interns worked as volunteers but, when FEMA funds became available, it was possible to pay them for their services. After the grant had expired, all of the therapists continued their work at both the schools and the clinic where students were treated without cost. This program is an example of a successful collaboration between a public school system and a nonprofit community agency. This relationship has continued long after the earthquake.

One of the community clinic's disaster counselors worked in two elementary schools in the northeast San Fernando Valley with largely Latino student bodies whose homes had been hit hard by the quake. She reported that the teachers had suffered their own losses and panic, and were increasingly concerned and upset as the aftershocks continued. Some schoolchildren had lost their homes, some had been trapped or injured, and some had seen parents in stark terror or injured. The loss of cars, plumbing, heat, water, electricity, telephone service, and familiar roads took its toll. Many families were forced to move in with relatives in already overcrowded houses or apartments. The children suffered classic symptoms of traumatic stress: irritability, hypervigilance, sleep and eating disturbances, nightmares, flashbacks, and regression to infantile behaviors such as thumb sucking, nocturnal and diurnal enuresis, and baby talk. Almost all refused to sleep alone, so many were sleeping with one or both parents at 7, 8, 9, and even 10 years old.

Teachers at the elementary school reported that some students could not be controlled in the classroom. Fights broke out daily as aggression and oppositional behavior made lesson plans impossible to carry out. A "round 'em up and rope 'em in" policy was implemented, but it did little to bring order. Repeated aftershocks upset both the teachers and the children. Counseling revealed that, prior to the earthquake, many of the students with marked distress from the quake had suffered from battering, molestation, abandonment, and, because the area was gang turf, observation of violence and death. The following vignettes provided by the clinic therapists illustrate the types of complicated issues that emerged during case-finding (actual names have not been used).

- *Raoul*, age 8, invented an aunt—"his mother's sister"—who was coming to "take him to his mother," even though he had been abandoned when he was 5. Raoul's "aunt" had lost his phone number in the quake and he had lost hers; however, he waited and worried.
- *Kari*, age 8, carried a tiny doll about with her, cuddling and comforting it continually, and saying nothing at all about the fire that had destroyed her home the year before. She sometimes had become the sole caretaker of the children of three blended families living in the small, two-bedroom duplex apartment she called "the house."
- *Fernando*, age 8, went truant for no reason and his usually prompt, though not exceptional, homework decreased in quality and quantity. He refused to take work home, and left art projects at school saying, "Just throw it away." He had been alone the night of the quake, afraid and recalling the secrets that he and his father had shared about corpses, violence, and molestation. He picked fights every day.

Counseling for the children depended on consent for therapy and the cooperation of the parents. This was a problem because many parents had a cultural distrust of "outsiders meddling in family business." Many already had been given advice by friends, teachers, school counselors, and school psychologists. For the most part, the children proved eager to talk to the counselors. The concern of their schools, and the dependability and the compassionate interest of the therapists, enabled them to talk to the community clinic's disaster counselors about their experiences and helped them to harness their acting-out behavior. Reports from the clinic's counselors who performed school-based interviewing have indicated that, through drawings, journals, or stories, prior child abuse experiences were revealed among the so-called "earthquake groups." The following cases were reported by counselors providing school-based intervention after the Northridge earthquake.

Trauma and Concealment in a Latency-Age Boy. Marcus, a 9-year-old Latino, was referred to counseling by his teacher for what seemed to be earthquake-related anxiety. An excellent student, he had withdrawn and refused to participate in class discussions.

His therapist worked with him once a week for 4 months. Marcus's drawings in therapy revealed nothing unusual about his family—a young mother (age 26) who worked, a father (age 28) who tended gardens, and a large extended family of uncles and aunts from Mexico. However, his reticence to talk about the past or about himself, except to say that he wanted to have a "real home," convinced the therapist that there were problems about which he was not able to speak. Marcus had assumed a "macho" stance: unfeeling, uncaring, untouchable.

Five weeks after his treatment began, Marcus ran into therapy in tears, babbling nonstop about a dead little girl. When calmed, he described a school bus accident he had just witnessed in which a tiny girl darted in front of a school bus and was "killed, with blood and everything." Many students had seen this accident and mayhem reigned in the halls because the girl, who was still alive, was to be airlifted by helicopter from the playground to the hospital. Her mother's and aunt's hysterical cries were terrifying for everyone. In the middle of a group initiated to lessen the anxiety of the schoolchildren, Marcus, wailing, spoke up.

A few months before the quake his mother had delivered a baby girl at home. The baby died the same night. This sister was to have been "his" to care for and he had done much planning for the event. He bought toys, arranged a bed, and arranged a care schedule for his involvement. His mother's screams, the late hour, and the secrecy and confusion surrounding the emergency delivery had traumatized him. During the earthquake, he lay in bed with "her" toys, thinking he might die, too. But, he said nothing for fear of hurting his mother who had fallen into a postpartum and grief-fueled depression.

The therapist separated Marcus from the group and asked him to talk about those nights in more detail. He also remembered being forced to spend time with a 19-year-old uncle who had fondled him inappropriately when he was younger. This, too, he had kept from his parents.

A report was made by the school counselor to the Department of Children and Family Services and Marcus's father was encouraged by the therapist to separate Marcus from the uncle unless they could be supervised. It also was determined that the parents' secrecy and noninvolvement in Marcus' school life was due to fear of reporting the father's illegal status in the country.

Marcus became more active in the discussions with the therapist, and his rage and fear became apparent through his drawings and his identification with an "uncaring, unfeeling" father. His withdrawal had echoed his mother's depression and his own sadness at losing a sister who would have loved him unconditionally.

Although Marcus became attached to the therapist, his treatment was discontinued by his parents, who moved to another school district in fear of being identified as illegal immigrants.

Loss and Abuse in a Latency-Age Girl. Nora, a 9-year-old Latina, who lived with her foster mother, was referred to counseling by her teachers and the school psychologist. She had become "clingy, needy, and affection-starved" after the earthquake.

Her therapist, who saw her twice a week for 1 year after the quake noticed a sexualized response to affection in which she rubbed her body on objects of her affection. The therapist learned from the Department of Children and Family Services social worker that Nora had been molested by her mother's boyfriend 2 years previous to the quake.

In the course of therapy, Nora told about the evening of the quake. She had learned that same night that her foster mother was pregnant. Nora mistakenly believed that, if her foster mother gave birth, she would be assigned to another home, so she had wished for the death of this baby. When their house was severely damaged in the quake and the foster mother was injured as she attempted to flee the house with Nora, the child suffered guilt from the feeling she had somehow endangered her foster mother with the wish.

Nora also told the therapist that the "ex-boyfriend" was still seeing her mother in rehab, and that her mother had sworn her to secrecy about these visits, telling her that, if the social worker knew, Nora would never be able to see her mother again. Nora feared that one day she would have to accept this boyfriend, whom she still feared, as a part of her life.

In the course of play therapy and art therapy, the issues of abuse, invasion, drugs, distancing, and codependency emerged. Nora was supported in telling the social worker about the boyfriend's visits, and the boyfriend was given a court warning through the Department of Children and Family Services. Nora had never been able to talk about the symptom of her anxious rubbing of her body on objects of affection. The therapist coaxed her to talk about the feelings associated with the rubbing and the fears that underlay them. After a few months, Nora was better able to understand her injury and to tolerate the anxiety associated with her molestation. Her teachers reported that she seemed to be "less needy and more giving, receiving pleasure from helping the teachers rather than constantly seeking cuddling."

The previous cases illustrate that many deep-seated problems surfaced because of the additional trauma created by the disaster. The treatment by the therapists enabled these children and their families to address both the disaster-induced and the family relationship problems.

Consultee-Centered Case Consultation

Consultation with teachers and other school personnel after a crisis is used to relieve some of their own emotional distress so that they can better help their students. According to Caplan (1964, 1970), the mental health consultation model focuses on program development or administrative problems. It is a "consultee-centered case consultation" model; namely, one that focuses on cases or clients of the consultee. The objectives of the model are: (1) to improve the work effectiveness of the consultee, which subsequently helps clients' performance and psychological development; and (2) to enhance the understanding of the psychological issues involved in the case, and thereby alleviate the emotional blocks that may be interfering with such an objective understanding.

The preparatory stage of the consulting process involves obtaining information on the formal organization and the informal power distribution of the consultee system—the school district, the individual school, and the surrounding community—through materials published by that organization, newspaper accounts, informal contacts, and interviews with personnel. The consultant thereby develops an understanding of the structure of the consultee organization that may help to delineate system barriers to the process of change. The key issue during this stage is the examination of the history of one's own relationship with the consultee organization; that is, previous experience and preconceptions that may affect attitudinal issues as they emerge during the consultation.

The entry stage of the consulting process involves formally initiating contact with the consultee, accepting the existing relationships, and gaining the respect of the peers within the organization. The consultant must develop a sense of intimate familiarity through direct and participant observation of organized activities (Schein, 1969, 1987). The consultant begins to clarify her or his role and, at the same time, engages in reality testing of that system's defenses. The key issue during this stage is the avoidance of co-optation by the consultee as an ally during the internecine conflicts that characterize a system in crisis. The mental health professional is a "consultant without portfolio" who is part of the process of change, yet lies outside of the system because of her or his professional identification. The mode of consultation is equally paradoxical, because the consultant must initiate an "informal interaction process" (Ketterer, 1981) in order to bring about formal changes in the consultee's organization. This process involves: (1) planning for program effectiveness, (2) identifying the potential problems in the consultee, (3) developing common modes of understanding these problems, (4) focusing on the stresses on the consultee, (5) clarifying concepts of strain with the consultee, (6) recommending options and strategies, and (7) assisting the consultee in overcoming resistances and attitudinal blocks.

Each school develops its own unique programs based on availability of trained personnel, location, and school population. The mental health consultant needs to take those factors into consideration in helping the school to adapt its program to the needs produced by the disaster. A school-community consultation modeled on Caplan's crisis intervention and secondary prevention theories is that of the Children's School Outreach Project in Pitt County, North Carolina, where mental health professionals provided outreach, training, and follow-up services to several schools after tornadoes ripped through North Carolina and South Carolina, killing 44 people, injuring 800 people, and leaving 2,200 people temporarily homeless (Mega & McCammon, 1992).

A disaster also creates unusual management issues for administrators who may be struggling with their own and their family members' emotional distress, as well as that of their staff. Problems that might confront the administrators in a disaster include staff experiencing higher degrees of stress, absenteeism, possible alcoholism, and decreased ability to manage or control their classrooms. Some school administrators may be reluctant to introduce new or unusual programs and activities. Some administrators may react to the stress by making every effort to reestablish the old order as quickly as possible. Other administrators might see this as an opportunity to expand school activities and to develop new programs to be implemented and staffed by school mental health personnel. Generally, administrators will more readily collaborate with disaster mental health experts in the community if they have developed prior relationships.

For example, in a recent situation in which a teacher at a local high school had been threatened by a student with a knife, the vice principal contacted a therapist who was known to the school because of previous consultations when there had been violent incidents on the school grounds. The consultant met with the school administrators and teaching personnel who were upset by the attempted knifing. A conflict within the staff quickly emerged with respect to the circumstances of the attack on the teacher. The student who threatened the teacher was well liked, but the "victim teacher" was regarded by some as "too strict" and some felt that she had provoked the attack. The school principal feared that the consultation would serve only to escalate existing tensions by calling attention to the problems that surrounded the event. When it became clear that, before any further actions could be taken, it was necessary to alleviate the principal's concerns and hesitations, the consultant met privately with the principal. The consultant was then able to initiate procedures for problem solving aimed at preventing subsequent friction among the teachers.

Postdisaster Interventions

Teachers and other school personnel are essential in helping to restore a sense of normalcy for children who have experienced a disaster. In recent years, schools have become a focal point of postdisaster activities for youth. Counseling staff provide on-site services, case-finding, and group interventions for youth and their parents. School counselors who have received specialized training in debriefing techniques following a crisis also have the skills and training to perform case-finding and provide referrals for the more serious cases to appropriate mental health agencies for treatment. In order for schools to function as postdisaster resources, school counselors need to take a proactive approach during predisaster preparation and planning that should include such tasks as consulting with teachers and administrators, defusing potential hazards, mobilizing essential resources, fostering social support, providing accurate information, and developing referral procedures for more serious problems and for further treatment.

It is necessary to enlist community support for postdisaster activities. School districts in smaller communities generally have parental involvement on a day-by-day basis and, as a result, the schools are trusted by community residents. But, in larger districts, especially where the populace has a high proportion of ethnic minorities and mobility, counseling programs offered by the schools following a disaster often are met by widespread feelings of distrust. It is difficult to gain family involvement and approval for counseling and other interventions to ameliorate the trauma that children experience after a disaster. When the schools have not worked closely with community residents to gain their trust and support, it is even more difficult following a disaster. The more responsive the school system is to the everyday needs of the community, the more successful the intervention programs are likely to be in the wake of a major disaster. The following types of interventions have been found to be effective in schools after a disaster.

Crisis Lines

When a major disaster occurs, emergency response plans mandate school districts to keep the children in school until their parents can fetch them.

Schools establish crisis hotlines that provide parents with information about the location and the safety of their children. Hotlines also keep parents informed about the status of the disaster, which helps to control the rumors and misinformation that are common after a disaster. The crisis hotlines may continue for some time to provide information to parents in helping them cope with children's problems that surface later.

Case-Finding

When children return to the classroom after a disaster, teaching personnel may be the first to observe adverse reactions. Teachers need to be alert to what are considered to be problem reactions, like marked changes from the usual pattern of behaviors, hyperactivity, and withdrawal. These behavioral responses have been found to arise in direct proportion to the degree of direct exposure to horrendous sights; the amount of damage sustained to their dwellings; the amount of destruction witnessed; and the extent of injury to the child, family members, and friends (Pynoos et al., 1993). The teacher's awareness of the children's individual vulnerabilities contributes toward understanding the effects of the current disaster, as well as the children's prior experiences of trauma and loss. Teachers can be instructed in case-finding skills and debriefing techniques, since these are very helpful following a school-based disaster. They also need to become aware of the school's resources and to become familiar with the emergency plan.

Small Crisis Groups

Group intervention techniques have been found to be useful in helping children cope with other traumatic events, such as bereavement and campus shootings. Such groups often are initiated by a request from a school administrator who is responsive to the need that has arisen within the school and is aware of the available service. Small group counseling activities are best conducted in the classroom, although bereavement groups include only children who have been affected. The familiarity of the classroom setting provides children with a sense of security and trust that enables them to speak freely. The following case illustrates the use of crisis groups in schools.

The 1983 Santa Cruz Winter Storms

In 1983, heavy rains and major floods battered the city of Santa Cruz on California's central coast, causing the death of several children in a mud slide and much damage to the coastline and to property. The principal of a local school was concerned about the impact of these deaths on the classmates and sought services from the local mental health clinic. He discussed the situation with the consultant from the mental health clinic, who then met with teaching personnel. First, the teachers reported that the children seemed to be unable to concentrate and exhibited heightened emotionality, restlessness, and anxiety. Then, the teachers revealed their own grief reactions, and discussed some of their feelings of inadequacy in not being able to calm the children. The mental health consultant recommended that a bereavement counselor from the clinic participate in future meetings, and further suggested that after school bereavement crisis groups be organized for the children.

Since not all children had experienced a sense of loss, participation was voluntary but only with parental approval. Before the classroom intervention was initiated, a meeting took place between the teacher and the counselor to discuss the major purpose of these classroom groups; namely, to encourage the children to discuss their feelings and to enlist the classroom teacher's participation as a discussant or as coleader of the group. Group dynamics techniques included encouraging the expression of feelings, identifying shared reactions, exchanging experiences, and understanding coping responses. The teachers found the groups to be helpful not only in coping with their own feelings, but also in understanding their students' reactions. The classroom-based groups gave the children opportunities to talk about their feelings of loss and sadness, and to share with each other their experiences and their sense of mourning.

It also should be noted that, in this same community, a program of the local mental health department—Project COPE—had developed special training materials for teachers to be used in the classroom to help children to deal with the widespread loss and displacement caused by the floods.

Specialized Small Group Interventions

Specialized small group interventions are most useful when there is a concern for the emotional well-being of particularly vulnerable children (for example, those who have lost a loved one, have been displaced from their homes, or who have remained living in homes that have sustained substantial damage). The small group interventions are conducted in the school, and participants are drawn from many classrooms. Such an arrangement also has been found to serve well in handling grief reactions of students who have lost a friend by suicide or by accidental or violent death (Murphy et al., 1997). Again, obtaining parental approval usually is required for these programs. The groups also provide the opportunity for case-finding of children who may need further individual intensive counseling.

Even when not directly related to a natural disaster, a suicide by one of the students causes problems for the school and its teachers, administrators, and other students, especially close friends of the one who died. Fears arise over the possibility of contagion, as evidenced by clusters of "copycat suicides" that have occurred in New York, Virginia, Texas, Nebraska, New Jersey, and Arkansas. Programs have been developed by the department of education in some states, such as New Jersey (Underwood & Dunne-Maxim, 1997) and California (California State Department of Education, Instructional Support Services Division, 1987), with the objectives, among others, of providing models of appropriate response in the event of violent deaths, suggesting strategies to facilitate the grief process for faculty and students, and establishing procedures for identifying students who may be at risk after a suicide or homicide. The "work" of bereavement and mourning has been found to be greatly facilitated by survivor groups in which close friends and homeroom peers can share their feelings of grief and loss.

Schools should be encouraged to offer on-site parent groups. These groups focus on the skills that parents need to develop to cope with a child who experiences distress after a disaster. The problems that parents generally have reported in such groups are sleep disturbances, agitation, clinging, and other familiar signs of anxiety. The parents of vulnerable children could be requested to attend groups that focus on the special needs of their children.

Individual Crisis Counseling

The school psychologist at the school or at the school district's mental health clinic sometimes offers individual crisis counseling. This type of counseling usually is short term. Children requiring more extended services may be referred to local child mental health clinics or to private practitioners in the community. In all cases, the parents also need to become an integral part of the treatment and the referral process.

☐ Emergency Planning in the Workplace

When a disaster strikes on a weekday, office and factory personnel will be at their jobs, sales personnel will be in their shops, and building trade and technical services personnel will be scattered throughout the community. Depending on the time of day, schoolchildren will be in their classrooms, enroute to their schools or their homes, and many will be away from their homes in before and after school activities. The immediate concerns of working parents will be for the safety of their children. The children themselves will be frightened by the disaster and concerned for the safety of their families. Teachers will be concerned about their own families.

Although a disaster imposes a severe strain on everyone in the workplace, those employees with children require special consideration. In designing a successful emergency preparedness plan, it is important to recognize that employees will be concerned about the well-being of their families. Their distress, worry, and concern can be disruptive to the functioning of the workplace and can affect the success of the emergency plan. It therefore is important to have an emergency preparedness plan that takes into consideration the special issues of those employees with children or dependent adults in their families.

Employees should be urged beforehand to develop effective family preparedness programs. These programs are offered in many local communities to assist families and neighborhoods to develop their own preparedness plans. Families that are well informed have greater competency by knowing what to expect and what to do. In an increasing number of households, both parents work away from home, and there is an increase in single-parent families, which also results in the absence of a parent or other adult in the home. This means that there is daytime separation of parents from very young children who frequently are cared for in child care settings or in schools for an extended day. Public and private schools and other child care settings are being required to develop their own contingency plans, and to have emergency equipment and supplies for caring for their charges for at least 3 days in the event of a major disaster. Schools and day care centers also require that parents provide emergency phone numbers.

Emergency training programs at the workplace should encourage and instruct personnel in ways to prepare for earthquakes, including family contingency planning for alternative meeting places if parents are separated from their children and if there is damage to the home. Plans should be developed for obtaining information about the child's safety, forwarding information to the child about the parent's safety, and making arrangments with child care center staff and babysitters so that they know what to do in the event of a disaster.

Employers need to be alert to the dilemma of their employees who have a conflict between the responsibilities of job and family. Parents will be eager to be with their children, something that may not always be immediately possible. This concern will be greater when there are young children or family members who have disabilities. Needless to say, these employees will require reassurance and support.

When a major disaster occurs, however, there is likely to be a disruption in communications for a period of time when information about the extent of damage and the safety of family members is limited or unavailable. Employers and emergency planners must be aware that, because of the severe stress caused by the disaster, personnel will show signs of emotional distress that will be exacerbated by family issues.

It is desirable company policy to allow employees to leave work early after a moderately strong earthquake, a flood that is spreading, or a fierce storm. When a catastrophic event occurs, individuals often will behave in a desperate way to get to their children. In a recent training session, for example, a young mother said that she was prepared to start walking the 20 miles from her workplace to her home to get to her child if roads were damaged.

In the first days following a major community-scale disaster, individuals with family concerns may have difficulty leaving their home and children to return to the workplace. Increased family demands will include meeting the emotional needs that children frequently exhibit after a disaster. Depending on age, children can be expected to show many fears and anxieties; have difficulty in sleeping; be fearful that another event will happen; object to going to school; and regress to clinging, bed-wetting, or similar behaviors. These symptoms of stress may continue well into the recovery period, placing an additional strain on the working parent. Children may cry, have tantrums, or be reluctant to separate from their parents, making it difficult for the parent to leave for the workplace. After a disaster, there may be frequent phone calls to parents at the workplace from older children who are seeking reassurance, and children may become ill more frequently. The adults themselves may be exhausted from interrupted sleep because of their children's sleep disturbances and increased demands. The distress reactions of the children may result in the parent's absenteeism, lessened effectiveness, and loss of productivity on the job. Generally, however, the passage of time helps reestablish equilibrium and improved functioning for most families, without the need for outside help as they learn to cope with the stress.

Clinical intervention may be desirable to speed recovery and, in many instances, to prevent serious problems and disruption of work routines later. Intervention programs will vary, depending on the disaster, the local situation, and the special needs of the community. Many organizations have found it helpful for their employees to participate in group sessions that deal with the disaster and family issues. Essentially, these sessions would provide information and support, help reduce fears and anxieties, recommend coping skills, and help quickly return the workplace to a more efficient operation. The types of counsel offered in these sessions include how to provide reassurance to children, how to understand one's own fears and how these fears are communicated to children, how to listen to children's feelings and effectively reduce their anxiety, how to communicate information about the disaster and its aftermath to children, how to modify normal expectations of the child at home during the recovery period, and how to rehearse safety measures to be taken in future disasters. These sessions also can serve a case-finding purpose and can inform parents, who are having unusual difficulty with their children, about counseling programs that become available in the community.

☐ The Media and Disaster Mental Health

Gaining Media Attention

Public perception and media reporting of the emotional aspects of disaster have improved considerably over the past two decades. Until the early 1970s, it was rare to find the media reports about the emotional problems associated with disaster. After the 1971 Sylmar earthquake in the Los Angeles area, the mental health activities for earthquake victims developed by the SFVCGC were reported by local and national media because of their uniqueness. *Newsweek*, for example, devoted a full page to a report on this program. A manual for mental health professionals during a disaster was published by NIMH (Farberow & Gordon, 1981). The manual stressed the importance of providing information to and developing a collaborative working relationship with the media. A subsequent brochure further elaborated on techniques to be used in working with the media, including sample press releases. However, throughout most of the 1980s, there still was relatively little attention paid to the subject.

Only as the number of programs focusing on mental health problems proliferated, did the media became interested in these activities. For example, the 1994 Northridge earthquake saw a huge increase in the involvement of the local mental health community in postdisaster services. The local press and television were very interested in these activities, publishing daily reports of programs that were established and publicizing the variety of services being offered in the community. In addition, media reports obtained through interviews with mental health professionals provided mental health education to the community by describing the experiences of survivors and the help they received, as well as other symptoms that might yet be expected. However, it is important to be very clear about the information imparted. For instance, 2 months after the temblor, one story featured the prediction of possible suicidal behavior among children, based on reports of experience from Hurricane Andrew. Unfortunately, the report presented inaccurate information about the relationship of depressive feelings and suicidal behavior. Research has shown that depression is a major element in suicidal behavior and also is present in disaster, but it does not automatically follow that disaster victims who experience depression also will become suicidal. For example, a study after the 1989 Loma Prieta earthquake described a wide variety of reactions by children that indicated the presence of moderate levels of post-traumatic stress disorder, with its symptoms of anxiety, jumpiness, and nervousness. While many of the children also were described as being depressed, there were no reports of suicidal attempts or suicidal thought among the children.

Mental health professionals need to exercise caution in the information that they provide in interviews with the media, which always will be attracted to the more sensational information (Ruben, 1992). Mental health specialists need to make sure that the information they provide is accurate, concise, and will not be sensationalized. The objective of the professional should be to accurately inform the press and the public about on the nature of the possible symptoms, without unnecessarily creating alarm. The guidelines for interviews with the media emphasize the importance of providing information that is concrete, instructive, useful, and generally supportive. Providing press information requires skill, and school districts and public agencies often strive to assign experienced spokespersons to meeting with reporters from the print and electronic media. It is desirable, for example, to have one person from a school district assigned with the responsibility for media liaison. This also is a useful policy for other agencies, such as mental health clinics and mental health professional associations.

The Media Image of Disaster Mental Health

A series of disasters experienced by southern California residents (riots, fires, floods, and earthquakes) has brought into sharp focus both a dilemma and an opportunity for local mental health departments and the professional mental health community. FEMA has responded to the mental health needs of the victims of those disasters with grants for education, training, and services to the community. FEMA funds were provided to LACDMH based on the required needs assessment made after each event. In the 1992 civil unrest and the 1993 fires (California State Department of Mental Health, 1994), for example, the projected needs for service exceeded the actual demands for services on the system. The department attempted to increase the utilization of services by contracting out funds to community-based organizations, such as Senior Peer Counseling Services and Family Service of Los Angeles. Even after extensive outreach efforts, LACDMH did not spend all the money that was available. The local press became aware of the fiscal inconsistency and sharply questioned why the mental health department was unable to use the large sums of money that still were available. Local officials added their critical voice to the story. Elected officials publicly criticized the fiscal management of the mental health authority, since this agency continually was reporting shortfalls in funding for its many routine responsibilities. Apparently, the LACDMH response had been more than adequate to meet immediate emergency needs, but officials had overestimated what the utilization would be in the longer term. While the department planners had carefully projected the continuing need for long-term postdisaster problems, the public had not availed itself of the resources. Not only was there not enough publicity about availability of the services, but there was insufficient effort to educate the public about the longer term effects and demands that begin to surface many months after a disaster. As a result, there was a lag in the utilization of the services.

Two months following the 1994 Northridge earthquake, there was an extensive critique of the FEMA-funded mental health program in the local press. The article featured a well-intentioned program that, despite low utilization, had continued to operate long after the disaster had become a dim memory. The article was correct in pointing out that an earthquake is different from other disasters and that the numerous aftershocks create recurrent feelings of distress. Difficulties occur because of the time frame imposed by funding regulations, although these policies have recently been modified.

The local mental health authority should develop an ongoing cooperative relationship with the media. It is helpful to inform the community that there is a connection between the original disaster and later problems. Community education activities should be incorporated into the request for funding, with a specific portion of the budget allocated for an ongoing aggressive campaign to inform the public about both the probability of long-term emotional effects and the availability of counseling services. This obviously requires a good relationship between the local mental health authority and the media. Many mental health department administrators are just beginning to recognize the importance of working closely with the local media. The local press association, reporters, and editors often will provide advice on how to establish and facilitate this collaboration. In Los Angeles County, representatives of the media now participate in planning sessions of the Office of Emergency Services.

An essential part of this collaboration is to assist the media in carrying out its educational function, as well as its reportorial function. This will include providing advice and information on emotional danger signs indicative of longer term problems. The emphasis in this public communication campaign (Rice & Atkin, 1989; Rogers & Storey, 1987) should be on service availability, seeking help, and other forms of self-care. An important secondary aim of such information would be to reduce the stigma associated with seeking help for emotional problems and to establish the acceptability of the use of the services. In pursuing this collaboration, the mental health administrators will need to be especially sensitive to the response of the media and to make sure writers and editors understand that the main purpose is to improve the mental health of the community and not to publicize and aggrandize the agency itself.

After the 1992 civil unrest, one of the most violent outbreaks of urban disorder in recent history, LACDMH with funds through its FEMA-NIMH grant (Los Angeles County Department of Mental Health, 1993, 1995), contracted with a public relations firm to manage its public information and education programs. The firm developed a public communications campaign to increase awareness about free services. It also created educational materials, posters, brochures, and flyers in several languages for the Project Rebound Crisis Counseling Program after a string of disasters impacted the 9 million residents of Los Angeles County in less then 2 years (the April 29, 1992, fires and civil unrest; the October 1993 southern California firestorms; and the January 17, 1994, Northridge earthquake). The firm handled media relations, press releases, media alerts, public service announcements, public affairs program presentations, speakers bureau presentations, and media interviews. The firm organized a direct mail campaign, placed posters on buses, solicited free billboard advertising space, and distributed millions of pieces of print material, including children's art calendars and milk caps ("POGs") stamped with Project Rebound hotline numbers.

The mental health community and the local media share participation in emergency preparedness activities. One such joint activity is rumor control that may be done through the establishment of a specific information center in which mental health professionals would play an important role. During the Watts riots in the 1960s, Los Angeles city agencies established an outstanding rumor control division that included involvement of mental health professionals. This same operation has been reactivated in ensuing disasters. A key feature has been the development of information hotlines, which are publicized by the media. The central phone number provided to the community serves as the major source of information and rumor clarification. For example, residents of a disaster-stricken community recently called the number to learn about their proximity to the threat of a raging wildfire, and the possibility of a flood or mud slide in their area. This hotline also provides information about available services and their locations.

☐ Summary

Communities are mandated to prepare emergency plans to respond to large-scale disasters and, since 1974, to incorporate mental health services in these plans. Both federal and state assistance is provided to communities for the design of their emergency mental health plans. Written materials and consultants help to identify and assess needs and to advise on integration of mental health services with traditional community emergency services, such as law enforcement, fire departments, and transportation. Steps in constructing a community plan include a thorough understanding of the structure of the existing mental health system; procedures for efficient mobilization; an effective utilization of resources; and the provision for staff training, especially in services for children and families, crisis counseling, debriefing, and outreach strategies. The plan must include procedures for working with schools and existing children's services at local health care and social service agencies. Most schools have developed their own emergency plans to respond to both community-scale disasters and localized events. Schools serve as excellent resources for community needs in a disaster because generally they already have been a focus for involvement and have gained the trust and support of the local residents. Helpful procedures are identified as critical incident stress debriefings, defusings, crisis lines, small crisis groups, specialized small groups, and individual counseling.

Public perception and media reporting of the emotional aspects of disaster have improved considerably over the past two decades. However, only as the number of programs focusing on mental health problems proliferated, did the media became interested in these activities. The local mental health authority should develop an ongoing cooperative relationship with the media. The local press association, reporters, and editors often will provide advice on how to establish and facilitate this collaboration. An essential part of this collaboration is to assist the media in carrying out its educational, as well as its reportorial function. This will include providing advice and information on emotional danger signs that are indicative of longer term problems.

Caregiving after a Disaster

Children and their families confront a changed world after a disaster. The child's world becomes a mass of confusion, possibly filled with destruction and the loss of objects that have served as a primary source of stability. Often the child's first sight of this changed world is the presence of emergency services personnel engaged in rescue operations, digging out the rubble, barricading damaged areas, searching for injured and deceased victims, and locating and reuniting family members. The children also see police and firefighters carrying out immediate rescue and safety tasks, and utility personnel working at reestablishing services. The presence of these strangers is both frightening and reassuring. For days or weeks after a disaster, the family's world remains disorganized, with the disruption of normal daily routines such work and school and uncertain mail delivery, telecommunications, and television reception.

Children and adults suffer immediate and longer term psychological effects from residential dislocation. Families should be encouraged to restore the usual activities of everyday life whenever possible. Most families have the resilience to restore some normalizing activities. However, families that already were overstressed before the disaster, such as single-parent households, troubled families, and families with older people or members who are disabled are likely to have less resilience and to experience more difficulty in restoring normal routines. Those who are newcomers to the community may have additional problems in coping with the event because they do not have extensive support systems within the community. Such families are likely to require assistance from community social services organizations.

The early emotional effects of dislocation are often observed at Red Cross shelters, disaster assistance centers, motels where families are given temporary shelter, and trailer parks set up by the Federal Emergency Management Agency (FEMA). Interviews with families in these new settings often reveal the presence of emotional problems and can provide the opportunity for outreach and case-finding for referral after early intervention.

The loss of a home, possessions, and the familiarity of everyday life disrupts a person's psychological functioning, which leads to anxiety and depression. New routines that facilitate reconstruction are needed to replace the familiar ones interrupted by the disaster. People forced to relocate must find temporary housing, and they may spend countless hours seeking assistance at the one-stop disaster assistance center. The disaster assistance center generally requires individuals to register for each of the different services that they need. This may result in long waits at each of the desks, and people often become frustrated with the length of time it takes to process applications and to actually receive the needed assistance. Sometimes a local homeowners association will assist the community by serving as a clearinghouse for recovery information. Community meetings are scheduled at a school or church to help residents conduct their rebuilding efforts by applying for insurance and federal entitlements. In the first weeks after a disaster, these informational meetings often serve as support groups for survivors to voice their gripes and ventilate their anger and frustration.

It is at this time that children are most in need of support and reassurance that they and their loved ones are safe. Despite the disorganization of their normal world, most parents will attempt to meet their children's needs. Some parents find it difficult to concentrate on their children's needs when they are burdened with the injury or death of a family member, or when their residence has sustained major damage. Adults sometimes will try to minimize their children's feelings or even deny that the disruption of their children's world affects their emotional functioning. A couselor may need all his or her professional status to reinforce the idea that untoward events which happen to significant individuals, places, and routines predictably affect a child's sense of security and well-being.

☐ Caregiving in the Early Stages of a Disaster

The Critical Event and the Aftermath

In the aftermath of a major disaster, the sights that are witnessed will be distressing, unusual, and likely will leave a lasting imprint on a person's memory. There will be damaged residential and commercial buildings in the more developed areas. In the countryside, particularly after a tornado, carcasses of livestock may be seen scattered in the fields, and farm buildings and machinery may be damaged and deposited in odd places. A variety of confused behaviors will be observed. Many people will be seeking information about friends or neighbors who may have been injured. Teenagers may seek information about their peers.

The circumstances that accompany a disaster are unfamiliar to most mental health professionals, and include witnessing death, injuries, widespread damage to property, disruption of transportation and communication systems, and sometimes even looting and violence. There is likely to be disruption of family units, with many distraught parents and children who are looking for each other and who need help. Children and parents may be separated because the child has been at school or the parent has been at work. There will be many frightened children and families who are experiencing difficulties in helping their children cope with their fears. Sometimes those who are providing services to the children and their families also will be attempting to cope with their own reactions.

Because the incidence of death in most recent disasters in the United States has been low, disaster mental health specialists have had relatively little experience with providing bereavement counseling in mass emergencies. When there are widespread injuries, extra medical care will be provided in hospitals and clinics throughout the community. There will be many people experiencing emotional distress because their loved ones have been physically injured or because they are searching for missing family members. Search and rescue teams still may be engaged in locating injured and missing persons. In a transportation accident, particularly those involving children, the process of locating survivors is stressful both for family members and emergency personnel.

Family members will be actively searching for their children and expectably will be distraught until they locate them. There may be physical damage to schools, child care facilities, and recreational centers. Telecommunications may be interrupted, and people may feel desperate because they have lost phone contact with family members. Unless a family has access to a battery-operated radio or car radio, they also may have lost access to news reports. Family members will make great demands on emergency personnel to help them locate their children. During this period, the primary concern is for the safety of family members, and for food and shelter. Those whose homes were damaged or destroyed will be busy taking steps to arrange for shelter and to restore order, and to retrieve as much of their personal possessions as they can. Others will be guarding what they still have from possible vandals, and may become aggressively possessive.

Coordination of Efforts

Large-scale disasters require coordination among every portion and every level of governmental and community functioning (Pynoos, Goenjian, & Steinberg, 1995). This includes planning for intervention and implementation by executive agencies at the national (FEMA and the National Institute of Mental Health [NIMH]), state, county, and city levels, and by municipal service agencies (such as transportation, utility, education, health care, and mental health). Predisaster planning is necessary to establish priorities, allocate responsibilities, and resolve turf issues.

Local officials will meet as soon after a disaster as possible. Federal officials from FEMA will meet with the state emergency services administrators and with key emergency services representatives to determine the status of a disaster, report on the extent of damage, and coordinate resources. Representatives of the local mental health authority also will attend these briefings, with the responsibility for assessing and coordinating mental health disaster services. Each agency is required to interface with the Red Cross and other organizations that comprise the emergency services network. These key agency representatives will provide information on the extent of damage to public utilities, roads, hospitals, schools, and other community facilities, and injuries to residents of the community at large. Each agency, including the mental health authority, also will report on the status of its own facilities and personnel.

To be effective after a disaster, local mental health authorities will have to become oriented to the needs of the community and the helping efforts being planned by the emergency services system. Those who are specialists in working with children and families should establish linkages with the local school district. Schools are the primary resource for helping children following a disaster, and they have their own disaster plans and crisis teams. Local comunity-based agencies, such as the United Way agencies and other organizations that provide counseling services, should coordinate with the local public mental health authority and school districts. This coordination can occur most effectively when the agencies are proactive and have participated in predisaster planning and training.

Delivery of Crisis Services

Mental health professionals will need to have access to Red Cross shelters, disaster assistance centers, and other community counseling agencies in order to offer crisis services. These emergency centers and shelters have limited access strictly to those staff who have been officially designated as "disaster workers." These professionals will have received identification badges if they have been so designated by their agencies or the Red Cross prior to a disaster. Referrals for counseling are made by representatives at the disaster assistance centers, by Red Cross shelter staff, and by other emergency services personnel. Individuals seeking services for themselves and their children come to these settings for help. These services usually are offered on a drop-in basis and at no cost to the recipient. In some instances, the local mental health authority will develop contractual agreements with local agencies to provide these counseling services. The local mental health authority will require documentation of these services in order for the agencies to receive reimbursement from federal funds and in order to provide information for possible follow-up care. In the confusion and accompanying pressure following a disaster, documentation of services frequently is overlooked. Required documentation is usually limited to demographic information, not clinical case records.

The mental health professional's primary task in the early postdisaster period is to assist families in coping with the most pressing personal aspects of the disaster, which may include locating immediate family members, identifying a deceased relative, or calming distraught children. Mental health professionals may need to assist with the application process at the disaster assistance center when people who are referred for assistance are confused, distressed, and unable to cope with the application process. Parents sometimes will seek assistance for a child who is in distress and who is behaving in an unusual manner. Play activities for children frequently are offered in these settings in order to help relieve parents who are pursuing the application process through its several steps.

Those seeking help also may be people who have suffered the death of a family member, a close friend, or a neighbor. Bereavement counseling that offers the survivors opportunities for comfort, support, and advice frequently is provided at hospitals, offices, and clinics, as well as at the morgue or the coroner's office and at mortuaries. In most, if not all, disasters where families and children suffer loss, the treatment offered will be short-term crisis intervention. In some instances, the crisis therapy may reveal the need for more extensive child therapy. Clinicians should apply the principles of crisis intervention, with a clear focus on bereavement and loss. Many families either are unfamiliar with or object to "psychological" intervention, and may not understand how such intervention will help them and their children. Therapists need to encourage the parents' cooperation. When it appears that a family is numbed by the experience and in need of psychological assistance, the shelter staff might help avoid some of the initial reluctance by introducing the therapist as "a person who is experienced in helping families."

The therapist listens to family members' narratives of their situations, and learns how the family is functioning, the strength of its resources, and whether it will require follow-up counseling. Some families may refuse the offer of follow-up interventions because of their strong objection to any association with mental health. They may believe that they should handle such matters themselves or, at most with the assistance of the clergy, which should be provided if at all possible. Faith organizations have been actively involved in disaster relief activities, providing pastoral counseling after many events (Larson et al., 1988; Malony, 1992; Pargament et al., 1990; Propst, Ostrom, Watkins, Dean, & Mashburn, 1992). Refusal to accept help also may be rooted in a strong independent approach to problems in which the solution always was done within the family by family members themselves. To these families, a referral implies that the family cannot manage on its own and may need some outside help with emotional problems, a suggestion the family members indignantly reject.

Therapists working with families in a disaster may feel at a loss in breaking through these barriers. Although therapists cannot insist that family members recognize the problem and accept the available help, they can provide information about services for the future. The therapist might find it helpful to seek consultation from peers to see whether they have any suggestions for further interactions with a family that declines clearly needed help. The clinician also might find it useful to seek consultation for his or her own feelings of frustration that may result from refusals of the offer of help.

☐ The Debriefing Process and Critical Incident Stress

Debriefing is a process that initially was developed for use with emergency services and rescue personnel. The format is to bring together individuals with shared experiences to talk about their personal reactions and to derive mutual support from this process. The leader of these groups frequently is a mental health professional who has been through specialized training. Debriefing methodology has been modified and applied to other professional and occupational groups (Mitchell & Everly, 1995).

The standard debriefing format includes: a review of the event; a description of each person's perception of the event; and a discussion of what each person's experience of the disaster entailed, including where each was when the disaster occurred, and what their role was during and after the disaster, the disaster's impact on their functioning, how they came to function as helpers, their experiences of the disaster as a mental health professional, and what each was doing in relation to children.

Debriefing of mental health personnel has two objectives. One is to assist them in sharing their own experiences and feelings, as with any other emergency services personnel. The second is learning what other mental health professionals may have developed as useful techniques in working with disaster victims. Mental health professionals may choose to participate in sessions with other professionals, or to attend debriefings specifically for their profession. When they attend cross-disciplinary debriefings, such as those with physicians, nurses, and teachers, they will have the opportunity of learning what other professionals experience and how they cope. With their own peers, they will have more of an opportunity to share their experiences and exchange information and techniques that others have found useful. Like many others affected by the stress of disaster work, they may be reluctant to discuss their experiences at the outset, and initially may be inhibited in admitting their own emotional distress. There may be a fear that this will reflect on their own professional competence before their peers. For the mental health professional who is inexperienced in working with children who are highly distressed, the impact of the debriefing experience may be unexpected and even embarrassing, especially when colleagues may share procedures and techniques of handling stressful situations with which they are unfamiliar.

The success of any debriefing depends on the skill of the facilitator in developing and promoting an atmosphere of trust within the group. Many professionals in the community have received debriefing training. The initial debriefings ideally will be conducted by such individuals. These trained facilitators can become available to other professionals involved in the emergency response. Leaders for debriefings can be found through the local mental health authority, mental health professional association, and the Red Cross.

Stress on Mental Health Professionals

In a major disaster, many children may be severely traumatized by the event, as well as being physically injured. Because such sights are not a routine experience, mental health professionals themselves may become emotionally distressed when they observe the injured and traumatized children. In residential settings where mental health professionals are more accustomed to the unpredictable demands of a child who is emotionally disturbed, a disaster will intensify the disturbed behavior and increase the demands that the child makes on them. When the facility itself is damaged or destroyed, children may need to be relocated, an event which itself is stressful, further heightening the difficulties of the caregiver.

In outpatient clinics, clients may not keep their regular appointments. When contact with their regular clients is impossible because of the communication disruptions, clinic staff may feel burdened both by concern about what has happened to their regular clients and by the stress of initiating treatment for a new group of clients. Many families will seek services for their children from pediatricians and other health care providers. In their attempts to alleviate the symptoms of distress, pediatricians may fall back on prescribing medication without also exploring the emotional aspects. Parents have to be informed that physical symptoms often are emotionally based and may be directly related to their child's experience of the disaster.

Mental health professionals working in a disaster will find themselves engaged in tasks that differ markedly from their everyday routines. A major source of stress on the clinicians results from conflicting and unfamiliar roles required by the overwhelming event. Those who normally work with patients in a calm, quiet, office environment are likely to find their disaster activities occurring in physically uncomfortable situations that are unstructured, chaotic, and disorganized, and in physical locations that are lacking privacy. For example, following Hurricane Andrew, mental health services were offered in shelters and tent city settings in south Florida. Therapists found themselves feeling only minimally informed and somewhat isolated. They lacked any background information about the children and their families, which routinely is provided by the usual referring sources, such as schools, social agencies, clinics, and medical sources. Under ordinary circumstances, they would have had a wealth of information and resources available to them before they began treating the children. But, in disasters, background information may not be available. In addition, information about support and other services that still are functioning may be lacking.

In addition to working without the support system ordinarily available to them, school counselors may also be called on to perform tasks outside of their realm of general expertise or experience. For example, they might find themselves asked to treat children who are severely emotionally traumatized, whereas normally they would be involved only with children with school- and family-related problems. Along with depression, one of the most frequent emotional syndromes resulting from a disaster will be post-traumatic stress disorder (Pynoos et al., 1993). This syndrome may present clinical symptoms with which a school counselor has little experience. Clinicians who customarily treat adults may be requested by community agencies to also offer services to children, which may arouse feelings of unease and uncertainty. Disaster programs, particularly federally funded ones, frequently will emphasize psychoeducational activities that clinicians are asked to perform. This may be especially stressful to the clinician who has limited experience in planning and implementing such programs. Also, the emergency system in a disaster generally considers mental health interventions as having a less important role than other services. This attitude may be offensive and irritating to a clinician and injure his or her self-esteem.

The demands of a disaster frequently inspire altruistic behavior that may prevent clinicians from recognizing their own physical limits and the fatigue incurred by these circumstances. Mental health professionals who have been working long hours under difficult circumstances also may benefit from debriefing and other psychosocial support activities. For example, Project Return in Los Angeles provided support services to its staff through stress reduction groups and job transition workshops in anticipation of the end of their assignments.

Stress on Teachers and Other School Personnel

Teachers and school personnel frequently find themselves in the roles of both victims and caregivers. Teachers may be required to keep children in school until their parents are able to come for them, which in some widespread disasters, may involve caring for children for several days. In addition, teachers may be separated from their own families for a number of days, and may be faced with the dual task of handling their own feelings resulting from the traumatic event along with the distress of their wards. Following the disaster, when children return to school, the children may have difficulty concentrating, and may express their fears and anxieties both through distressed behaviors and physical symptoms. To address the children's distressed behavior, teachers often will avail themselves of interventions provided by the school's nursing and mental health staff members, such as in-classroom crisis groups. Teachers often are determined to get on with business as usual and may be uncomfortable with encouraging children to talk about their disaster experiences and related feelings, even when consultants advise them that this is helpful. Teachers might not know how to respond to the emotional distress that could surface.

Because teachers might become overburdened by these increased demands, psychological debriefing should occur as soon as possible. Debriefings are valuable in a number of ways. They provide the opportunity for teachers to share their own disaster experiences with their peers and to hear from others about what is occurring in the classrooms as the children return to school. Teachers will have the opportunity to discuss their experiences, the problems that they faced, the complications that resulted, and the emotional impact of the disaster both on their personal lives and on the classroom. The debriefings will help teachers get through this stressful period by providing them with an opportunity for catharsis, mutual support, and coping skills. The sharing of these experiences is therapeutic and will help them move on to their primary educational task.

Teachers may find themselves pressured by the variety of demands on them. They may resent the caregiving role when they feel it interferes with their primary educational task because it requires them to perform an additional task in which they do not feel secure. They may object to attending debriefing groups, which may be viewed as an extraneous demand. Because of these objections, it is recommended that debriefings be conducted during work hours and that they be made mandatory. Participants in these groups are likely to express anger over this additional demand that is being made on them. A trained facilitator can constructively use this expression of anger by acknowledging its justification and by helping teachers to recognize that, at least in part, it is the result of their feelings of being overburdened.

Following a disaster, the usual issues that surface in a debriefing with teachers is their wish for things to return to normal, their frustration with increased demands on them, and their feelings of inadequacy in coping with children who are distressed. Teachers in disaster-impacted areas may comment on their personal frustrations in relation to rebuilding their own lives, and literally having to rebuild or repair their own homes. Sharing these feelings in the debriefing, and learning that others are experiencing similar feelings of frustration, can be cathartic and can help to relieve some of their own distress. There are topics, especially problems with classroom management, that many teachers find difficult to share with their peers. Managing a classroom is even more difficult following a disaster. Some teachers may feel that having such a problem implies inadequacy as a teacher and may be uncomfortable discussing such problems in a group. The debriefer can help by introducing the question and encouraging discussion within the group.

Some teachers may resist receiving mental health information, fearing that they are being asked to assume the responsibility for handling children's emotional difficulties. It is reassuring to teachers to be informed that many mental health resources are available in their school or in the community to support them in handling such problems. Teachers also appreciate recommendations about the variety of educational interventions that they can use in the classroom, such as games, drawing, and other expressive activities. They also will see that some of the techniques used in the debriefing can be easily transferred to the classroom. It is important that the debriefers acknowledge and support the key role of the teacher as an educator, and not as a primary caregiver.

Although teachers are experienced in dealing with children, they may not have experience in dealing with children who have been traumatized by a disaster. In order to involve teachers during these debriefing sessions, the facilitator will need to offer concrete advice and specific information that can be applied in the classroom setting. One of the tasks of these sessions is to help teachers recognize that distressed behaviors they are seeing in the classroom are a result of the children's disaster-related experiences and not the result of their own classroom skills. By helping teachers understand the normality of these behaviors, they also will learn that, for most children, these behaviors are transitory. During a debriefing, teachers often will complain that the children seem driven to constantly retell their disaster experiences.

Simply learning that this is both a normal and a helpful reaction of children to severe trauma is useful toward understanding the behavior. Teachers also can help younger students to discharge their disaster-related fears and anxieties through the use of expressive techniques, such as play activities and drawings. They can conduct brief group discussions with older students so that they can express their feelings. The older children can benefit from journal writing, which they can share in the classroom. Teachers frequently express a dilemma of deciding when to begin the regular classroom routine. The support that they receive from their peers in the debriefing will be especially helpful in resolving this question.

After a debriefing, some teachers may feel uncomfortable with what they have disclosed, and may need additional support from the facilitator. It is important in the debriefing period to have available additional counseling resources for teachers and their families, such as individual counseling or referrals. Large-scale debriefings normally are a one-time service, so it often is advantageous for a school to provide ongoing smaller groups on a voluntary basis, particularly in the aftermath of a major disaster when they are more likely to be needed. The small groups can be psychoeducational, dealing with both classroom and personal concerns. These groups are generally conducted by a school psychologist or other mental health professional, and are time-limited with termination by mutual agreement.

Stress on Emergency Services Personnel

This section is included in order to better understand the kinds of pressures and stresses experienced by this special, highly focused, group in the community: the emergency services personnel who are among the first people to come in contact with children after a disaster. Their ability to handle the stresses of a disaster may have special significance in the rescue and safety of children. Emergency services personnel, such as law enforcement officials, firefighters, emergency medical personnel, and utility personnel face critical situations on a daily basis (Mitchell, 1985). Emergency work is both challenging and rewarding, offering the individual a sense of personal accomplishment and competence. Those who serve in these roles possess a sense of dedication, altruism, and courage and a public service orientation. Their jobs frequently require split-second decision making, and a commitment to the safety and well-being of others.

During a disaster, particularly one involving a larger community, there is a great potential for stress reactions in the frontline personnel. Their work organizations have certain expectations regarding their behavior in emergency situations. During a major disaster, their working conditions are erratic, and may include lack of lodging and support services, abrupt changes in procedure, and even exposure to widespread injury and death. The personal characteristics that lead to career choice and success in these occupations may prevent emergency personnel from recognizing and acknowledging the internalized effects of stress engendered by their work. They often will maintain a facade of self-control, and suppress anxieties and fears during emergency operations in order to concentrate on the tasks at hand. Keeping personal feelings under control usually is necessary for effective job performance. Furthermore, they often are reluctant to discuss their personal experiences with others.

Those attracted to emergency services are reported, as a group, to be more emotionally stable than the general population, and to be less likely to break down under intense pressure. However, they are subject to an increased incidence of stress-related ailments, including cardiovascular and gastrointestinal symptoms, migraine headaches, and neuromuscular pains. Mental health professionals only recently have been enlisted to serve the needs of emergency services workers. Many emergency services departments have their own psychological services for their personnel. Local fire departments, for example, have volunteer peer counseling available. Law enforcement agencies have a staff of mental health professionals to serve their employees.

Involving, as it does, the responsibility for the well-being or the lives of others, emergency services work is a source of stress. There is considerable agreement that the stresses of this work derive from two sources. The first is job related, originating from physically hazardous conditions and other extraordinary work demands. The second source of stress is somewhat more personal and oftentimes is exacerbated by family relationships. Job stress that affects a person's physical and emotional well-being reciprocally affects family relationships. The stress of caring produces feelings of anger, embarrassment, anxiety, frustration, fear, and despair. Among the behaviors observed in emergency personnel under stress are withdrawal, distancing, and decreased sensitivity to others. They may be even more reluctant to share their work-related experiences and feelings with friends and family members than are nonemergency personnel.

Emergencies in which children are the primary victims, and where rescue personnel are directly involved, bring about a special kind of response. There are heightened feelings of grief, helplessness, and frustration. Relief personnel have reported intense feelings of identification with the child victims and their families, sometimes visualizing their own children and families in the same situation. If relief personnel are from the same area that has been impacted, they will have valid fears for the members of their own families. Sometimes, emergency personnel are overcome by the horror of handling burned or charred remains or dismembered parts of the bodies of children. In the rescue efforts of some disasters, especially plane crashes, there may be no survivors, so that rescue personnel are forced to deal with only the dead, who sometimes are horribly dismembered. The feelings of frustration are heightened by the fact that there are no survivors to rescue or save.

The debriefing procedure for emergency personnel optimally should be held within the first week of a critical event. All line personnel should have the opportunity to participate. The organization can help personnel and their families by setting up an early meeting to provide them with information on the status of the event and the potential emotional effects on the emergency personnel. It should be emphasized that a debriefing is not a critique of the way that an emergency situation was managed. Rather, it serves as an opportunity for all employees to deal with the emotional aspects of the experience. For example, a debriefing session may bring together personnel from different organizations that have been involved in an event. A session that includes the participation of law enforcement officials, firefighters, and paramedics, reinforces both effective teamwork and shared goals during a critical incident. Many emergency services departments have begun to make a debriefing mandatory after a critical incident. Thereby, the debriefing becomes regarded as a natural, routine procedure, avoiding the possibility that personnel would not attend due to fears of being stigmatized.

Stress on Medical Personnel

Medical personnel experience high levels of stress in the normal performance of their jobs. The routine stressors in medical settings derive from the literal responsibility for the patient's health and well-being, chronic time urgency, and the necessity of working closely with a large number of different people. The kinds of stresses that develop in medical settings during a disaster result from working with victims who have sustained physical trauma and accompanying psychological trauma.

A disaster impacts the medical setting by requiring immediate action and by overloading the demand on existing personnel, supplies, and equipment. The health care facility must deal with markedly greater numbers of victims during an emergency event. An incident with only a few victims can be handled by the existing medical system. A multiple casualty incident, with many victims, requires a coordinated communication system to manage casualty distribution. A mass casualty incident, which may have generated hundreds or thousands of victims, requires the coordination of all local resources, those of neighboring communities, and potentially state and federal assistance as well.

Medical emergency personnel are subject to a variety of stressors arising out of the disaster itself, as well as from various aspects of the job, from uncertainties in the person's role, or from conflicts at the workplace. These stresses include the experience of witnessing the loss of lives and injuries that accompanies a mass casualty incident. Medical personnel who are responsible for life-and-death decisions, for example, in triage situations, are considered to be highly vulnerable to traumatic stress reactions. They have high motivation to perform their jobs competently and successfully. When the high expectation of saving lives cannot be met, they may experience feelings of disappointment and a sense of personal failure, even when there is no rational basis for the belief.

An additional major source of difficulty for medical personnel is that the nature of the work may require highly stressful environments, with their attendant physical and emotional discomforts. When a disaster is widespread, emergency medical personnel at area hospitals are called on to work long, difficult, hours without relief, resulting in physical exhaustion. A mass casualty incident may cause changes in work routines for an extended time period and, although medical personnel are accustomed to irregular shifts, excessive work hours can become seriously draining during a disaster. Hospital personnel are familiar with work overload, but they may be burdened with increased responsibilities during a disaster. Supervisory personnel, in particular, may be temporarily overwhelmed by the multiple tasks that seem to require simultaneous attention.

During a massive disaster, medical personnel may spend hours cut off from their usual sources of support. The organizational setting and its problems affect them to a greater extent than during ordinary times. Issues, such as organizational conflict and change, become pertinent because both standard procedures and the ability to adapt to unusual circumstances are critical. During a disaster, medical personnel from other settings are mobilized. Conflict may occur when people or organizations work together for the first time. Each emergency unit has its own style of work, and conflicts may result when organizations cannot absorb new personnel or adjust rapidly to differing operational styles. The regular medical staff also may be recruited to assist emergency personnel. Medical personnel may be asked to work outside of their specialties, often for the first time since their internship. The demand, then, is both physically and emotionally taxing. These organizational factors can be a source of stress for the individual, particularly in such incidents where the differences that exist may go unresolved.

Medical emergency protocols normally specify strict time limits between injury and the start of surgery; an optimum time window presages the victim's best chance of surviving a severe accident. Knowing this, and being unable to provide the immediate care within the "required" time in a disaster, can be a major source of anxiety. In large-scale disasters, where many people are injured, medical facilities will find it necessary to initiate a triage procedure. Triage is the assigning of priorities for treatment of injured persons according to their extent of injury and a judgment as to who has the greatest possibility of survival. Sometimes this includes a judgment on the part of emergency medical personnel that may result in allowing an injured child to risk death in order to concentrate medical capabilities on those who have a greater chance to live. In a disaster, with hospital facilities overtaxed, the triage process may occur outdoors on the hospital grounds. Even with highly experienced emergency personnel, the process of decision making in triage can become overwhelming, particularly when facing massive injuries to children.

Job burnout is a significant problem in the delivery of emergency services during a disaster. Personnel in all phases of emergency medical services are exposed to unprecedented physical and emotional demands in their desire to aid the victims. The burnout syndrome is a state of exhaustion, irritability, and fatigue that gradually emerges, sometimes goes unrecognized and undetected, and markedly decreases an individual's effectiveness and capability. The best way to forestall this syndrome is to expect it, to be alert to its early signs, and to prevent and alleviate stress reactions. However, encouraging health care personnel to avail themselves of the relief from debriefing, or of taking some time away from the scene, may itself present a challenge because of their already overburdened time situation.

Medical social workers are the most appropriate personnel with whom other mental health counselors can seek to develop liaison because they are familiar with the hospital disaster plan and with its diverse person- nel. They usually are assigned the role of providing both information and emotional support to survivor families. The hospital chapel often is the des- ignated point of information where individuals and families can gather to await news about their loved ones. The information about a patient's status usually is brought to them by a physician or nurse, together with a social worker. Medical social workers frequently orchestrate the debriefing of their fellow hospital employees.

Increasing attention is being given to the psychological needs of medical personnel. Through debriefings facilitated by mental health professionals, medical personnel can learn to recognize and deal with the stresses inherent in their work and to develop their own preventive strategies for mitigating these stresses. They should be able to recognize early signs and symptoms of stress and develop plans for managing such stress. They should learn about resources available to them in dealing with disaster-related stress, including counseling interventions. Prior awareness of the effect of personal stress and emotional reactions during mass casualty incidents should help medical personnel to be more sensitive to their own emotional needs, as well as be more effective in their treatment of survivors and their families.

☐ Summary

Children and adults suffer immediate and long-term psychological effects from residential dislocation and destruction in a disaster. In the early stages of a disaster, chaos, confusion, injuries, possibly death, will be observed, as well as anxieties, fears, fright, panic, depression, numbing, withdrawal, and other symptoms. The task for the mental health professional may call for bereavement counseling, calming of emotional distress, and support for people with missing family members. These services may be offered in the field in Red Cross shelters, in disaster assistance centers, in schools, in hastily set-up emergency shelters or tents, and in unfamiliar offices. Large-scale disasters require coordination across community institutions, including government agencies. The first stage requires a meeting of all officials to determine the status of the disaster and to coordinate resources. Community-wide needs assessment is required from each of the agencies represented. Procedures for interfacing with Red Cross, schools, and other agencies in the emergency network are determined, preferably based on predisaster planning. The mental health professional needs to arrange access to the emergency centers, such as the Red Cross shelters and disaster assistance centers, so that crisis counseling can be provided and families can be assisted with their most immediate needs. Contacts in the emergency centers may serve in identifying cases which will require follow-up care and referral, persuading reluctant parents to use the help provided, and educating parents and emergency personnel about the kinds of reactions and behaviors they might encounter in children.

Stress not only will occur for the victims and their children, but for teachers and other school personnel, for the medical and emergency services personnel, and for the mental health professional. Sources of the stress may be individual and common. For all caregivers, a severe disaster may require working in the midst of extensive environmental damage with destruction, wreckage, damaged residential and office structures, denuded agricultural fields, or the mud and water of widespread flooding, and working with individuals and families who have received serious medical injuries and are experiencing severe psychological shock. The mental health professional may not have any experience with injured or traumatized children, and may have to work in unfamiliar venues without the usual support and backup of information and consultation. Stress also may be experienced when the parent rejects available psychological help and persuasion is ineffective. Teachers may be forced to work with children who are yet unable to function in school because of continuing fears and anxieties, and may feel overburdened and pressured by the variety of unfamiliar demands that are being made on them. Teachers often need reassurance that the problems they are encountering are the result of the disaster and not of an inadequacy in their own teaching skills. Medical and emergency services personnel experience stress from the very nature of their work, which is hazardous and life threatening.

A disaster increases the demand for medical and emergency services, requiring personnel to work long hours, cut off from their usual sources of support and respite. Debriefing is an important source of relief and support for all emergency personnel. Mental health professionals and human resource managers need to guard against burnout in their personnel and in themselves, and to prevent or forestall it in others through education and alertness to early signs, by treatment, primarily with changes in schedules of work hours, and with debriefings.

CHAPTER

Program Design and Training Issues

☐ The Need for Disaster Mental Health Training

Over the past two decades, there has been increased awareness of the need for disaster mental health training for emergency services personnel, mental health personnel, school personnel, and caregivers. Previously, disaster training emerged only after a major event had occurred and only as part of programs supported by the Federal Emergency Management Agency (FEMA) and the National Institute of Mental Health (NIMH). In recent years, with the increased interest and awareness of disaster mental health effects, professional associations, the Red Cross, and local mental health departments have provided training programs in disaster mental health, proactively. The training often is provided as part of community-wide disaster preparedness activities, as well as during both the rescue and the recovery phases following an emergency. In many communities, training is required for anyone who wishes to volunteer their services in a disaster response.

Training is now required of mental health professionals in Los Angeles who volunteer or wish to participate in local Red Cross and Department of Mental Health disaster interventions. In the early 1990s, when a number of sequential emergencies befell the region, many volunteers had to be turned away because they lacked the approved training experience. It is of interest to note that, in the 1994 wildfires in southern California, many clinicians in private practice offered their services without charge through ads in local newspapers. It is not clear whether these professionals had received prior disaster mental health training, nor is it known to what extent the community availed themselves of these offers. However, these efforts reflect the current interest and willingness of the professional community to offer its services, a kind of response that is likely to occur in many urban communities. Professional associations in disaster-prone areas can be of service by helping to screen and monitor their members' efforts, surveying the experience of volunteers, providing disaster training, and maintaining a registry.

In the midst of a disaster, it is essential to update the mental health professionals and to prepare them for the uncertainties that they are likely to experience in the particular event. A disaster most likely will require them to carry out many activities with which they are not familiar and about which they have neither information nor experience. To be effective in a disaster assignment, they will need to be flexible and creative in adapting themselves to the unique demands. For example, mental health personnel may be called on to participate in such unfamiliar activities as "ride-alongs" with emergency services personnel; outreach to shelters and soup kitchens; debris clearance; transporting water, food, and supplies; and advocacy with insurance companies or FEMA. Law enforcement officials may ask them to assist in escorting families out of the disaster area, as they did in the Oakland Hills fire, or to assist in calming children who are separated from their families and are traumatized, or to console bereaved families at the coroner's office or morgue. Disaster assistance center staff routinely request the help of everyone at the center who is not busy to assist in serving refreshments, calming people in lines, and listening to their problems. These activities help to establish therapists as trusted helpers and team players when mental health problems arise in the centers. Training at the initial stage of the crisis should emphasize the special needs of children and families, and provide trainees with a working knowledge of resources available.

In-service training should continue after the counselors have participated in their initial fieldwork, and when they return to the coordinating unit for information sharing and discussion of experiences. At the end of their shift, they are expected to document services and identify children and their families who exhibited specific problems and should be considered for referral. Mental health professionals frequently are hampered with shortages of materials, equipment, and other resources. The training session becomes the vehicle for coordinators to work together with field-workers to identify their needs and to recommend outreach strategies. The informal meeting also serves as an opportunity for the mental health professionals to ventilate feelings. Counselors have reported that the meetings, with their sharing of personal experiences, have provided emotional release and have enabled them to conduct formal debriefings more efficiently.

Predisaster Training

The primary goal of predisaster training is to develop clinical skills appropriate to working with disaster-impacted families, especially children. The objectives are to recognize children who are traumatized and their symptoms and to facilitate communication with children and their families. The training should include a review of age-typical behaviors and how disasters may affect children in their developmental stages. Many mental health professionals will need to update their information with respect to children, particularly those who are not child specialists. Teachers and other school personnel also would benefit from learning the characteristic behaviors of children in disasters.

Training coordinators should be familiar with children's mental health needs, as well as being skilled in using specialized materials, such as those developed by prior NIMH-funded disaster intervention programs, and well trained in disaster mental health interventions. If available, training coordinators should recruit experts in child therapy (including art and play therapists) and family therapy, who could explain and demonstrate the application of their techniques. For example, trainees would learn the importance of communicating facts about a disaster to children because it has been found that conveying this information helps to reduce a child's anxiety.

The staff of child care programs also will benefit from training in techniques and strategies for handling the emotional issues that arise in a disaster, particularly post-traumatic stress reactions. Following the 1992 civil unrest in Los Angeles and the 1994 Northridge earthquake, the California Department of Education, Child Development Division, developed extensive curriculum and intervention guidelines for Project REST—Reducing Exceptional Stress and Trauma (California State Department of Education, Child Development Division, 1997) designed to instruct providers on how to help children deal with disaster-related trauma, stress, and grief. The curriculum guide provides activity and intervention strategies generic to any traumatic event, as well as suggestions about coping with specific catastrophes, such as fire, earthquakes, floods, violence, and death. The curriculum techniques and guidelines are designed for providers who work with children between the ages of 3 and 8. The materials are applicable to both large and small center-based programs and to family child care homes. The facilitator's manual is designed to assist program administrators in preparing and supporting staff to identify and help vulnerable children and to build partnerships with mental health professionals in the community. The curriculum stresses the necessity for a process involving self-expression tools, parent partnerships, community networks, supportive staff teams, and dispute resolution.

School personnel attending a predisaster training session would learn that increasing the children's understanding of disasters which might occur in their community would increase their competence in dealing with them. School-based personnel would be advised to familiarize themselves with their district's policy and to participate in their school's prevention activities in order to become familiar with its emergency plan. For example, the policy in many school districts in earthquake-prone communities requires schools to provide shelter for their residents in the event of an earthquake. The schools need to be prepared with food, blankets, cots, and other emergency supplies for a period of several days.

School psychologists could present information regarding the school-based crisis teams and how they operate after an emergency. In increasing numbers, schools have been incorporating the crisis team model into their administrative support system, and have been formalizing training modules. The crisis team usually includes the school mental health personnel, nursing staff, and school administrators. Consultants are sometimes included, on request. Once they are familiar with emergency procedures, crisis team members orient and train other school personnel. There are many workbooks, training manuals, and curricula available at this time (see Appendix).

Post-Traumatic Stress Disorder

An important part of the predisaster training should be directed toward training mental health professionals to address and relieve the emotional stresses of emergency services personnel and others who work long hours under difficult circumstances and great emotional strain. The strain is particularly noticeable when the victims are children. Emergency personnel tend to become more upset in these instances because they identify with the victims and with their families. The sense of compassion is heightened by the emotional anguish of the families when children have been injured or killed. The stressful demands of natural disasters and other major emergencies are accompanied by psychological reactions, regardless of the experience or level of competence of emergency personnel.

A significant concept for understanding the reactions of both victims and emergency services personnel in major disasters is post-traumatic stress disorder. In 1980, the American Psychiatric Association recognized the growing scientific evidence of traumatic stress reactions by incorporating the diagnosis of post-traumatic stress disorder in their diagnostic manual. The concept first emerged from the study of certain types of extreme situations, such as war combat experiences, and the intense emotional impact that they have on those who experience them. Research on the persistent psychological symptoms occurring among Vietnam veterans led clinicians to a better understanding of this syndrome. Survivors of major disasters have similar psychological reactions, which include such symptoms as reliving the event, social withdrawal, anxiety, sleep disorders, nightmares, and feelings of guilt about surviving the event.

Those experiencing these event-related reactions have been diagnosed as having some form of post-traumatic stress disorder. There is recent evidence that symptoms of post-traumatic stress disorder occur among rescue personnel and other emergency services personnel. Studies of air disasters in San Diego and Chicago in the late 1970s have shown that emergency personnel who worked at the scenes and the medical staffs who provided postdisaster care were experiencing the effects of these tragedies months and years after they occurred, with symptoms of fatigue, irritability, and anxiety.

Critical Incident Stress Debriefing

One of the most widely used procedures for helping persons who have been exposed to large scale disasters is critical incident stress debriefing (CISD), a procedure developed and refined by Mitchell and Everly (1995). While it originally was designed for use with emergency personnel, it has been adapted for use in many other situations, such as schools, community groups, businesses, and industries.

The authors differentiate CISD from psychotherapy, which generally claims affective, cognitive, and behavioral changes over a period of time. Rather, CISD is used specifically for the relief of severe stress in normal, emotionally healthy, people who have been subjected to a severely traumatic event. Those affected in a disaster might be classified into three groups: the victim, emergency services personnel, and family or friends of the victim. The primary aims for the procedure are to mitigate the impact of the disaster and to accelerate the recovery process. Ideally, CISD should be provided within 24 to 72 hours of the event, for maximum benefit. The recommended format for the debriefing is a team of three or four people, when possible, made up of trained peers and a mental health professional. Teams members have roles, with the peers providing the stress education and handling most of the one-to-one contacts with fellow emergency services personnel, as well as follow-up and defusings. The team leader, a mental health professional, should have received special training in CISD techniques and group leadership skills. The advantage of using trained mental health professionals is that they can assess people quickly and can manage intense emotional situations which may happen spontaneously at these debriefings. Recovery from exposure to the traumatic situations often is difficult, and can be optimally accomplished in collaboration with mental health professionals.

The process was described by Mitchell and Everly (1995) as having seven steps:

1. Introduction, in which the purpose and process is described and the rules are presented, such as confidentiality; participants do not have to speak if they do not want to; ask questions anytime. The process and the rules are aimed at gaining rapport and motivating the group.
2. Fact, in which each participant describes their own experience and the leader validates the emotions expressed and offers reassurance of appropriateness of reactions.
3. Thought, in which the individual is asked what was the most prominent thought about the event.
4. Reaction, in which the questions are: "What was the worst thing in this situation for you personally?" and "What causes you the most pain about the situation?"
5. Situation, in which the participants are asked about any kind of symptom they have developed as a result, such as fears, intrusive thoughts, startle reactions, feelings of dread, etc.
6. Teaching, in which the symptoms are normalized, not only those encountered, but also those that might be expected, and instructions may be given on diet, rest, exercise, sharing of feelings with family, etc.
7. Re-entry, in which closure is effected, summary statements are made, questions are answered, reassurance is repeated, and handouts are offered, if available (pp. 110–114).

The debriefings often are highly charged, emotionally laden, sessions with many such feelings expressed. The reentry phase is viewed as a gradual return to normal feelings and functioning. The authors recommend that, if possible, snacks be made available to further the return to normalcy. The debriefing also is seen as a means by which persons in need of further help can be identified and referrals can be made if necessary. This is best done on a one-to-one basis during the more relaxed postdebriefing atmosphere.

Although CISD has been used widely since its introduction in the 1980s, research on the efficacy of the procedure has been sparse and the evidence of its effectiveness has been mostly clinical and anecdotal. This is understandable as the procedure is one to which it is difficult to apply standard research methodology. Most of the published reports describe a wide variety of critical events in which the subjects are opportunistic and rarely are chosen at random, and where it often is difficult, if not impossible, to obtain appropriate control groups for comparison. Some researchers who have challenged CISD's dominant status in the field have suggested that there are factors besides psychological debriefing in the recovery environment that determine outcomes for individuals exposed to traumatic stressors (Avery & Orner, 1998). A call for greater attention to the procedure's implicit assumptions, along with careful consideration of factors that differentiate those persons who benefit with the use of CISD from those who do not, should lead to refinement and improvement in this highly regarded technique for individuals been subjected to the trauma of severe disasters.

Defusing

Mitchell and Everly (1995) also recommended defusing as an earlier process that differs from the CISD in timing and type of response. As a shortened version of CISD, it is more immediate, less organized, and designed to render the stress reactions harmless before they can do immediate damage or, at least, to reduce their potential. It thus is viewed as a primary intervention technique, to be provided as early as possible, usually aimed at small groups that work together. The goals are a rapid reduction of intense reactions, "normalizing" of the experience, reestablishment of the social network, and a means of assessing the need for full-scale debriefing. It also may be useful to provide practical information, affirm the value of the personnel, and establish linkages for additional support.

The timing for the defusing is seen as crucial, with the process being most effective if offered from 3 to 12 hours after the event. Similar to the CISD, the process is seen as having segments, consisting of the Introduction, which describes the process, encourages mutual support, emphasizes confidentiality, and alleviates group anxiety; Exploration, in which the participants discuss their experiences, followed by the Fact, Thought, Reaction, and Symptom steps, all in a more or less conversational style; and Information, which combines the teaching and reentry phases, with summaries, and teaches practical survival skills if necessary. One-to-one consultations after a defusing also are common. If need continues in any or all of the participants, full CISD is most often seen as the next step.

Recognizing and Avoiding Burnout

The term *burnout* is used to describe the effect of the stresses of job performance that reach a critical level. Burnout refers to the inability to perform at a person's usual level of competency because of too much stress for too long. The most frequently observed symptoms of burnout include: detachment, excessive fatigue, irritability, anxiety, impatience, decreased job efficiency, possible cognitive impairment, increase in alcohol and other substance use, and increase in family disputes. Emergency services personnel, for the most part, function at a very high standard of performance that is very sensitive to changes in personal task efficiency. Burnout will occur in those who perform demanding physical or emotional tasks to the point of excessive fatigue. Long hours of unrelieved intensity in attending to or rescuing victims of a disaster will take their toll. Hospital and mental health personnel often pay insufficient attention to the long hours and the stress-inducing circumstances of their work, and may deny their own resultant signs of stress. The condition results in impaired decision making and a lack of clear judgment that will continue unless recognized and treated.

The potential for emotional distress increases markedly when there is a lengthy aftermath, with symptoms extending over several months and even years, and also when disasters follow each other closely in time so that they expose emergency personnel to event-related stresses with little interim relief. For example, in late October 1993, two major wildfires swept through two southern California communities, Laguna Hills and Altadena, within a week (California State Department of Mental Health, 1996a). With repeated exposure to traumatizing stimuli, emergency and rescue personnel did not have time to fully recoup from the demands of the first disaster before they were subjected to those of the subsequent one.

The sources of burnout are both physical and emotional. The physical causes are long shifts and exposure to uncomfortable working conditions. The emotional exhaustion comes from feelings of helplessness, dealing with gruesome and gory injuries and death, and with victims' reactions to separation or loss of their loved ones. It is increased by ongoing concern for the safety of their own families, and by witnessing injuries and death to colleagues. Other sources of stress and potential burnout are the frustrations involved in treating children and families during a disaster. A specific issue for mental health professionals is the reluctance of families to engage in needed therapy. The subsequent frustration experienced by the therapist can be great. In addition, psychological services offered to children may be more difficult to deliver because of distrust of the mental health professionals. Therapists become frustrated when their helping skills are poorly utilized. The professional begins to feel a sense of rejection, helplessness, and sometimes anger when viewing children who clearly are distressed and who would profit from their help, but the families refuse it. It may become difficult for the mental health professional to continue his or her helping efforts when his or her repeated recommendations are rebuffed.

Training programs need to identify and define the concept of burnout as a risk factor in disaster; indicate the potential origins of burnout; describe the symptoms of physical and emotional burnout; and suggest procedures for prevention, mitigation, and treatment. Content should include ways that burnout decreases effectiveness in a disaster, and provide information about what can be done before and during the disaster to avoid burnout. Training sessions also should address the nature of disaster work which involves high-stress tasks and the potential for overload. Attendees will be instructed in stress reduction and relaxation techniques that are helpful to mental health professionals, survivors, and emergency services personnel. A wide variety of options include experiential exercises, such as progressive relaxation, breathing, meditation, guided imagery, autogenic training, biofeedback, body work, and exercise techniques. Time away from the assignment should be considered seriously when burnout occurs.

☐ Helping Families in a Disaster

A major disaster is disruptive of family functioning because of displacement of families, damage to the home, injuries to loved ones, and, in extreme situations, separation of family members and death. Therefore, the training program needs to include discussion of family dynamics theory. Fragile families will reveal the extent of their dysfunctioning through their children who are more likely to be irritable, have difficulty sleeping, and be more demanding. The increased demands placed on the families by children who are experiencing stress may be more than it can handle. Conducting an evaluation of the families that seek help after a disaster also requires assessment of their existing coping skills and mobilization of family members to utilize these skills.

The disaster-impacted family has multiple needs and strengths. Clinicians working with families in a disaster setting need to understand the structural makeup of the family, including its belief systems and problem-solving styles. Their training should focus on the application of the family crisis model, including how to identify and prioritize presenting problems, discuss rapid assessment techniques useful to assess family coping skills, and refer to available resources for family therapy. The training will inform the therapists on methods of community consultation and introduce issues not likely to appear in family counseling, such as relocation; special concerns of single-parent households; the impact of parents' reconstructive efforts on family life; and especially the concerns of families that have experienced loss of loved ones, property, and communal life. The therapist should engage the entire family, including the children, in defining the needs and the tasks necessary to establish new patterns and thereby restore a sense of cohesiveness and balance. This is particularly desirable when the surrounding environment has been changed considerably as a result of disaster damage, with accompanying loss and family displacement.

The training will emphasize crisis therapy, a treatment approach with which some therapists may be unfamiliar and one which requires interaction with other agencies. Therapists working with families will need to familiarize themselves with community resources and how to make their services available to disaster survivors. They will need to help the family use its own coping skills so that it can take advantage of the resources to reestablish its own functioning. Distressed families will likely require practical assistance in meeting their multiple needs. Clinicians will have to be creative in applying their skills in the interviewing, diagnosis, and treatment planning phases. They will need to apply their knowledge of psychodynamics and skills in cognitive and behavioral approaches in addressing the special needs of disaster-impacted families. Those whose experience primarily has been in treating individuals will be encouraged to extend their skills to treating families as a unit. Those skilled in group therapy will find multifamily groups a useful form of intervention because of the common experiences and concerns of families in disaster. The groups will provide disaster victims with the opportunity to discuss family problems and solutions, and will also reduce the isolation that may be the result of relocation and separation from their neighborhoods.

Certain therapeutic techniques, such as cognitive therapy combined with crisis intervention, have been found to be highly effective in treating families. Cognitive appraisal techniques require individuals to identify their current functional level. The individual is led to recognize the idiosyncratic way in which he or she thinks and how he or she organizes his or her coping behavior to solve problems. The cognitive therapist applies these techniques to help a family identify its coping strategies in order to solve family problems and to facilitate strengthening the family so it can again function as a unit. Families with children that have had to relocate often experience difficulties because of disruptions in their routines, especially at bedtimes and mealtimes. The cognitive therapist might focus on helping these parents to restabilize their family routines.

Mental health professionals will need to develop skills in working with families from diverse ethnic and cultural groups—a task which calls for sensitivity, information, and specialized training. Effective assessment and planning of the work with such groups requires sensitivity to the special problems that these families may confront in the reconstruction period. The following cases illustrate some of the issues and pitfalls inherent in this task.

1989 Loma Prieta Earthquake

After the earthquake struck the San Francisco Bay Area and central California, the predominantly Latino community of Watsonville—the hub of an agricultural area—was reluctant to seek assistance from governmental agencies. Their status as undocumented immigrants caused the residents to be wary of governmental agencies, and their poor English language skills already had made for unhappy experiences in their contacts with agency bureaucracy. Understandably, they also were reluctant to seek counseling for themselves and for their children. When teams of bilingual professionals from southern California mental health agencies were recruited to assist the outreach efforts to the Latino populations, they found the entire emergency system in disarray.

Although 3 weeks had passed since the initial temblor, the staff of the emergency services still was not meeting the ongoing needs of people who were now living in shelters. The emergency services personnel had not received adequate training on what might be the special needs of the new immigrant populations. Food preparations in the shelters, for example, did not take into account dietary preferences, and the municipal fairgrounds shelter site was located 5 miles or more from familiar ethnic neighborhoods, resulting in a heightened sense of disorientation for these recently immigrated families who lacked transportation. FEMA and Red Cross personnel who were helping these populations appeared to be frustrated and suffering from burnout. Because many of the personnel lacked Spanish-language skills, translators were needed for all their contacts and this seriously handicapped their helping efforts. There also was an inadequate medical component. Thus, the disaster relief efforts in this situation were complicated because planners had not recognized that the survivors spoke only Spanish, were for the most part unassimilated, and were unfamiliar and distrusting of the services available to them.

The example points to the importance that clinicians and emergency personnel be aware of existing conditions in the community that will affect the disaster response efforts, such as language, food preference, and distrust of authorities. It is necessary to be sensitive to the cultural differences and specific needs, particularly when working with disaster-affected families. Training personnel to be aware of the ethnic and cultural differences would have pointed out the desirability of maintaining community life intact to the extent possible when planning shelter sites and of utilizing personnel with similar backgrounds who would understand the special needs of these groups, such as special diets and different cultural styles.

1994 Northridge Earthquake

Many of the earthquake victims in Fillmore, California, a small town northeast of Los Angeles which is 59% Latino, were monolingual farmworkers with minimal education. Two contract agencies, Catholic Charities and Clinicas Del Camino Real, provided services to these survivors, along with regular staff from Project COPE (Ventura County Department of Mental Health, 1995). Catholic Charities had been delivering services for many years to the town of Fillmore, inasmuch as the population is predominately Roman Catholic and their cultural and social life revolves around the church. The monolingual and bilingual population trust the church and use the church instead of the government for most of their needs. With the help of Saint Francis Church in Fillmore, Project COPE workers linked up with Catholic

Charities to provide counseling, including a bilingual psychologist who met with the farmworkers in the packing houses during their lunch hours.

Clinicas Del Camino Real, a nonprofit health care agency that operates clinics for the farmworkers and others in the Latino community, integrated crisis counseling with their medical services after the earthquake. People who came in for their routine visits and exhibited quake-related stress reactions were screened for crisis counseling. Some of the patients told counselors that they had left Mexico City and other parts of Mexico because they were victims of earthquakes in those areas, and many believed that "the earthquakes were following them." Children asked counselors whether "the earth monster is going to kill my family." Some even believed that the earthquake was caused by their own sins.

It is within this context that the trusted contract agencies were used to alleviate the distortions and to dissipate the fears. These agencies provided a humane response to the earthquake victims by communicating to them in their own language and cultural style. Because of Proposition 187 in California, which requires the reporting of illegal aliens, many legal as well as illegal immigrants were terrified of going to anyone for counseling. But, these trusted agencies helped overcome both stigma and fear.

1996–1997 Winter Storms in Yuba and Sutter Counties, California

Yuba and Sutter Counties in California's Sacramento Valley include agricultural areas that have experienced repeated flooding during the winter. The Sutter-Yuba Mental Health Services operated its Project CARE crisis counseling program at the flood resource center, a one-stop location for all flood-related needs and concerns (Sutter-Yuba Mental Health Services, 1998). Large ethnic populations, specifically Latinos, Hmong immigrants from Southeast Asia, and East Indians, were affected by the flooding. The mental health agency initiated a proactive effort that included outreach in the flooded communities, direct crisis intervention, and information dissemination about material resources and emotional responses to disaster. English- and Spanish-language brochures describing Project CARE services were distributed at the Yuba-Sutter Fair and at local health fairs. Sutter County also developed a brochure, entitled *Important Information in the Event of Flood Danger*, in English-, Punjabi-, Hmong-, and Spanish-language versions, and Project CARE distributed copies of the brochure widely. Most of the Latino, Hmong, and East Indian families encountered during the outreach were able to communicate in English, or had someone in the family who spoke or read English. The few Latino families in need of an interpreter were referred to a Spanish-speaking staff member who followed up with home visits.

The agency's ties with community-based agencies yielded continued referrals of victims from ethnic minority groups needing Project CARE's assistance. The California Rural Legal Aid Center had long-standing contacts with migrant farmworkers and disseminated information about Project CARE in its service area, especially to those who had resided in migrant labor camps destroyed by the flooding. The U.S. Department of Agriculture's Cooperative Extension Service and the Farm Bureau assisted Project CARE in its outreach efforts through their contacts with farmers and others who employed immigrant farmworkers. Project CARE counselors also stayed in close contact with faith-based organizations, such as Disaster Relief Interfaith, Craftsmen for Christ, and Mennonite Disaster Services, whose workers were skilled in identifying distressed individuals and referring them to crisis counseling as they worked on rebuilding their homes.

Outreach Strategies

A disaster assistance center (DAC) is opened in the first days following a federal disaster declaration. The local mental health authority has the responsibility of staffing a counseling station at the DAC as mandated by Section 413 of the Disaster Relief Act of 1974. The exact format is determined by the local mental health authority. The public mental health authority is expected to provide the staff for these on-site crisis counseling services. It also has the latitude to develop innovative outreach services in the community. Although the local mental health authority has the primary responsibility for servicing the community under the federal mandate, other mental health providers may offer their services. In many communities, the resources and potential contributions of nonprofit agencies are overlooked both in predisaster planning of mental health interventions and in their mobilization when a disaster occurs. Community-based organizations (CBOs), such as family service agencies, routinely provide counseling services to families and individuals in need, yet these agencies often have not been included in the planning for emergencies. However, these agencies can and should be viewed as an additional resources for the community. Recently, the trend has been to include community-based organizations in disaster planning and in the coordination of postdisaster activities, a move that would require recognition from federal agencies and local governments (Benini, 1998; Wallrich, 1996).

Outreach following a disaster involves bringing services to the people in a variety of settings, such as Red Cross shelters, DACs, temporary housing, schools, playgrounds, and child care centers. The Red Cross operates in both major and localized disasters. The Red Cross chapter generally is the focal point for ongoing emergency services activities and coordination, with its emergency shelters located in undamaged public buildings to provide food, clothing, and overnight housing. Under its charter with the federal government, the Red Cross works with public and private mental health agencies. It is valuable for mental health professionals to familiarize themselves with their local Red Cross chapter's diverse activities and to become acquainted with its personnel. Mental health professionals would find it useful to take courses offered by the Red Cross in disaster mental health training and shelter management.

Temporary shelters are set up in community settings, such as schools, gyms, armories, and other public settings which have large open spaces. A shelter manager controls the comings and goings of the Red Cross personnel and volunteers, as well as the victims. Disaster victims in the shelters have been displaced, their homes have been damaged or destroyed, and they are there on a temporary basis. There is usually a large, open room with rows of cots, where families stay together with whatever small possessions they have brought with them. A nursing station is set up for emergency medical needs. One of the primary tasks for the Red Cross is to facilitate communication in a disaster, and a message center is available at the shelter to serve as a link for disaster victims and their families and friends. After communication is restored, the telephone company frequently will set up a bank of phones at the centers.

Red Cross shelters vary according to the nature of the disaster, the locale, and the anticipated length of recovery. Families whose residences were lost or damaged may be temporarily located in the shelter. In the first days after a disaster, the visitor is likely to observe a great deal of distress among those currently residing in the shelter. There often is a quiet atmosphere, as the Red Cross personnel will attempt to establish an atmosphere of calm and security—a "safe haven." After a few days, however, the families will have set up their own space, will have gotten to know each other, and may even provide mutual support for each other. However, the shelter is set up as a short-term, temporary arrangement, and the Red Cross will attempt to relocate families to motels and other available housing as soon as possible. Red Cross volunteers often will be available to provide organized play activities for children at the shelter because these activities help reduce the stress on the child, as well as offer respite to parents. Ideally, a mental health volunteer will be available to provide support to the parents, along with concrete advice on coping with both adults' and children's fear reactions. The Red Cross normally will establish a referral process for counseling assistance to victims, and shelter personnel will help identify clients who may need such assistance.

The potential locations for outreach to disaster victims are numerous, and successful outreach often will depend on the ingenuity and flexibility of the mental health professional. In gaining entrée to nontraditional settings, it also will be necessary to assure confidentiality in working with children and their families, particularly since they are not clients seeking clinical services. At a DAC or Red Cross shelter, physical arrangements do not usually offer much privacy. The DAC frequently consists of a large room with many tables where different emergency service providers are sitting; the mental health counselor is usually one of them. These arrangements, with their lack of privacy, are not conducive to personal disclosure of emotional distress. The shelter manager will attempt to find a private corner for counseling. It is important to make prior arrangements with the DAC manager for some private space, if at all possible. It may require considerable ingenuity to find this private space.

The DAC consists of the multiple providers of services to disaster victims. Clients routinely pass from station to station. They are required to have their paperwork initialed by each agency at the center. Each service represented at the center has a sign identifying itself, such as Salvation Army, Red Cross, and emergency housing. The mental health provider in this setting has a special challenge. The seeking of counseling services continues to imply emotional pathology in the public's mind. The challenge is to avoid the stigma by developing neutral titles for crisis counseling services which avoid that implication (for example "disaster counseling," "someone to talk to," "support groups," and "problems with children?"). Very often, mental health personnel stationed at a disaster assistance center are frustrated in fulfilling their assignments because their services often are overlooked or ignored by those in need, and they may be reluctant to initiate a consultation. It does not work to sit at a table and wait to be approached. Chatting with disaster victims informally can be very helpful. It also is desirable to mingle with the other service providers so that they become familiar with the mental health services offered.

Although families are more likely to seek help because it's "for their children," the reluctance to seek help persists, requiring mental health personnel to be specially trained in how to interact in outreach locations. For example, the mental health professional may need to approach a person who appears distressed and strike up a conversation rather than wait to be approached. The mental health system also could be more successful in gaining access to the public if it publicized its services more widely. The optimal arrangement would have the mental health professional provide a routine screening as an integrated part of the center's procedures. This has been tried successfully in some centers.

Nontraditional Crisis Activities

Mental health professionals have performed a variety of nontraditional activities in disasters. After a hurricane in Houston, Texas, staff of the local mental health center assisted the Red Cross in managing a shelter for older people and people with disabilities. Prior to the hurricane, they had volunteered for Red Cross shelter management training. They also were involved in helping to locate family members, assisting them to evacuate, enabling them to confront the loss of their personal possessions, and counseling them to adapt to the strangeness of the living situation in the shelter.

Since the early 1970s, mental health professionals have become an established part of the disaster assistance response in a variety of ways and have taken on many nontraditional roles. Following the 1971 Sylmar earthquake in the Los Angeles area psychologists organized parent meetings in the community, joining with geologists and seismologists in what were publicized as informational meetings. They also used these meetings to meet members of the community and as an opportunity to provide psychological support to parents whose children were experiencing emotional distress.

Informational meetings were organized after the 1978 winter floods in the San Fernando Valley of Los Angeles, when residents of the community appeared to lack information about the availability of the mental health services offered to them and therefore did not utilize them. After a couple of months had passed, the center staff sponsored a community meeting to inform residents about the availability of these services. At the time of the meeting, many families still were displaced as a result of mud damage to their homes. Representatives of the federal agencies were invited to the meeting, providing an opportunity for residents to make their needs directly known to them. The president of the local homeowners association presented the community's complaints that the services offered by federal agencies were inadequate, insensitive, and insufficient. Parents complained that their children were forced to be transported long distances to their local schools from the temporary housing sites where the families had been relocated. The mental health disaster project staff had focused on offering individual counseling to those that appeared to be suffering from the stress caused by the mud slides. It became apparent that group meetings in the community would be more useful.

In the 1991 Oakland Hills firestorm, mental health staff assisted emergency services personnel by accompanying families into the burned out area to view the damage to their homes, and providing comfort and support during this process. In the same disaster, the local mental health authority dispatched staff to the coroner's office to provide bereavement counseling.

When Hurricane Andrew hit south Florida in 1992, mental health personnel helped disaster housing personnel relocate disaster victims to temporary tent quarters where particular attention was paid to resettling neighbors in the same area. In the wake of Hurricane Andrew, they also identified the problem of parental stress and attended particularly to the potential of child distress. They helped set up "child care" in emergency centers to provide respite for the parents, freeing them for the multiple tasks they faced in restoring their households, and providing diversion for the children.

After the 1994 Northridge earthquake, Project COPE counselors accompanied FEMA workers on home visits for various certifications and damage reports. The home visits met with success, because people who normally would have been suspicious of opening their doors for government officials were relieved to know that counselors were present to help them in this disaster (Ventura County Department of Mental Health, 1995).

To all of these nontraditional activities, mental health professionals bring their compassion, as well as their clinical training and experiences, including diagnostic and communication skills. While providing many services supportive to the other emergency personnel, they bring professional skills and a background in case-finding and crisis intervention. Mental health professionals engaged in these activities must recognize that disaster victims are different than "patients" to the extent that they have not identified themselves nor formally requested professional help. In other words, they need to recognize that survivors are ordinary functioning people who are subjected to severe, but usually temporary, emotional strain. This includes children, who have become confused as a result of their dislocation, the magnitude of loss, and the disruption in their lives, but who still possess the coping skills developed in the past.

In more recent disasters, the value of the assistance that mental health professionals can provide has been more generally acknowledged by emergency services agencies. In the past, there was hesitation by some emergency services personnel to any involvement of the mental health community since it implied a stigma. This attitude has diminished since emergency services personnel have personally experienced the help in coping with their stress provided by mental health professionals within their own organizations. The acceptance of counseling also has increased in the general population, and this has affected the willingness of many victims of disaster to avail themselves of help from mental health practitioners. Despite the decrease in stigma associated with interactions with mental health counselors, the attitude of embarrassment has not been completely erased. Therefore, when case-finding has identified problem behavior that merits further treatment, the recommendation should be presented privately and discreetly, assuring the family of confidentiality and that they can make their own decisions. In the Teton Dam disaster in Idaho, for example, mental health professionals who were engaged in outreach activities would refer cases to still-functioning mental health agencies where the family could obtain the recommended treatment. As usual, it was left up to the family to follow through on a recommendation. This does not differ much from the experience that mental health professionals have in nondisaster situations.

Despite the variety of settings where crisis counseling may occur, the principles of crisis intervention are applicable. The focus of treatment should be the reported or manifest problem behavior of the child and family functioning as a result of the disaster. Since the opportunities to work with clients are limited by the circumstances, the practitioner needs to maximize the opportunity by providing immediate supportive advice to the family. Although the dynamics and underlying conflicts that are affecting the reactions of the family may be recognized within the initial interview, the major effort should focus on the presenting problem and the relief of stress. For many families, this will be their first experience with a mental health practitioner, so it is important that the encounter be viewed as helpful and not threatening. A number of professional organizations are involved in efforts to improve services for children who have experienced trauma. For example, the American Psychological Association has introduced a brochure for the general public, *Managing Traumatic Stress: Tips for Recovering from Disasters and Other Traumatic Events*, which describes many steps parents can take to relieve the emotional consequences that their children may experience after a disaster.

☐ Designing Postdisaster Programs for Children and Adolescents

Play and Expressive Activities

Play and expressive art therapies have a long history of usefulness in child therapy. They are especially applicable in working with children traumatized by disaster. These techniques have been used extensively following traumatic events, such as residential fires, school yard shootings, school bus accidents, and civil disorders. Following a shooting that occurred in Los Angeles at the 49th Street School, a team of mental health professionals provided interventions for school personnel and children and their families. These classroom programs used artwork as a screening tool then, and also later for therapeutic interventions. In another example, in the Ash Wednesday fires in Australia, crisis teams provided outreach to children and developed a variety of interventions and specially designed materials, including storytelling, drawings, and coloring books. Coloring books have been used widely since their introduction following the Omaha, Nebraska, tornado in the early 1970s. These coloring books, containing topically relevant material, are designed to assist the child by providing both information and a creative outlet. Children enjoy using the coloring books as a way of expressing feelings through color and accompanying comments. In this way they are useful to the therapist in relating to the child.

Play

Young children express their feelings through their play. Playrooms staffed by the Church of the Brethren and other volunteer organizations frequently are available at disaster assistance centers to provide recreational activity and respite for parents. Volunteers from the church groups staff these child care centers, provide play material to the families, and set up a playroom to occupy the children while their parents are involved with the business of receiving disaster assistance. The mental health professional should meet with the playroom staff and offer information to them about available counseling services. The play groups may be a rich source of case-finding. The play materials should be chosen so that the emotions the child has experienced can be expressed in coloring materials and clay. Materials should be easily acquirable. Building blocks allow children to reenact their disaster experiences. There are a wide range of toys that represent emergency services personnel and their vehicles (ambulances, fire trucks, patrol cars) that may aid in this task of reenactment. In selecting toys, it is important to consider both their recreational and their therapeutic value. Dolls and family figures are useful for play activities. Preschoolers who survived the blast of the 1995 Oklahoma City bombing used toy figures with missing limbs to play "hospital." Commercially produced toys are not always necessary. Children who survived Hurricane Hugo found that broccoli could be used to represent trees and pouring gravy all over them could mimic the water rushing all over the landscape. A therapist who intends to do outreach with children following a disaster will find it valuable to assemble a portable kit containing play materials. These materials are valuable because they can be used diagnostically and therapeutically in a variety of settings, and can break down the barriers between therapist and child.

Therapy with a Child Who Has Been Traumatized. Subsequent to the Northridge earthquake, Alice, an 8-year-old Hispanic girl, was referred to counseling by her teacher. Ordinarily a docile and compliant child and an excellent student, she had begun bursting into quiet tears and quarreling with her classmates over trivial infractions into her "space." Her grades dropped and she began missing an unusual number of school days due to "illness." Her mother reported that she experienced anxiety attacks and diurnal and nocturnal enuresis. The therapist treated her once weekly for 8 months.

The family picture that Alice drew in art therapy depicted a story of trauma, alienation, and dispossession: Her home had been condemned after the quake. She had been trapped in a room with her aunt and infant cousin as the doorjamb skewed. She narrowly missed being flattened by a chest of drawers. Gas had leaked from broken lines and there was an imminent threat of fire. Her mother's hysterical cries from outside and the noises of her house imploding had stunned her to silence. She enacted this scene again and again in dollhouse play, with wordless compulsive repetition.

The therapist used hand puppets to help Alice talk about her feelings and played games, such as Monopoly and Four Across. Twelve members of her extended family were now living together in a three-bedroom apartment, one family per room. She often was compelled to skip school to care for the five smaller children (age 5 months to 3 years) during the day, since all of the adults worked and Alice's 16-year-old sister refused to care for them.

The school counselor filed a report with Los Angeles County Child Protective Services. The mother was encouraged to join a neighborhood preschool cooperative with other working mothers. She was given support in moving Alice out from her bed at night and comforting her until she fell asleep in a separate bed. The regression to infantile behavior resolved with adequate attention; the enuresis diminished, then ceased.

The therapist helped Alice start a diary. She began to write poems about her wish to have a home, to have free time, and to have a father again (her father had been incarcerated for gang activity). Teacher approval and encouragement of these activities helped her to come out of her disturbed, dissociative shell. Her grades improved and, during the 8 months of therapy, she became more vocal, relaxed, and congenial.

Expressive Activities

The child often depicts family problems in drawings and other expressive techniques. By studying children's drawings following a disaster, therapists can observe how they have accommodated to these catastrophes. The drawings often are of the disaster experiences, such as burning and broken buildings. The traumatized younger child can be encouraged to engage in drawing activities, where the content of the child's drawings in terms of both color and subject matter may give some insight into the child's emotional state. For the latency-age child, who has much more language facility, the play techniques can serve as an adjunct to verbal interaction. The verbal techniques useful in child therapy, such as storytelling about the event and recounting of their own experiences whether individually or in groups, are applicable at this age. Dream analysis, dramatic play, and expressive movement also have been useful in working with adolescents. Some therapists have found that journal writing is useful for a child in recalling the event.

After the 1992 Landers-Big Bear earthquakes (San Bernardino County Department of Mental Health, 1993), the counseling team used a puppet show to validate younger children's thoughts and feelings associated with the earthquake and its aftershocks. The interactive exercise attempted to build a sense of confidence in the children by reinforcing self-protective responses to future disasters. The format of the show is as follows.

The puppet show stage is set up before the children arrive. The show's main character is Elmo from *Sesame Street,* and his performance is based around the song, *Beatin' the Quake* which was produced by the Children's Television Workshop. After the children come in and sit down on the floor in front of the stage, one of the counselors talks to them and gets them "warmed up" by asking them what they call the earthquakes and aftershocks explaining that some children have other names for them. The counselor then asks some of them to talk about how they felt during the earthquake and aftershocks. After this, the puppet show begins and the puppets talk about how they feel during an earthquake and that it is okay and normal to feel afraid, and how even adults feel frightened, too. The puppets also talk about indoor and outdoor safety spots where children can go to keep safe in an earthquake. After the puppets finish, the counselor leads the children in a train around the room and has the children point out safety spots. During the show, the puppets and the children sing the *Beatin' the Quake* song together.

Throughout the show, the children's expression of feelings is validated by the puppets, the presenters, and by the other children. The parents' feelings are validated by the puppets when the puppets mention that even parents get frightened, too. As the children talk about how they feel, the teachers and parents who are watching learn about the children's fears and how to encourage their children's expressiveness.

Desensitization exercises also are useful with children who have been traumatized. This form of behavioral modification, or deconditioning, serves to decrease fears and anxieties by gradually increasing the tolerance for sound and movement. Behavioral modification techniques have been useful in reducing fears stemming from traumatic events. A child may react fearfully for example, to the sound of a passing truck after having experienced an earthquake. The fear of the sounds of an earthquake become generalized to the fear of other loud noises. Desensitizing techniques include reassurance and cognitive awareness of the association between loud noises and the original noise of the earthquake to reduce the child's reactivity. The parent is an important ally in helping this fear reduction process to occur.

Desensitization techniques were used to help children cope with southern California's earthquakes. The Los Angeles City Council funded the construction of a vehicle designed as a playhouse by Hanna-Barbara Productions. Children would enter the playhouse where the movement and the sounds of an earthquake were simulated. The familiar cartoon character of Yogi Bear would then inform the children about how to both prepare for and behave during an earthquake. Behavioral techniques also were used following the 1971 Sylmar earthquake at the San Fernando Valley Child Guidance Clinic. Therapists used tape recordings of sounds, at differing volumes, to simulate the thunder-like sounds of an earthquake. They also used a platform that would shake when a child would walk on it to simulate differing types of movement suggestive of an earthquake. The children would be exposed in graduated measure to these stimuli to reduce the fear experienced during the disaster. Therapists have to be especially careful in applying these techniques to assure that desensitization occurs, rather than additional traumatization.

Group Techniques

The use of group techniques is particularly effective in working with latency-age through adolescent children who have experienced trauma from a disaster. These techniques provide children with an opportunity to talk about their experiences and fears, and to recognize that other children have reactions similar to their own. The sharing of feelings and the opportunity to hear what other children have experienced is a useful therapeutic process. The child frequently is unaware that other children have the same fears. Recognizing that other children have similar feelings encourages a child to express them. Parent-child groups are a valuable treatment modality to use in working with younger and latency-age children. The parents will learn how to help the child cope with his or her fears and also will learn that other children have similar reactions so that their child's reactions are not atypical. The group helps parents to recognize and allay their own fears, and to receive advice on managing their own fears as well as the child's fears.

Dramatic play, expressive movement, and journals are some of the activities found useful for expressing feelings with groups or individuals. Many of the techniques that are useful in working with latency-age children are applicable, with some modification, to adolescents. These techniques are developed to take advantage of the adolescent's increased expressive and intellectual abilities. Rap groups, both scheduled and drop-in, are advantageous in helping teens to recount their feelings. Drawings of their disaster experiences, perhaps accompanied by a written narrative, serve a similar purpose. Sometimes, adolescents will enjoy developing a play which incorporates the disaster and the events subsequent to it.

Groups of adolescents are able to talk more about the experience because they have the cognitive capability which allows them to process the information about the event and to express experiences and their reactions more clearly. Adolescents, however, also may use denial more often than children or adults, and thus often will attempt to appear unaffected and "cool," particularly with their peers. The use of denial as a defense is more prevalent in this particular age group than in adults. The group leader will need both to explore the teenagers' actual perceptions and feelings regarding the impact of the event on them and to differentiate between what is actually "real" and "not real" to the adolescent, and not be put off by what appears to be detachment, disinterest, or callousness.

The teenager may attempt to handle loss with a great amount of suppression, and with a more stoic attitude regarding the universality of death. Youth raised in areas dominated by gang violence, where shootings are commonplace, revenge actions are obligatory, and deaths of family members or close friends are frequent, may seem to have become desensitized. They develop a coping style of denial and bravado regarding death. This is a stance that is difficult for adults to understand because it appears as callousness. This stance is particularly evident in communities, like southcentral Los Angeles, where the teenagers showed little concern for property loss or compassion for injury after the 1992 Los Angeles civil disturbances. Some youth who were interviewed on television appeared to be unconcerned about the damage to property in the community and the loss of community facilities and services. However, when losses were personal, expressions of caring and feelings of bereavement surfaced.

Group counseling may not work as well in rural communities where stigma frequently is attached to attending a support group, as was the case in Big Bear, California, after the 1992 Landers-Big Bear earthquakes (San Bernardino County Department of Mental Health, 1993). The atmosphere of self-reliance often is strong in rural communities and this creates the risk of stigma, and even ostracism, if a person is viewed by his or her neighbors to be weak or in need of mental health services. The preferred mode of treatment was individual counseling in the office or in the homes. The schools were enlisted as the main venue for reaching children and their families after the earthquake because they had gained the trust and support of local residents. Family sessions were provided, on request, to educate parents in helping their children to cope with their fears and concerns.

Pynoos, Sorenson, and Steinberg (1993) felt that the treatment issues specially addressed by group techniques are most useful in reinforcing the normative nature of the reactions that the group members are experiencing, the sharing of mutual concerns, and the identification of common fears and traumatic reminders, and also provide an opportunity to increase the tolerance for disturbing emotions and to provide problem-solving suggestions.

Peer-Based Activities

Natural disasters create a different set of experiences for adolescents. It is a common experience, not provoked by any subgroup in the community, and the impact is shared by everyone. Adolescents may have difficulty acknowledging the impact of the disaster on the community and may seem to be lacking compassion and concern for other disaster victims. However, at this stage of life, injury or death of family members is traumatic. The teenager may feel helpless, angry, and confused by such experiences. Some will present a facade of callousness and lack of concern, behaviors which should be explored as evidence of denial. Members of the family may become angry by the teenager's apparent lack of concern. The role of the mental health professional is to help families understand these age-specific reactions. In working with the teenagers themselves, it is important to provide clear, accurate information. It therefore is advisable to consider informational groups targeted specifically to teenagers. These groups can be offered in community settings, such as schools, youth centers, and clubs. Teenagers are more likely to respond to informational programs than to the relatively less structured "rap groups," except when they are peer led.

Teenagers differ in the ways that they express themselves. Some will demonstrate concern for their families and neighbors by helping in the cleanup efforts. Other will simply continue in their normal, everyday activities with their peers. Still others will withdraw and become isolated. Parents of teenagers may be frustrated with the seeming lack of involvement by their adolescent children with the family's losses and repair efforts. Adolescents can be important assets to the community after a disaster, and it is worthwhile to organize activities for youth to participate in the cleanup efforts, providing them with the possibility of social interactions with their peers. Through such organizations as the Girl Scouts and Boy Scouts, 4-H, and Camp Fire, "teen lines" have been set up following a disaster to provide information about service opportunities, peer support, and counseling. Mental health professionals can provide support to these peer-focused efforts. Youth who seek help from teen lines, in addition to being assisted by the contact with the peer counselor, may be offered help and advised when further services are available in the future.

☐ Summary

It is now recognized that it is essential to train mental health professionals so that they are prepared for the many unfamiliar activities they will have to carry out, such as "ride alongs" with emergency service personnel, calming people in lines, and escorting families in and out of the disaster area. Predisaster training is aimed at developing the necessary clinical skills in working with families and their children during and after a disaster. The training is provided for mental health professionals, child care program staff, school psychologists, teachers and other school personnel. Training would include review of age-typical behaviors; how the disaster might affect children at varying developmental stages; how to deal with disaster-related trauma, stress, and grief; identification of children who are vulnerable; development of parent partnerships and community networks; and familiarity with specialized materials and procedures, such as art and play therapies. The training also would include skills in conducting CISD, recognizing and preventing burnout, and in using stress reduction and relaxation techniques. Other important training would focus on specialized skills in working with families, such as discussion of family dynamics; the effects of a major disaster on family functioning; issues associated with relocation; and the concerns of families who have lost a loved one, property, and communal life. A presentation would be included on the availability and utilization of community resources, especially those targeted to diverse ethnic and cultural groups.

Outreach activities for the mental health professional include being stationed in the disaster assistance center, and providing counseling in Red Cross shelters, temporary housing, schools, child care centers, playgrounds, and other places. Mental health professionals will be challenged to offer their services in ways to avoid the stigma of implied emotional pathology, and thereby increase utilization. For many families, these encounters will be the first experience with a mental health professional, so the practitioner has to be alert to the reluctance of the parent to seek help and to make the encounter as rewarding and nonthreatening as possible. Among the techniques found most useful in working with children are art, expressive activities, storytelling, and play therapy. For younger and latency-age children, parent-child groups are effective, while "rap" groups for older children and adolescents are useful. Teenagers typically volunteer their time at peer-staffed agencies providing postdisaster services and respond to requests for assistance in community cleanup and rebuilding efforts.

CHAPTER

Children's Reactions to Disaster

☐ Attachment Theory and Human Behavior in a Disaster

Attachment

Attachment theory, developed by Bowlby (1982), is applicable to human social behavior in response to disaster. Bowlby integrated psychoanalytic concepts of child development with parts of cognitive psychology, ethology, and human information processing. He defined attachment theory as a way of conceptualizing "the propensity of human beings to make strong affectional bonds to particular others, and of explaining the many forms of emotional distress and personality disturbance, including anxiety, anger, depression, and emotional detachment, to which unwilling separation and loss give rise" (Bowlby, 1980, p. 39). Attachment refers to the affectional bond that forms between a nurturing figure, usually the mother, and child in the course of time and in response to consistent care. Bowlby stated that there is an innate tendency within the human baby to seek and maintain proximity to an attachment figure. This behavior has the function of protecting children from the risk of harm. The repertoire of activity that enables children to contact their mother is called "attachment behavior." It includes certain patterns of behavior, such as crying and calling by the infant, and clinging and following by the young child. Complementary to this, the care given by the mother, especially the readiness to respond to the baby's signals, helps develop a secure attachment which becomes the foundation for future mental health.

Attachment behavior is a fundamental part of human nature and is considered equal in developmental theory to sexual and feeding behavior. It is first directed to a specific individual, the caretaker, then gradually extended to other family members, and later to peers and other people. Though less intense after the third birthday, attachment behavior exists—ready to be elicited—throughout life. It is especially apt to be aroused when a person is ill, fatigued, or afraid and, at such times, it is natural to search out the care and comfort of a person, a family member, or even a place that holds promise of being "a secure base." Because attachment behavior is more readily elicited in childhood, the young are especially prone to distress when there is no one available and responsive when needed. Separation or threat of separation from an attachment figure is a particular vulnerability of children.

Separation

Separation is the other side of the coin of attachment. Bowlby stated that human beings are genetically constructed to attach themselves to others and also to respond with anxiety to an unwilling separation. Bowlby (1973, p. 405) defined separation anxiety as "how we feel when our attachment behavior is activated, and we are seeking an attachment figure, but without success." This behavior is a natural, instinctive, response to separation. Anything that signals the threat of separation is apt to cause anxiety. There are a series of "natural" cues that indicate a possibility of danger: isolation, exposure to strange people or strange situations, darkness, sudden movement, or noise. Safety is sought by responding with caution or taking appropriate action when confronted by any of these conditions. When children of any age are frightened, such as by a sudden loud noise, they not only will attempt to withdraw from the alarming condition, but will attempt in some way to reach an attachment figure or a safe location. A family together is a more solid base, ready to provide comfort for each other.

A disaster may be looked on as a sudden and unexpected situation which threatens safety and also threatens separation of family members from each other (Sable, 1995). Separation anxiety can be expected to be greatly heightened at such a time. As family members find each other, or learn the whereabouts and safety of each other, they feel reassured. However, feelings of fear, worry, and concern may linger. The more severe a disaster, the more serious is the threat and the greater the chance of actual separation and loss. It is natural for children to be afraid of being alone or of sleeping alone in the dark for a period of time following a disaster. How they are helped through this period of stress will play a part in determining their recovery from the stress and resumption of their usual activities. Parents can be reassured that they are not spoiling their children when they respond to a child who is frightened. It is not overdependency or regression to want added comfort at such times. If children's attachment behavior is rebuffed, feelings may go "underground" only to surface later, possibly as an emotional problem. Children who know a reliable attachment figure is available and responsive will be less prone to chronic fear and will be able to move through a period of stress more easily.

☐ The Child's World after a Disaster

Children experience the devastating set of events wrought by a disaster as a confusing, threatening, disruption. In disasters where damage extends to schools, playgrounds, and parks, the probability of children being traumatized is increased. The lives of the adults within a destroyed and damaged community also are seriously disrupted, and their capacities to respond to their children's social and psychological needs are greatly diminished. As part of a functioning community, parents bring their children to activities where they participate, feel secure, and are comfortable—activities that occupy a large part of a child's day, but also provide adults respite from their caretaking role. After a disaster, the community no longer can provide these resources to the family. Therefore, one function of the emergency system, is to offer substitutes for these "lost" institutional resources.

The dynamics of family life may be discontinuous after a disaster because the event disrupts the homeostasis of the family and alters the interpersonal relationships that underlie family life. The family's social routines are upset because of destruction or damage to the residence and injury sustained by family members. The economic effect of a disaster on children and their families includes temporary housing and displacement, and the loss of familiar and prized possessions, such as toys. Interactions will be altered by the need to attend to damage to the home, injury to family members, and by the emotional impact on the family at large. The focus of concern is forced to shift then, from the management of everyday affairs to meeting the demands for survival created by the disaster. When parents are burdened with these immediate, unfortunate, demands, it is difficult for them to meet their children's increased demands for support and attention.

Disruption of family functioning also has longer term effects on a child's emotional life. How a family recovers from a major disaster will depend on both its own integrity and the availability of personal and community resources. The more functional family will cope better with these new demands because of an already well-established relational and personal support system in the community. When displaced from their homes, these families may not find it necessary to seek shelter from the Red Cross because they have an extensive network of family and friends available to them. By utilizing their support network, they can somewhat mitigate the emotional impact of the disaster on children who will be with familiar people and will be in familiar places. In a major disaster, however, damage may be so widespread as to make even this kind of extended support unavailable. In such cases, the functional family will also lose the normal support system that generally is found within a functioning community. For the less functional families who are attempting to cope with the new situation, preexisting problems in communication and interpersonal relations will become exacerbated. Such families will lack the resources to redirect their coping activities, and therefore will find it difficult to mobilize their minimal resources in the face of disaster.

Separation and loss have long been recognized as key traumatic events that occur in a child's life. In the everyday life of the child, there often is the fear of leaving home and of separating from parental figures. When a family relocates under normal conditions, the child experiences anxieties and feelings of loss, and the home as a secure base diminishes. Even though the child may feel unsafe in the new home environment, it still is relatively familiar and remains a "secure base." When the home is destroyed or severely damaged after a disaster, the child may feel there is no physical place that is secure and safe. Nevertheless, while the child may be saddened by the loss of cherished objects, toys, and familiar surroundings and may express the wish for the restoration of these things, material loss is less traumatic than separation experiences from cherished attachment figures.

In an extreme situation, such as a disaster, when separation as a result of injury and loss to one or more members of the family occurs, the impact on the emotional functioning of the child causes reactions that closely resemble those appearing in grief and mourning situations. Behavioral manifestations take the form of regression (that is, behaviors most characteristic of earlier stages of development), apathy, clinging, whining, and irritability. Emotional responses may appear as depression, sadness, anxiety, agitation, and guilt. Cognitive reactions may appear as loss of concentration and attention abilities, accentuated startle responses, and distorted reactions to stimuli in the environment which are interpreted as the recurrence of the disaster itself.

The child is more likely to develop such responses in the absence of the support of parents or familiar primary caretakers. Rapid restoration of the family unit thus will serve to diminish the traumatic effects of the disaster on the child. How the family experiences and mediates a disaster is central to how the child makes sense of it, especially in the ways that fear and security are communicated to the child. Displacement to the shelter environment or to temporary housing interrupts parental control. In the absence of primary caregivers, other close family members and friends can help the child deal with the tragic impact of the loss. Trusted people can diminish the impact of the tragedy by recreating a sense of a secure base in a child's otherwise shattered world, thereby helping the child to reestablish a familiar and secure world again. The situation is worsened when the adults are overwhelmed with their own mourning and therefore are not emotionally available to the grieving child. Parents may become preoccupied with the paperwork necessary for insurance claims and federal entitlements after a disaster, and be too exhausted to be emotionally available to the child.

Schools provide a sense of regularity and order to the child's day, guiding activities by an ordered schedule in the company of familiar persons. They play a major role in the process of building the sense of safety and security that is so important to children. Parents also regard the school as a safe place, and entrust educators with their children daily into what they come to regard as a secure environment. The fact that the community at large looks to the school as a normalizing context emphasizes the need to reopen schools as soon as possible after a disaster. However, in the past, community leaders have been more likely to begin by restoring basic services and, only after this, will they turn to the problems of reopening schools. As a result, many school districts not only will plan for the safety and protection of students in a disaster, but also will make extensive plans for providing continuing care for children in the immediate aftermath and not releasing the children from school until their parents call for them.

Schools in disaster-prone areas frequently are prepared to provide for children's immediate needs for as long as 3 days, by stocking enough emergency supplies, food, blankets, and bedding. Carrying out postdisaster tasks at their schools requires great dedication and commitment from the teachers who often are separated from their own families. In some situations, school personnel may have made arrangements to be reunited with their own children at the schools where they teach, but this may become difficult because of the physical destruction and the chaos that occurs during a disaster. This points to the need to plan for effective emergency communication networks to keep teachers as well as parents informed about the safety of their children.

The school also is the locus of activities that anchor the lives of older children and youth, providing venues for sports, clubs, and informal peer interactions. The older children's lives also are disrupted by a major disaster because the school plays a regulating role in their lives. A school's earliest reopening therefore will help restore the emotional support that comes from informal interaction with peers, and participation in usual school activities can serve to reinstate a sense of the familiar and the routine in children's disrupted lives. The middle schools and high schools also can provide support groups and specialized crisis services for older children, such as developing a peer counseling program within the school setting. In addition, community volunteer efforts to aid in cleanup and reconstruction can enlist youth through existing organizations within the schools. Teenagers can staff information lines, help with child care, be messengers, and perform other helpful roles. In this way, the school and community can positively direct the altruistic energies of youth that frequently are found in the period immediately following a disaster.

School absences commonly are reported following a disaster because children will be kept at home by their parents for fear of additional disasters. Older youth may remain absent because they are needed at home or in the community as helpers. Children may be fearful about leaving their parents and returning to school, and parents share their fears. Because this occurs, school-based parent meetings become very important. The meetings should be both informational and supportive to keep the community informed about the status of the disaster, and to become a source of information regarding helpful strategies in coping with children's problems. They also should provide information to parents on how to deal with school avoidance behaviors.

Following a disaster, there frequently is a phase where apathy sets in, which is fed by discouragement, frustration, and disappointment as the residents wrestle with the tasks of restoring its community life. The "pulling together" that characterizes the earlier phase of the disaster creates a sense of camaraderie for the families who have experienced a common loss. As the reconstruction proceeds over time, and residents struggle with their own individual problems, there frequently is a reported sense of "let down," resulting from the loss of this sense of a common cause. It is important for mental health professionals and teachers to be aware of this and not to become discouraged should such change occur.

Children Who Have Been Traumatized by a Disaster

As soon as school and community routines become reestablished in the early months after the disaster, the majority of children will return to their normal predisaster patterns. However, some children will continue to require more attention, with behaviors that are more common in the immediate postdisaster phase. Behaviors, such as sleep disturbances, anxious attachment, and withdrawal from other children and family members may indicate that a child is experiencing a persistent post-traumatic stress disorder. The longer that the symptoms persist over time, the more frustrated the parents may become in being unable to meet the child's needs.

Disaster experiences may result in persistent fears for children of all ages. The fears are renewed by reminders, such as loud noises, rainstorms, howling winds, and smoke. Younger children who are unable to verbalize, cry and cling to adults to indicate fear and distress. Older children and adolescents are better able to express their fears verbally and are more likely to seek out information about the event and be aware of the probability of its recurrence. If a child has experienced a trauma (such as an earthquake, tornado, or civil disturbance) in a particular setting, then he is likely to perceive that place to be unsafe. Very often, children who are traumatized will demand adult protection because they are afraid to be alone even in places that had not been regarded as "unsafe" in the past. In an actual war zone, by comparison, certain behaviors are learned that are more protective and more vigilant than in communities that are not under siege. The term, *war zone*, has been used to describe inner city neighborhoods where there is a proliferation of aggressive and criminal behavior, such as shootings and gang wars. Similar behaviors have been reported in actual war zones.

Post-traumatic stress symptoms may be confusing to parents who have difficulty understanding the emotional distress manifested by a child's actions. They may be unfamiliar to the family that has not had any problems in handling a child's behavior in the past and, for the first time, needs to deal with a child who is now exhibiting strange new behavior disturbances. Parents who have seen a child through previous developmental crises may be particularly upset by the regressive behaviors that are one of the more common signs of disaster-induced stress. They may expect that the child's behavior will return to normal over a short period of time and, when regressive behavior persists over time, there is both concern and anger that it has not ceased. Parents may become irritable, punitive, and rejecting, when it seems to them that the child should have "gotten over" the effects of the disaster more quickly.

Many parents will seek advice about their concerns with friends, family members, their child's pediatrician, and school personnel. It often is the teacher who first identifies the child who is traumatized, and who requests to see the parents. The teacher often will confirm the parents' concern, having observed the same pattern of behavior in school as in the home, and may recommend that they speak with the school counselor for a possible referral for counseling. Some parents will accept the recommendation for help and will welcome the referral. Others may reject this advice because of their need to deny the existence of a "stigmatizing" emotional problem.

For the family already feeling overburdened as a result of having to deal with the rebuilding process, bringing their child in for special assistance may be seen as an additional burden. It becomes important for the parents to understand that the helping process also will offer support for the entire family. It is particularly important to avoid attributing guilt or blame to the parents for the difficulty that the child is having, even when it is apparent that the child's behavior may be modeled after their parents' (Allen & Rosse, 1998). The parents are much more in need of reassurance and support in their situation. They also need compassion with their struggle to meet the needs of a child who is traumatized. The goal is to enable parents to identify the emotional distress the child is experiencing and to initiate the steps necessary to rebuild their shattered lives.

The child who is traumatized and who comes from a dysfunctional family will have much more difficulty recovering from the disaster. The child's development has been hampered by the prior demands of coping within the family. The family's supportive functions may have been inadequate prior to the event, so the child has less resiliency to cope with the trauma of a disaster. The dysfunctional family also will lack the emotional resources to support the therapeutic process. Children who are traumatized also may appear in families that distrust psychotherapy, that are unfamiliar with the benefits of counseling, and that do not welcome outsiders intruding in their personal lives. These families deny that the child's problems are serious and resist the recommendations made by teachers and school counselors. As a result, the schools can offer only limited support to their students and often only after they have obtained grudging approval from the parents.

A Child, with Limited Family Support, Who Has Been Traumatized

Fernando, a 9-year-old Hispanic male, was referred to therapy by his teachers, the principal, and the school counselor. Fernando's mother, who is 25, and his 10-month-old brother had abandoned the boy and his father some months before the earthquake because of his father's drinking and aggression. Fernando's behavior following the Northridge earthquake had become aggressive and defiant. After he had been in several major skirmishes with classmates, his father was informed, but paid no attention, so the school became concerned. A report to the Los Angeles County Children and Family Services in the previous school year had made the father wary of outside intervention.

The therapist worked with Fernando twice weekly for nearly 1 year. In initial sessions, his drawings showed alienation, fear, and lack of self-esteem. The therapist learned that during the temblor he had been alone in his "bedroom" (which was a closet of the bachelor apartment his father had rented) from which Fernando had run out into the streets to caution his friend downstairs, a 6-year-old, who also was alone. Fernando could not understand what caused the floor to shake, the ceiling to fall, and the dishes and mirrors to break.

The fights that he picked were seen as behavior he used to express his rage at absent parents and to attempt to draw attention to his terror which, at first, he denied. The therapist encouraged him to voice his fears of abandonment, to talk about his father's rigid discipline that included beatings when he cried, and to speak about his terror when there were continued aftershocks. The therapist helped Fernando to develop a support network, made up of a buddy system, to assure his personal safety. He was placed in a therapy group with three other similarly acting-out boys, where the focus was on problem solving, cooperation, and anger management.

Through his drawings, Fernando revealed that he assisted his father in nighttime pickup of corpses for delivery to the mortuaries. As a result of his poor sleep schedule, he showed fatigue, irritability, and dissociation in school the next day. When he was absent from school, his father told the principal that Fernando was ill. However, Fernando's therapist learned the next day that actually Fernando had "assisted" until dawn. His therapist called his father and the father promised to acquire an adult assistant for his business. The therapist and the father discussed the problems that Fernando was experiencing because of his acute sense of abandonment by his mother. In hopes of providing parenting skills and support for the father, the therapist offered therapy sessions at the clinic for both Fernando and himself, and the father accepted.

After a year, Fernando's grades had improved and his relationships with his peers were more cooperative. He had acquired a best friend—his first— from the group therapy and the group members monitored each other's angry moods by providing peer support, identity, and understanding.

When considerable time has passed since the disaster, the family may fail to make a connection between the disturbed behavior displayed in response to a new crisis and any prior trauma that the child may have experienced. Certain recent situations may trigger all the old memories and fears that accompanied the memories, and the current behavior may be a renewal of the old traumatic symptoms. It therefore is important for the clinician to explore for traumatic events that the child has experienced in the past, and to be alert to "residue reactions" of such crises. For example, thunder may recall fright of an earlier frightening violent storm, or vibrations caused by passing trucks may feel like an earthquake and startle the child. In such cases, the fragments of the most recent experience have served to awaken a full-blown response that had first appeared as a response to the original disaster.

The symptoms that parents are concerned about, such as sleep disturbances, irritability, excessive clinging, and problems with siblings, may be new symptoms or ones that have been persistent over time. The fact that the child has developed "new" symptoms in the late aftermath of a disaster may be enough to concern the parents so that they will seek help from pediatricians and child therapists. Very often, the child's symptoms disrupt family life and affect the child's school performance, and the seeking of help is precipitated by the parent's recurrent frustration and feelings of helplessness.

Help-seeking also may be provoked by the persistence of heightened arousability and regressive behaviors. For example, a child may have achieved independence, but regresses to clinging after a disaster. Parents often will expect that these disturbing behaviors will be short-term reactions but, when they persist over time, they feel frustrated in their attempts to comfort the child and may become desperate enough to seek professional help. Another example is that of a young, school-age child with whom there may have been difficulty reestablishing healthy bedtime behavior and sleep patterns.

Parents also may become concerned about their older children and adolescents whose school performance and social relationships have suffered. Separation from their peers as a result of the disaster disrupts their usual social and athletic activities, and they become harder to manage at home because of the diminished support systems. Emotional problems may take the form of aggressive behaviors toward peers and siblings, somatic symptoms, school avoidance, and family problems. Obvious signs of depression and anxiety, such as sleep and appetite disturbances that are more prevalent in the younger child, may appear. There also may be a disrupted home life due to damaged houses, or to living in temporary quarters in new or strange environs. Moreover, the parents who are involved in reconstruction of home and family life may be less involved because, even under normal circumstances, parents often feel that they no longer have to be as available or attentive to the needs of a teenager as to the needs of a younger child. Another source of distress to teenagers may be the loss of work that frequently follows major disasters. One way independence develops for a teenager is in the after-school job, and this may be lost permanently or may not yet have been restored. In addition, families may not have money available for the usual allowances and luxuries that children demand.

Competence, Resilience, and Vulnerability

Competence, or the pattern of effective adaptation that results from complex interactions between the individual and the environment, often will determine a child's emotional response when a catastrophe poses a significant threat or challenge to that environment (Masten & Coatsworth, 1998, p. 206). However, a child's reaction will also depend on the impact of the event and will vary in relation to a number of situational factors. When a child experiences the death or injury of a family member, or is exposed to gory, gruesome images, these create a longer lasting trauma and place the child at high emotional risk. Regardless of the age of the child, personal injury to the child will cause emotional upset; if the injury is extensive, it will remain a lasting reminder to the child. Destruction or damage to the home and the loss of familiar objects, such as toys and books, can be more traumatic than adults realize. It is not unusual to see a child clutching a doll, a stuffed animal, or a cherished toy as a source of comfort. The extent of damage to the community at large will affect the child's ability to engage in play and to participate in social activities with peers at school and in the neighborhood. The effect of situational factors is that children of all ages experience the disruption of a formerly safer and more secure world, factors which, in turn, have contributed to the presence or absence of functional family and social support systems.

The probability of longer term psychological effects of a disaster on children and youth generally varies with the magnitude of the disaster and the extent of the dislocation (Green et al., 1990). However, it is important not to form judgments about the traumatic effects on a child solely on the basis of the severity of the external disturbance. The child who is more psychologically vulnerable generally will be more severely affected by disasters of lesser severity than the less vulnerable child. When the disaster has resulted in deaths of family members, friends, and peers, there is a greater likelihood of longer term emotional distress. One of the factors that will determine the degree of emotional distress is the resilience of the child. *Resilience* generally refers to manifested competence in the context of significant challenges to adaptation or development (Masten & Coatsworth, 1998, p. 206). Some children do not become traumatized by the different events in their lives and are able to adjust in the face of change and crisis. Resilient children have the capacity to "spring back," or to recover rapidly, from the disruptions that they experience. Resilience is, in part, related to the child's disposition, familial strengths and resources, quality of parenting, and stability of the home environment.

Garmezy (1991) and Garmezy, Masten, Nordstrom, and Ferrarese (1979) identified three protective factors found in resilient children: dispositional and personality features, family cohesion, and the availability of external support systems. According to Masten and Coatsworth (1998), the following qualities characterize resilient children and adolescents: (1) *individual*—good intellectual functioning; appealing, sociable, easygoing disposition; self-efficacy, self-confidence, high self-esteem; talents; and faith; (2) *familial*—a close relationship to a caring parental figure; authoritative parenting: warmth, structure, high expectations; socioeconomic advantages; and connections to extended supportive family network; (3) *extrafamilial*—bonds to prosocial adults outside the family; connections to prosocial organizations; and attending effective schools.

The construct of resilience, derived from developmental stress studies (Rutter, 1979), has been applied specifically to catastrophic trauma, including natural disasters, war, and family violence (Garmezy & Masten, 1994; M. O. Wright, Masten, Northwood, & Hubbard, 1998; Zimmerman & Arunkumar, 1994). Resilience seems to be one of the key factors in the development of coping patterns that play a role in effective adaptation to the challenging circumstances brought about by a disaster. The child's resilience is affected both by experiences within the family and by personal hardiness. This form of individual competence appears to determine how well a child copes with a new, overwhelming, traumatic event.

One can conceptualize who the most vulnerable children are likely to be. From a practical point of view, intervention should be targeted to those children who are behaviorally indicating stress reactions. In general, children who are vulnerable have a difficult time coping with the disruptions that occur in their lives. They are more fearful and more easily traumatized by day-by-day life events. They are more irritable, clinging, and difficult to comfort; more afraid of being separated from their families; and often unable to resume their normal sleep patterns. Psychodynamic indicators of vulnerability in children are experiences of prior separation or loss of a nurturing figure, physical or sexual abuse or neglect, and psychological or neurological impairment. As a result, they generally have greater difficulties in coping, and an unusual event, like a disaster, would be even more difficult for them.

Children who are vulnerable therefore require more attention in a disaster than other children. They depend to a greater extent than other children on the consistency and predictability of their environment and the people around them. Their emotional needs are likely to be exacerbated by a disaster of any magnitude. Their parents usually have problems in just coping with their children's needs on a day-to-day basis. They may find it more difficult to function when their usual home environment is damaged or if they are moved to strange surroundings. Disasters and periods of disruption to the home bring additional burdens on the families of vulnerable children. In fact, the therapist might find that the child's problems sometimes parallel the level of anxiety in one or another of the parents, most often the mother, who usually has the primary responsibility to care for the child. If the mother is highly anxious and overburdened as a result of the a disaster, she often is not able to provide a sense of emotional security for the child.

☐ The Developmental Approach

E. H. Erikson viewed individual development as occurring across eight stages in a person's life cycle. At each stage, there is a psychosocial crisis brought about by the need to resolve a significant developmental task or conflict. Psychological development emerges from the manner in which the individual resolves the crisis. According to Erikson's (1963) epigenetic model, personality arises from the interaction between the individual's biological needs and social demands during key points in development. Table 1 follows

TABLE 1. Stages of psychosocial development

	Stage 1 Oral Sensory (Birth to 1 year)	Stage 2 Muscular-Anal (2 to 3 years)	Stage 3 Locomotor-Genital (4 to 5 years)	Stage 4 Latency (6 to 11 years)	Stage 5 Puberty & Adolescence (12 to 18 years)
Tasks	Trust vs. mistrust	Autonomy vs. shame and doubt	Initiative vs. guilt	Industry vs. inferiority	Ego identity vs. ego diffusion
Crisis	Can I trust the world?	Can I control my own behavior?	Can I become independent of my parents and explore my limits?	Can I master the skills necessary to survive and adapt?	Who am I? What are my beliefs, feelings, attitudes?
Needs	Support, provision or basic needs, continuity	Judicious permissiveness, support	Ecouragement, opportunity	Adequate training, sufficient education, good models	Internal stability and continuity, well-defined sex models, and positive feedback
Typical problems	Lack of support, deprivation, inconsistency	Overprotection, lack of support, lack of confidence	Lack of opportunity, negative feelings	Poor training, lack of direction and support	Confusion of purpose, unclear feedback, ill-defined expectations
Psychosocial outcome	Trust or distrust	Autonomy or doubt	Initiative or guilt	Industry or inferiority	Indentity or role confusion

Note. From *Children Today* by G. J. Craig and M. Kermis, 1995, pp. 68–69. Copyright 1995 by Prentice-Hall. Adapted with permission of the authors.

Erikson's classification of the stages of psychosocial development from infancy through adolescence, emphasizing age-specific tasks, expectable transitional crises, typical needs and problems, and psychosocial outcomes:

When stressful events, such as disaster and other catastrophies, impact a child in the middle of a developmental stage, or in transition from one stage to the next, there will be regressive behaviors and changes in the usual behaviors. Changes in behavior are seen when children react and do things that neither are typical or in their usual style. They may, for example, change from lively children to apathetic ones, or from being independent to being clinging and refusing to let the parents out of sight. Regressive behaviors are behaviors which were common in earlier phases of development, such as thumbsucking or soiling, and which reappear in periods of emotional distress. Stress manifests itself in different ways at each stage in a child's life. Some symptoms of disaster-related stress prevail across age groups, such as fear of separation and changes in eating and sleeping patterns. Other symptoms are more age-specific, such as regressive behavior related to toilet training and soiling. It is more common to observe anxious attachment and clinging in the younger child. When it appears in the older child, it can be a sign of serious regressive reactions.

The most frequently occurring reactions of children in response to a disaster are presented below according to three age groups: early childhood and preschool age, elementary school age, and preadolescence and adolescence (Farberow & Gordon, 1981). There is much overlap of symptoms among the groups. The behaviors described may appear immediately after the disaster or after the passage of days, or even weeks. Most often they are transitory and disappear within a short period.

Early Childhood and Preschool
(Children 5 Years Old and Younger)

Generally, the world of small children is based on predictable events in a stable environment, peopled by dependable persons. These provide security for further development and growth. Any disaster that affects this familiar combination may result in emotional distress, which will vary in almost direct proportion to the degree of disruption in their world. Most of the symptoms appearing in this young age group express in a nonverbal way the fears and anxieties that the children have experienced as a result of the disruption of their secure world. These symptoms include continuous, unrelieved crying; whimpering; screaming; excessive clinging; immobility with trembling and frightened expressions; and running either toward the adult or in aimless motion.

Regressive behaviors, namely behaviors that were considered acceptable at an earlier age and that had been regarded as passed, may reappear following a disaster. They include thumbsucking; bed-wetting; excessive clinging and whining; loss of bowel or bladder control; fear of darkness; fear of being left alone; fear of crowds or strangers; fear of animals; night terrors, nightmares, inability to sleep without a light or unless someone is present, inability to sleep through the night; marked sensitivity to loud noises; weather fears, including lightning, rain, and high winds; irritability; confusion; sadness, especially over loss of persons or prized possessions; speech difficulties; eating problems; and asking to be dressed or fed. Pynoos et al. (1995) pointed to cognitive confusion that may appear along with a general decrease of verbalization and a failure in appropriate use of fantasy.

The symptoms listed above may appear immediately after the disaster or after the passage of days or even weeks. Most often they are transient and soon disappear. When the symptoms persist, however, it should be recognized that a more serious emotional problem has developed. Professional mental health counseling may be sought, but many of the above symptoms can be diminished by the parents themselves through understanding of the basis for the behaviors and giving extra attention and caring.

Elementary School (Children 6 to 11 Years Old)

Fears and anxieties continue to predominate in the reactions of children in this age group. However, the fears show an increasing awareness of real danger to self and to significant persons in the child's life. The reactions also begin to include the fear of damage to their environment along with imaginary fears which seem unrelated to the disaster. As with the preschool group, regressive behaviors appear, some of them marked in degree. Problem behaviors include bed-wetting, night terrors, nightmares, sleep problems, inability to fall asleep, interrupted sleep, need for a night light, fear of sleeping alone, and fears of darkness or animals, weather fears, and irrational fears such as safety of buildings or fear of lights in the sky. Additional behavior and emotional problems may show as irritability, disobedience, depression, excessive clinging, headaches, nausea, and visual or hearing problems.

Loss of prized possessions, especially pets, seems to hold special meaning to children. The school environment and the increasingly important role of peers lend another dimension to the above behaviors. School problems begin to appear and may take the form of refusal to go to school; behavior problems in school; poor performance; fighting; withdrawal of interest; loss of ability to concentrate; distractibility; aggressive behavior, such as frequent fights with siblings or friends; peer problems, such as withdrawal from playgroups, friends, and previously enjoyed activities; and refusal to go to the playground or to parties. School-age children may show even more disturbance than preschool children subsequent to a disaster. This may be because the younger children remain closer to the family—their safe base. The older children, who are in the community and in school, are more aware of the extended world and that some of that larger world also has been disrupted. Pynoos et al. (1995) have described for this group a selective inhibition of thought and nonreflective daydreaming, thus compromising their potential for further development of communication skills.

Duration of the symptoms, which generally can be considered "normal" if they occur for only a short period during or immediately after the disaster, again indicate, in part, the severity of the reaction. When these symptoms persist beyond several weeks, professional consultation is indicated.

Preadolescence and Adolescence (Children 12 to 17 Years Old)

Adolescents are faced with two main developmental tasks: to integrate and adapt to the physiological revolution within themselves and to prepare themselves for the tangible adult tasks ahead of them. They are concerned with how to connect their roles and skills with the occupational prototypes of their culture and are hampered by concern over how they appear to be perceived in the eyes of others. Conformity is the outstanding characteristic of adolescents, but it is essentially conformity with their peer group and its standards.

Adolescents have a great need to appear competent to the world around them, especially to their family and friends. They are struggling to achieve independence from the family and are torn between the desire for increasing responsibility and the ambivalent wish to maintain the more dependent role of childhood. Frequently, struggles occur with the family because the peer group seems to have become more important than the parental world. Critical transitions in establishing peer relationships may be affected (Pynoos et al., 1995) In the usual course of events, the struggle between adolescents and family plays itself out and, depending on the basic relationship between the adolescents and the family, the trials and problems are resolved. A disaster disrupts this process, just as would a major crisis in the family, such as divorce or loss of a parent.

A major disaster may have a number of impacts on adolescents, depending on the extent to which it disrupts the functioning of the family and community. It may stimulate fears concerning the loss of family members, or fears related to their own bodies and their physical intactness. A disaster disrupts their peer relationships and perhaps their school life. It threatens their growing emancipation from the family because of the family's need to work together; and it threatens the adolescents with reactivated fears and anxieties from earlier stages of development. Ability to recover from the severe effects of the disaster will depend to a considerable degree on the level of development of their perceived coping self-efficacy. *Coping self-efficacy* is defined as a person's subjective appraisal of his or her ability to cope with the environmental demands of the stressful situation (Bandura, Reese, & Adams, 1982; Benight et al., in press).

Behavioral trouble signs include withdrawal and isolation; physical complaints, headaches and stomach pains; depression and sadness; suicidal ideation; antisocial behavior, such as stealing and aggressive behavior; school problems, such as truancy, disruptive behavior, and academic failures; sleep disturbances, sleeplessness, night terrors, and withdrawal into heavy sleep; and mental confusion.

Most of these behaviors are transitory and last only for a short period. When these behaviors persist, they are readily apparent to the family and to teachers, who should respond quickly. Teenagers who appear to be withdrawn and isolated, and who isolate themselves from family and friends, are experiencing emotional difficulties. They may be concealing fears that they are unable to express. Like many adults, adolescents often show their emotional distress through somatic complaints.

☐ Enhancing Competence in Children and Their Families

Disaster is an extraordinary event and the child's reactions to it have to be understood as being different from other experiences in quality, quantity, and form. All children who have lived through a major disaster, or even one limited in scope, are likely to be traumatized to some extent. However, not all children will require treatment. Some children are able to seek assistance from adults and express their need for comfort, support, and information, an ability that very much depends on the age of the child. However, children at all ages who are less expressive and more withdrawn may have their needs go unrecognized by adults in their world. Reactions of children differ according to age, stage of development, and the level of cognitive awareness.

Very young children, of course, are unable to express their needs verbally. Very young children, who may not appear to be aware of changes in their physical environments, may suddenly have difficulty sleeping in their own bed (they may associate being in their bed with the disaster that had occurred). The fears of young children often are reflective of the fears of the adults in their world. The adults will need to understand the basis of their own fears in order to help their children. In many cases, these fears will take the form of an unwarranted apprehension of continued danger, and an unreasonable anxiety for the safety of the child even when the threat has passed. Parents will need to be provided with the requisite skills on how to handle the anxious clinging, the sleep problems, the eating problems, and the like, and how to calm the child.

The older child who is more aware of the environment may express fears of separating from the family and losing the protection that the parents provide. After a disaster, older children often appear to be anxious, worried, and fearful that the disaster will recur. They are likely to have a generalized sense of apprehension that is expressed through difficulty in concentrating, irritability, and fear of being alone. Older children can talk about the losses they have sustained, and can request comfort from familiar adults in their world. A way to reassure older children after a disaster is to provide both accurate and complete information of what has happened, to indicate that attempts are being made by the adult world to protect them, and to explain to them the nature of these efforts.

Adolescents are more able to verbally express fears, worries, feelings, and concerns. They have a more cognitive understanding of the world around them, and may be more informed about the cause and the effects of the disaster than many adults. Adolescents appear to be more aware of the long-term effects of the disaster on both their family and the community. However, damage and injuries to friends and families may cause emotional distress that may be difficult to express. Teenagers are likely to conceal their predicament from adults, but will more readily share personal information with peers. This pattern of concealment from the adult world makes it more difficult to determine need among adolescents. It may be found that group-level interventions are effective both for case-finding and for providing emotional support for youth. There may be adults at school or in the community whom the adolescent trusts and will seek out.

Children and youth depend on the awareness and sensitivity of the adults in their environment to recognize and respond to their emotional needs after a disaster. This requires an awareness on the part of adults of all the potentials for disaster-induced stress in the child's world and the symptoms indicative of their distress. Parents need to understand their child, and to try to think the way the child thinks. Parents also will need both information on how to recognize, assess, and provide help for their children, and support and advice in applying their parenting skills to their children in this atypical situation. When the parents' usual approaches to the child cease to be effective, outside assistance should be sought. Since the parents themselves are undergoing considerable stress, they may find it difficult to provide even the basic qualities of parenting. By educating parents to recognize the potential emotional sequel of disaster and trouble signs in children, and in themselves, they can mobilize familial resources and community resources on behalf of their child.

☐ Summary

Bowlby's theories of attachment (1982), separation (1973), and loss (1980) are useful in understanding child and family behavior in disasters. Attachment is recognized as the process by which humans make strong affectional bonds with particular others. It is considered a fundamental part of human nature. Children are especially prone to distress when their attachment bond is disrupted or broken resulting in separation anxiety and emotional distress. How children are helped through the resultant stress plays a large role in their recovery and in the prevention of potential emotional problems. The child's world is disrupted and confused because family life and interpersonal relationships are altered. The degree of disorganization is dependent on the extent of destruction to the community and whether there is injury to or loss of family members. Parental focus often is shifted from promotion of family relations and growth and development of its members to the immediate pressing needs for survival and relocation. Disasters can cause reactions that resemble those found in grief and mourning, with regression, apathy, clinging, sadness, anxiety, agitation, and loss of cognitive abilities such as concentration and attention.

Restoration of the family unit in familiar places, if possible, along with early resumption of routines in school and other "safe environments" within the community, help in diminishing the impact of the disaster. Mental health professionals need to be familiar with the customary phases of recovery from a disaster so that they are not discouraged by the "ups and downs" that frequently accompany a family's struggle with the long-term reconstruction projects. While most children are able to recover to the normal predisaster patterns, some children will require more attention, eventually exhibiting a persistent post-traumatic stress disorder. Such symptoms may be confusing to parents who have had no difficulty with their children before the disaster. The family needs to be able to recognize the basis for the regressive or disturbing behavior. Dysfunctional families will generally have more difficulty recovering from the disaster but still may resist the help available. The concepts of vulnerability, resilience, and competence are helpful in understanding the reactions of the child and family in the disaster situation. Other factors are the developmental level of the child, personality features, and the degree of functional competence of the individual and the family. Stress manifests itself in different ways at each stage of a child's life, the major indicators of which are changes in the usual behaviors and regressive behaviors. Although all children who have been through a major disaster are likely to be traumatized to some extent, not all children will require treatment. To a large degree, this depends on the awareness and responsiveness of the parents to their emotional needs. Providing support and educational advice to the parents, along with help in resolving their own emotional distress, may meet the needs of the child enough to recover emotional stability.

Helping Children and Families in Disasters: A Crisis Intervention Approach

A basic principle to recognize in working with problems of children and their parents who have experienced a disaster is that they are essentially normal functioning individuals who have been subjected to sudden unusual and great stress. Although there is always the possibility of prior psychopathology that might exacerbate their reactions, most often the problems which appear are likely to be directly related to the disaster. The process recommended for helping the children and families often starts with *crisis intervention*, which has as its primary goal to identify, assess, and relieve the stresses developed as a result of the hazard (disaster) and thereby to reestablish the level of previous functioning as quickly as possible (Caplan, 1980; Wainrib & Bloch, 1998).

☐ General Steps in the Helping Process

Establishing Rapport

The first task is the establishment of rapport between the therapist and the children and their families as they initiate an interaction that is based on a genuine concern for them and for their problems, which will facilitate feelings of acceptance and trust. It is important to let both children and parents know that the therapist is informed and experienced with the kinds of difficulties that they are having and that he or she is able to help them. It is also important that there be mutual understanding in the course of the discussion. This often requires frequent checking throughout the encounter with the children to make sure that the therapist has understood what they have been saying, and that they have understood what the therapist has been saying.

Identifying, Defining, and Focusing on the Problem

Children going through a crisis often become confused and chaotic in their thinking. It is helpful both to the children and the families to identify and focus on one specific problem out of the many that are presented and seem to be overwhelming the family and the children. If possible, the problem should be one that can be quickly resolved, so that the children and families can feel that they are regaining control over their overwhelming problems. Selection of the problem to focus on will be determined by discussions with the family and evaluation of the family's capacity for successfully coping with the problem.

Understanding Feelings

A basic principle of communicating with a child is using language that the child understands, maintaining a friendly and supportive role, and avoiding interrupting the child. Frequently, the child's prior experiences of adult listening has been unsatisfactory. Working with children requires empathy and a copious supply of attention. Being empathetic with children requires extensive patience because children often are unable to express their feelings and adults need to infer from other cues, such as behavior, play, and drawings.

Adults may need to listen to a child's account of a disaster many times, as the child "works through" the disaster by repeatedly talking about "the loud noises" or the "fearful shaking." They also need to understand that the child's body language may be nonverbally expressing the anxieties and fears. The presence of the family generally is helpful at least in initial interviews with the children because the families will be more familiar with their behavior and will be able to interpret idiosyncratic expressions or behaviors. In addition, families may learn how to interact better with their children after observing the interaction with a mental health professional.

☐ Assessment Methods

Case-Finding and Screening

For the most part, families are receptive to offers of help and guidance after a disaster. However, a recommendation from a known and trusted person, such as a physician, a teacher, or a family member, may be required to assure a family that a counselor is someone who will help them with their child. Referrals to the counselor may come from a wide variety of sources. Medical personnel, at times, may identify a child who rouses concern during a physical examination when the child exhibits disturbing behavior or symptoms without a physical cause. Teachers and school counselors also may identify children who are having difficulty in their school adjustment because of changes in behavior or through drawings, play, story-telling and other expressive methods.

Early case-finding typically occurs as mental health personnel conduct their activities in emergency settings, such as Red Cross shelters and Disaster Assistance Centers (DACs). Every interview with an adult in one of these settings should explore for information about children in the family and inquire about how the children are adjusting. When the parents express concern about the child's behavior, full details about the behavior should be obtained. It also is important, at this time, to determine the extent of the adults' distress and to assess their capacity to assist the child in coping. The parents of children who are traumatized are themselves frequently unable to cope with the disaster and are in need of help before they are able to address the child's fears and difficulties.

The Crisis Interview

Crisis interviews are likely to be done in nonoffice settings such as Red Cross shelters, DACs, schools, and evacuation centers. When additional assessment is necessary and feasible, it may take place in more traditional settings like offices, hospitals, and medical and pediatric clinics. In emergency situations, when the traditional settings may have been destroyed, one can "set up shop" anywhere. The aim would be to establish a treatment and assessment venue as soon as possible.

The crisis interview is the key assessment tool on the effects of the disaster on the child's functioning. It should consist of at least three elements: an evaluation of the child's current status, the child's predisaster status and vulnerability, and the need for further assessment or referral. The purpose of the interview is to obtain information from the child, the parent, and, at times, from other informants. When necessary, a brief symptom checklist can be used to determine the child's current status. If such a checklist is not available, the evaluator may find it useful to develop a checklist of his own to help organize the observations of the child (see below).

The following questions are useful in developing a checklist for the effects of a disaster on a the child's functioning:

- What happened during and following the disaster?
- What memories does the child repeat about his or her reactions at the time of the disaster?
- Who was with the child at the time?
- Are there persistent and recurring thoughts about what happened that the child talks about?
- Are the thoughts scary?
- When do they occur?
- When are they the worst?
- To whom can the child talk about these feelings?
- Have things changed in the family, the living situation, and the school?

The purpose of such questions is to allow the child to review the precipitating event and subsequent experiences in the presence of supporting figures when possible and to observe the availability of emotional support within the family. Although primarily information gathering in purpose, the process also is the beginning of a "working through" of the child's fears and anxieties.

Questions to be asked of the parents or adult who is familiar with the child in the crisis interview include:

- What was the child's experience of the disaster?
- What behaviors is the child presenting?
- What are the presenting problems?
- How is the child functioning at this time?
- What was the child's previous level of functioning?
- What changes have occurred?
- How has the child been acting with you?
- How has the child been acting with his or her playmates?
- How has the child been acting with his or her siblings?
- How have his or her siblings been acting since the disaster?
- What are the child's capabilities at this point in time?
- How is the family coping with child's problem?
- Has the child or the family experienced any death or loss as a result of the disaster?

- Has the child or the family experienced any death or loss before the disaster?
- What is the availability of familial support?
- Where will this child or family be if a follow-up is necessary?

The objective is to identify the current sources of stress, the prior stresses in the child's life, the losses the family has experienced, the level of support available, and the most effective response to meet the child's needs. To accomplish this, the interviewer begins with the present time to determine the extent of the current difficulties, and then inquires about stresses that have occurred in the past and how the family coped with them at that time. The interviewer explores losses in the child's support network and who is available for current support, especially someone whom the child trusts and turns to when support has been needed. The interviewer will then discuss with the parents the steps helpful to relieve the child's distress. As stated earlier, a useful principle in this procedure is to focus on the one problem of many that is readily solvable. This helps both children and parents to regain some measure of control over what, for the moment, has become a disordered life. For example, a child fearful of separation from the parents should be kept informed where the parents will be at all times when they are not with the child.

Every effort should be made to interview the child with the family members present. This reduces the child's fear of the interview situation, allows the opportunity to gather information from the parents about the child's interaction within the family, provides information about the interactions in the family system, and provides an indication of the parents' level of fear and anxiety. Parents should be encouraged to talk about what they regard as the main problem and clarify who is taking responsibility for managing the crisis. The interviewer should look for and confirm positive actions the family has already taken, such as seeking help, rescuing the family from a damaged home, finding a shelter or a DAC and meeting what additional needs that they have.

The success of crisis intervention rests on the restoration and strengthening of the family's sense of competence (Figley, 1989a,b). Its primary aim is to reestablish a sense of order in a personal world that has been disrupted. Asking the family to review and prioritize its problems and then to focus on an immediate problem that can be solved quickly will help in penetrating the numbness and regaining a feeling of control. The suggestion of an action designed to help restore control serves as well for the family, as it does for the child. For the parents, the task is compounded by the need to care for the children while, at the same time, attempting to restore a safe physical environment for the family. With damage to the familiar home and community environment, it is not unusual for the entire family to react with a defensive numbness.

Experience has shown that the opportunity to provide mental health interventions during or immediately following a disaster may be limited. Practitioners cannot assume that the family, in light of all their pressing problems, will avail themselves of continuing counseling. The initial crisis interview often may be the only opportunity to provide help, especially if this initial contact successfully meets one of its primary goals and mitigates the sense of crisis. Indeed, it is useful to assume that this most likely will be the case and to consider the interview as probably the only opportunity to provide concrete advice and clear information. This is one way in which crisis therapy differs from the traditional approach of psychotherapy. With the prospect of many sessions of psychotherapy, the therapist's objective in first and early sessions is to observe, to listen, and to obtain as much diagnostic and case history as possible. In contrast, the goal of crisis therapy is to provide helpful intervention quickly, based on as much information as it is possible to obtain in only one or a few sessions.

Most young children find talking about feelings difficult. Developmentally, they do not yet have the skills to verbally process their fears. However, friendly, supportive adults can help the children who need to talk. Trained child mental health professionals know how to provide reassurance and emotional support to children who are beset with natural fears and anxieties. The skilled crisis counselor takes pains to be informed about the event so as to be able to provide clear, factual information regarding the disaster, along with emotional reassurance. The disaster often has the effect of destroying the sense of the security and predictability of the children's world, and the counselor's task is to help them reestablish a sense of a secure world. The skilled crisis counselor works toward this through the parents, and along with the parents in most instances, especially when the child is very young.

With the child who is blocked or has difficulty expressing herself or himself during an interview, the evaluator must proceed cautiously, taking care not to exert pressure on the child and create further resistance. It may be necessary to obtain the information through nonverbal techniques, such as the child's play and drawings. The clinician uses his or her observation skills to note the child's demeanor, expression, affect, and interaction with the parents. Such information always is evaluated within the context of such factors as age, culture, and language skills.

Drawing and play techniques will be particularly useful in interviews with the younger child, since many young children are not able to verbalize their difficulties, even at a superficial level. Play is a natural mode of communication for children, and their fantasies and games can provide much information about the psychological processes that are involved in their problems.

The way that children play with paints, clay, dolls, and water also provides outlets for their feelings. Often their play will incorporate their experience of the disaster, for example, when they build towers out of blocks and have them collapse or when they build towers and then deliberately knock them down, mirroring the events of an earthquake. Children's drawings will depict, on a more or less realistic level, the feared hurricane winds or tornadoes. Fortunately, children's play often discharges fears and anxieties that have been bottled up, serving both as therapy and a source of information. Skilled child therapists have learned it is best to allow the children to make their own interpretations of their play or drawings, rather than impose adult interpretations on them and possibly disrupt these valuable expressive avenues.

☐ Helping Techniques

Crisis Therapy

Crisis therapy by trained, experienced, therapists is undertaken to help a family whose equilibrium has been so upset by the stresses of a disaster that it is no longer able to fulfill its usual functions. Time and informed interventions help in reestablishing the family to its critical role in facilitating the developmental tasks of its children. This critical role underlies the basic principle in therapeutic work with children; namely, that the emotional problems of the child are not just the child's problem, but they are the family's problems. The family is considered the unit to be counseled, not just the distressed child, and as many family members as possible should be involved in the process. In many instances, the counselor also will be able to take advantage of the assistance provided by the concern and availability of members of the extended family and close friends. Sometimes adult members of the family may be experiencing emotional distress themselves, but have hesitated to seek help. However, they are more able to seek help on the children's behalf, and may, in fact, also use the children's problems as a way of asking for help for themselves. In school settings, the family may not need to be so continually involved and the therapy for the child may be able to proceed with less, or even minimal, family involvement.

When it has become apparent that the child and family are able and willing to attend further counseling, the number of therapy sessions provided will depend on such factors as the accessibility of services, the availability of the family, the motivation of the family to engage in the treatment process, and the persistence of the presenting symptom(s). The first therapy session is used to explain the goals of counseling and the procedure involved, in order to encourage the family's commitment. The counselor will explain why involvement of the family is essential. The presenting problems are explored from the point of view of the child or the family, and the family is encouraged to describe the attempts they already have made to cope with their problem situations. One objective of this first counseling session is to provide the family with at least one recommendation that will provide a feeling of regaining control of their lives. The family, in collaboration with the therapist, can determine what efforts will best help the child.

When crisis therapy is an ongoing process, further exploration takes place regarding the status of the child and the family. Through this exploration, there is a shift in focus. While in the first session the emphasis was on the child, the second session can begin to explore the family dynamics. This may take the form of questions about how the family functions on a daily basis, interpersonal dynamics, familial support systems, and the sense of competence in dealing with other life events. Information is sought about:

- Who is the spokesperson for the family?
- How different is the behavior that the child is showing now from his or her predisaster behavior?
- Have there been other uncommon stressful events that may be contributing to the present distress?
- Is the family in agreement about the identified problems?
- Is there a shared concern for the child's situation?
- How participatory is each parent or family member?
- What is the family communication style?
- What is each family member feeling?
- How does each member express these feelings?

The therapist reviews with the family the recommendation of the first session and its outcome, which also will provide further insight into family dynamics and problem solving. This will indicate the motivation and the competence of family members to cooperate in the treatment process.

Some of the formalities of crisis counseling may have to be modified, or even abandoned, in a disaster. For example, full documentation and formal diagnostic procedures frequently are set aside in order to provide the interventions. The urgency of the moment may require the relaxation of the policy regarding extensive record keeping. Whereas the necessity for adequate case recording is well recognized, these requirements are not always possible to complete in the emergency counseling situation. In addition, clinicians may be instructed to maintain the anonymity of the clients and to maintain minimal documentation specified by the sponsoring agency or funding sources, such as time records, and age and sex of the children. School district personnel, for example, may be instructed to maintain minimal records because they do not have the parental consent required for counseling intervention.

The following is a description of a collaboration between several school districts and a mental health agency. After the 1994 Northridge earthquake, Family Service of Los Angeles (FSLA) developed a program to help children. All case examples have been changed, where necessary, to protect identification of the clients.

The 1994 Northridge Earthquake

FSLA provided counseling to children attending elementary schools in several disadvantaged communities. School personnel referred children who had developed fears and anxieties and were acting out in school to FSLA counselors. The counselors then contacted the families and arranged to meet with children and parents individually, or as a family unit, at the school. Experience has indicated that even hesitant families are more likely to access services when offered in school settings, because the school is regarded by most families as a nonintimidating, positive environment. Counselors worked with children and their parents to identify possible post-traumatic stress disorder (PTSD), existing support systems, and outstanding needs. The counselors provided the family with updated information about the disaster and associated emotional distress, such as PTSD, including how to recognize physical, cognitive, emotional, and behavioral symptoms, and suggested strategies for relieving stress reactions, addressing maladaptive coping mechanisms, and improving communication of feelings.

Child counseling methods included storytelling; games; puppets; dream analysis; sentence completion (for example, "If I could be ..."); drawing and painting (family, self, and tree); writing a secret message; using feeling words; using faces with statements to represent feelings; discussing feelings about things (with pictures of faces of children in class, in the neighborhood, playing games, reading, and writing, as well as of teachers and other grown-ups); and discussing feelings about "how I look."

The following cases are examples of children who were seen only once in school by FSLA counselors (identifying details have been changed to protect privacy).

Luis.   Less than 2 months after the Northridge earthquake, Luis found it difficult to remember what happened during the temblor. He was reluctant to discuss any of the circumstances. At the time of the earthquake, he was with his aunt because his parents were in the hospital with his younger sister who was having serious surgery. He did not see his parents until the day after the earthquake and was "very scared." Luis was shy and friendly, although reluctant to talk. It was apparent that the child felt alone and abandoned by the absence of his parents. His drawing was of an automobile with a tiny child inside described as "during" the earthquake, and, in a separate panel, of a bed with a figure sleeping described as "after" the earthquake. The child's reaction to the earthquake was compounded by the absence of the parents and the hospitalization of his sibling that served to intensify his fears.

Jane.   Jane was at home in an outlying community when the earthquake hit. She stayed with her mother and watched television all day, and was scared when she was bussed back to school and away from her mother. Jane is the oldest of four children, quiet and confident, with strong parental figures; nevertheless, being separated from them following the quake caused her to become very anxious.

Emily.   Emily is a charming, verbal, and social child who is able to express her feelings of sadness and fear. She found the earthquake to be very scary and "cold." Emily talked about family problems and fears of her mother's boyfriend. Her grandmother is the positive strength in her life, inasmuch as her mother's social life with boyfriends upsets her. She appears to have some serious boundary issues, but seems competent. Her drawing depicted the family (her mother and three children)—all done in red crayon—outside of the family home, and the boyfriend—drawn with horns in blue crayon— separate from the family, reflecting her fear that her family also might be disrupted.

Ellen.   Ellen was reluctant at first to draw or talk, but then warmed up. She described how the family went under the table during the earthquake, and how she was very scared and still often is nervous. Her parents were offered an opportunity to participate in a group to help them adjust.

Geraldo.   Geraldo stated that the earthquake did not bother him at all, even though his drawing depicted the dresser falling on his foot. He also said that his friend was injured from falling down the stairs. His drawings revealed strong fears, despite his denial that the earthquake had frightened him. Although he appears to be a bright, verbal child, he refused to follow directions. Geraldo seems to be suffering strong anxiety and more assessment was recommended to explore beneath his denial.

Bobby.   Bobby is a bright, verbal, and friendly child and eager to relate his earthquake experiences. His parents protected him when the earthquake struck and took him outside the house that had suffered many cracks and much damage. His father now is unemployed because his workplace sustained damage as a result of the temblor. He said he was very frightened by the aftershocks. He also appeared upset by his father's loss of work and wanted to talk about this.

Toni. Toni described the earthquake as being very scary and how her parents came into her room. However, her parents were not there during the subsequent aftershocks that really frightened her. Toni is a very open child who could express her fears and earthquake experiences. She appears to have nurturing parents.

Bruce. Bruce described how the lights went out during the earthquake, and laughed when he described himself rolling in his bed. He is a quiet child and self-contained. There are no people in his drawings. He may be in denial, but also seems to be functioning adequately and there are no behavioral symptoms.

Renee. Renee was very jovial, friendly, and verbal. She laughed while she described the earthquake. She admitted that she was frightened and talked about her dog and her garden, and not of her family. Renee talked about her mother leaving home, and how she does not see her very often because of her mother's involvement with a boyfriend. Her father is the primary parent. She refused to draw her stepmother because she hated her. She seemed eager to talk to an adult about her situation.

The following cases are examples of children who were seen three or more times by FSLA counselors.

Miguel. Miguel is 9 years old and is "afraid of earthquakes." Before the Northridge earthquake, he was behaving well in school. Miguel was referred when he hit another child because he "just felt like it." His home is crowded. He is sharing a bedroom with uncle, and three other bedrooms are occupied by 10 relatives. He has dreams of his mother and father trying to kill him. After a large aftershock, Miguel said he was very afraid of earthquakes. He thought earthquakes appeared because there was "a devil underground making them happen." He dreamed the earthquake was a monster. Even after explanations were given, Miguel continued to have persistent fears of earthquakes and nightmares, although a year has passed since the Northridge earthquake. Now he dreams that a woman kills his parents and he then has to live with her. Fifteen months after the initial temblor, Miguel says he is "not afraid of earthquakes any more."

Jorge. Jorge is 7 years old, and lived with his parents, three siblings, and an uncle during the earthquake. Two children in his apartment building, who were friends of his, died. Jorge is afraid of earthquakes, and is afraid to be alone at night and to sleep alone. In order to fall sleep, he covers himself up and prays. A family session was arranged for the following week because of the child's intense fears. When his mother came in with him, she was given advice on parenting. In a subsequent family session, his mother and younger brother came in with him. His mother was given advice on how to handle all the children. He was "very scared" during an aftershock nearly 1 year after the initial temblor. Jorge's fears have been exacerbated by the fighting of his parents.

Marie. When the earthquake occurred, the family was very scared and got out of the house and into their car, where they slept for the next few weeks. The parents and younger brother came in with Marie for a family session 2 weeks after the first meeting. They reported that they had moved back into the house, but that the children still were sleeping together. Marie has resumed her social activities and wants to sleep alone, but her brother continues to express fears of the earthquake and demands that they sleep in the same bed. The family continues to feel uprooted, with the father showing irritability and the brother having trouble in school. The mother says they are considering moving to a different part of the country. Marie's drawing reflects her fears of the earthquake and the safety offered by their car in which they all slept together for a while.

Neil. Neil is a friendly child who described the earthquake as "fun." His narrative was disjointed as he described the damage to his home, still insisting that the temblor was fun. Neil is a child who is developmentally delayed and is from an intact family. In the second session, Neil's mother described how nervous she was. The following week, Neil's mother and sister spoke about ongoing fears, flashbacks, and having trouble sleeping. His mother also reported marital problems. Play activities were recommended for the mother to carry out with the children.

Billy. Billy was seen 2 months after the earthquake because of his severe fears when an aftershock occurred and caused things around him to fall. Two weeks later, the babysitter came to the school to report that Billy had come home very upset by the earthquake drill held in the school on the previous day. When Billy came to school the next day, he reported continued flashbacks, and a family session was arranged. The session focused on ways to help Billy overcome his fears by having him draw pictures and tell stories, encouraging him to talk about his fears, and reassuring him that he is safe. Billy's drawing reflects his fears of the unstable (red) earth beneath his home, which he describes as "falling apart." In his picture, Billy stands in the doorway seeking safety, but the blackened windows do not indicate safety.

The preceding cases illustrate the variety and richness of material encountered when psychotherapy was undertaken in a school setting with children referred by teachers and other school personnel. The initial crisis therapy focused primarily on symptoms of distress generated by the disaster, but the continuing therapy sessions indicated preexisting problems that contributed to and exacerbated the impact of the disaster itself.

Group Sessions

Children's Groups

Group interventions usually are effective for children of latency age and older because of their similarities to the daily experiences in classroom settings. After a disaster, they gain a great deal from a group where they can talk openly and honestly about their feelings. Peer involvement even encourages withdrawn children to talk about their feelings. Children frequently are afraid of appearing foolish in asking questions, but a peer group encourages them to ask their questions. Group intervention with children is especially useful for expression of their fears, because they are able to talk about them in front of their peers, once they are reassured that having fears and anxieties is normal and acceptable and that other children—"even the bravest ones"—also have these feelings. Children tell their experiences with great enthusiasm in group discussions with other children of similar age levels. The group therefore is a good resource for providing emotional support to children with whom it is difficult to communicate. The group also serves an informational purpose, especially because children will uncritically accept any rumors that may be circulating and need clarification. These may even include superstitions and fantasies about what happened. The counselor can use the group as an opportunity to provide the children with updated, accurate, information about the disaster.

The group ideally should have no more than 12 children. The attitude of the therapist is critical. Children respond when therapists are empathetically democratic and indicate their concerns about all the children. If the adult runs the group in an authoritarian manner, the group will not function well and children will not feel free to talk about their feelings. Children find that talking about a disaster, or drawing pictures about it, helps dispel their fears about such happenings. The following describes the processes and procedures in a group set up in a child care setting.

The group was told that meeting together gives everyone an opportunity to hear about each other's experiences in the disaster. Each of the children was asked to describe what happened to them and their families in the disaster. The leader made sure that everyone spoke and, if any child went on too long, he or she was asked to end in a sentence, with the explanation that everyone had to have a chance to talk and that he or she will have an opportunity to fill in more details later in the meeting. As the stories appeared, the children were asked to tell about their own fears, and perhaps even to act them out in dramatic play. In the course of the discussion, factual information about the disaster was interspersed. Members of the group were asked to take turns being helpers. The children were paired and then took turns, alternating asking for help with a problem and then acting as helpers with the others' problems. Two of the children were assigned as coleaders to help control restlessness and distractibility among the children. The children were provided with paper, plastic materials, clay, or paints, and asked to depict the disaster. Where children were verbal, their drawings and assemblages became a catalyst for conversation with the therapist. For the less verbal children, art and other types of expressive therapy were the methods used to explore for further insight.

The following are additional specific techniques that can be used in classrooms and in groups of three or more children. Each can be modified for age appropriateness.

Telling the Story.   Arrange for the children to tell a story of the disaster as often and in as many ways as possible. Telling and retelling helps the child to focus on his or her feelings and to be heard and validated. Vary both the groupings (individual, partners, small groups), and the ways (out loud, picture format, comic book, radio play). The children can be asked to write a story of the disaster, starting with "Once upon a time there was a terrible _____, and it scared us all _____. This is what happened _____." End with, "And now we are all safe."

Ask the children to bring in something that reminds them of a moment in the disaster. Ask what was the worst thing that happened? The best? The scariest? The funniest? Who lost a pet? A car? A house? A friend? A toy?

Ask the children: Where were you when it happened? Why? Was luck any part of the story? What did they do? What were they thinking? Feeling? Wishing? Who helped? Who got in the way? Were they feeling abandoned? Did they feel excited? Was it fun? Does anyone have photographs of the aftermath? Was their home damaged? Looted? Broken? Off its foundation?

Ask the children: Are they are still afraid? Do they have dreams? What do they do now that is different because of the disaster? In the case of shy, frightened, or nonverbal children, ask them to show answers with puppets or a doll house, or have them draw the answers. Invite everyone to do the same and share them with each other.

Ask the children to talk about behaviors and activities they have found comforting, such as eating special treats, wearing a favorite shirt, carrying a special toy, watching television, sleeping with an adult, rocking on a rocking chair or rocking horse, thumbsucking. Encourage each child to talk about how this works for him or her. Explore the ways that the children might comfort themselves, and normalize whatever they have done to comfort themselves. In normalizing, explain about the ways that familiar objects, warmth, tastes, scents, and motion provide comfort in troubling times.

Talking About Feelings. Introduce "glad, mad, sad" feeling charts with appropriate faces. Many children may not be aware of what they feel or why. Ask the children to pick a face that expresses how they feel, or to draw an entirely different one—a picture of themselves at the moment.

Ask the children: What does a feeling *feel like* in your body? Have the children take turns. Start by giving an example: "When I'm afraid, I know, because my neck feels all creepy and my back has ice up and down and I get goosebumps on my arms, and my stomach jerks around, and I don't breathe very well. Sometimes, I can hear my heart in my ears, and sometimes my hands shake or my knees are wobbly."

Ask the children: How can you tell when someone else is having a feeling? Can you tell what kind of feeling it is? How? Is it different for grown-ups and children? In what way?

Address the physiological changes in body chemistry, in simple words, such as the fact that smiles release "feel good" messages throughout the body and fears release "get ready to fight or run" messages. This can help to normalize feelings and put thought between feelings and action—an aim in treating reactivity in trauma.

Talk about what each child can do to modulate feelings such as anger, helplessness, loneliness, sadness, mourning, fear, frustration, and anxiety. Explain that feelings tell us how we are and what we need. Then promote discussion of one of the following: action versus inaction, suppression of feelings, help-seeking. Follow with a behavioral intervention, such as "count to 10" when angry, and acting-out is to be avoided. Form smaller groups to discuss stressful situations and solutions that promote peer support for troublesome feelings.

Teaching Disaster Survival Skills. Before addressing the causes of a disaster or introducing safety drills, encourage the children's storytelling. As questions occur, answer them realistically, but with care not to erode whatever sense of denial helps the children to cope and to sleep at night.

Incorporate a discussion about the causes of the disaster. For an earthquake, begin with discussion of the feelings of movement. Explain why people in some places feel the movement more than people in other places, and why some houses are intact while others fall. Make a game of having the group consider unusual places of safety as well as the familiar ones at home.

Ask the children to draw pictures of their homes (current and former, if applicable) and mark exits and escape routes. Ask them: What can you do if you smell gas? What can you do if you are caught in a fire? In a flood? In a tornado?

Ask the children to draw pictures of a house rearranged for safety, glass and heavy furniture well away from beds; halls, doors, and exits clear; extra keys, shoes, eyeglasses, and flashlights near the door; provisions for pets; water storage; bolted foundations; marked gas and water mains (have them find these with a parent's help). Send the pictures home with a note to parents about the thoughtful concern of the children in providing ideas for home safety. Follow-up in a few weeks to see if any changes were made.

Ask the children to make a list of what they might need if they have to be away from home for 3 days. Ask them: Can they gather these belongings themselves? What is their favorite belonging? Would it fit in a kit? If not, would a photo of it fit in a kit? Ask them to arrange what they need in a box and bring it to school, or to draw it. What would they have to leave? Why? Ask those who have had to leave belongings behind, how they decided what to leave. Have them tell their stories of loss.

Parent and Family Groups

Parent groups are an excellent means of helping parents understand their child's behavior, and also of providing them with specific advice on how they can deal with problems (Heft, 1993). A group enables parents to share their concerns with other parents who may be having similar problems and thereby provide mutual support. Advice from other parents frequently is more acceptable than advice from experts. However, caution must be taken to monitor the advice that some parents may give. The therapist needs to be in control at all times and must reiterate that the group is to be helpful, not critical, and encouraging to other members. A parent group also can be educational in focus. Parents often want to be given concrete techniques for handling specific problems, such as fears and anxieties, sleep problems, school difficulties, and behavior problems. Such a group also is a place where the parents can express their own fears. Helping the parents understand their own fears makes them more effective with their children. The group and facilitators are most supportive to the parents when they reinforce existing strengths present in the families and point out how they have been able to deal effectively with difficult problems in the past. If additional help is needed from other resources in the community, the facilitators should have this information available.

The mental health professional can initiate the formation of multifamily groups at a variety of locations, such as schools, Red Cross shelters, mental health clinics, family service agencies, churches, and disaster relief centers. When any group is formed, the participants need to be assured of privacy and confidentiality. It is useful to clarify the objectives of the group at the beginning: (1) the sessions will be crisis centered, problem oriented, and educational in nature; (2) the focus will be to provide information that will help them cope with their children's problems; and (3) the aim of the sessions is to be supportive of families struggling with disaster-related issues. The number of sessions should be specified. Sometimes the families will request additional sessions. If the decision is made to continue, it is imperative that the therapist and the group redefine the purpose of the further meetings.

A useful technique is to identify a common problem from the accounts of the group members and to solicit solutions either attempted or initiated by the various families. The facilitator can identify the most common concerns of families after a disaster, such as worries about their children, difficulties experienced in managing their own fears and anxieties, and specific concerns like the temporary sleeping arrangements that have been made to accommodate the children's fears and their demands for closeness. Families will learn from each other ways of solving common problems. However, when a problem surfaces that the group has difficulty dealing with, the facilitator should not hesitate to assume a more directive, advisory role.

Therapists need to develop a policy regarding how they will handle complaints that families have with the Federal Emergency Management Agency (FEMA) and other disaster agencies. It may be desirable to have representatives from the agencies present at a special group meeting, or have the names of ombudsmen who can help them with these problems. These complaints can disrupt the focus of the group. The parents are often suffering a great deal of frustration and distress because of the realistic problems they are having with the agencies. Children attending a multifamily group also gain a sense of family cohesion through participation with their families. They will learn how to identify their own reactions and difficulties in family relations when they hear them expressed by children in other families. When families have been relocated, children are likely to feel a sense of loss and miss their familiar surroundings and interactions with familiar schoolmates. In talking about their feelings in the group setting, children find affirmation through learning that similar feelings are shared by their peers. Parents may understand, for the first time, that the reactions are not unique to their children. They may even learn about problems that their children had not talked about within the family.

☐ Special Problems and Their Management

Loss, Death, and Mourning

Major disasters result in widespread disruption and destruction with multiple losses of homes, pets, and familiar surroundings. There also is the danger of death and injury to others in the child's world, such as family members, peers, and teachers. In some cases, children may become separated from their families for a period of time. This multiplicity of chaotic and traumatic conditions further complicates the threat that children experience. In a disaster, the child may not only lose the security of the physical environment, but also may lose one or more loved ones (Raphael, 1983, 1986). The more extensive the loss of both personal and material resources, the more traumatic the experience is for the child when a death has occurred.

According to the Harvard Child Bereavement Study, school-age children who have lost a parent are twice as likely to experience serious emotional and behavioral problems as their nonbereaved peers (Worden, 1996). The process of normal bereavement cannot begin until some stability is restored in the child's life. Once the child and the family are in the safe surroundings of a home or shelter, or in the presence of a trusted adult family member or a comparable other caregiver, helping the child through the slow process of grief and mourning can begin.

It is not unusual for a disaster, particularly a major disaster in which there has been loss of life, to trigger children's questions about death and dying. Some children will be silent as though they have been numbed by the experience; others may ask for minute details about the death, displaying an intense curiosity. The quiet child will need to be encouraged to speak; and the inquisitive child's questions concerning the death should be answered directly and honestly. The fear of the loss of a parent underlies many of the questions a child asks and symptoms a child may develop, such as sleeplessness, night terrors, and clinging behavior. Often, when a death has occurred in the family, the children's problems are overlooked and no one remembers to assist the children in handling their reactions to the loss. When one parent dies, children generally become fearful that they will lose the remaining parent. This fear also may occur with the death of a friend or other family member. Children should be encouraged to voice their questions and concerns about death and dying, and the adults should try to be as honest as they can with their answers. For example, questions about what happens to a person after death can be answered with the statement that, "We don't know. The wisest men and women through the ages have tried to answer this question, but there is no sure answer." Explanations dealing with heaven or hell, or afterlife, or the flat statement that after death there is nothing, are confusing to the child because they may contradict what they had been taught in the family.

After a death in the family, the sight of adults being distraught can be very distressing to a child who has never seen this behavior. It is equally confusing if the family acts as though nothing had happened. Generally, a child will understand if told that the adults are feeling pain and showing it in their own way. It also is not uncommon for children to act as though the deceased parent is still alive. They may call the remaining parent or family a liar and deny their parent's death. Some children may alternate between believing and not believing that the parent has died and may ask such questions as, "When is Daddy coming home from being dead?" or "I know Mommy's dead, but when is she going to make my supper?" Young children may not realize that there is no return from death, not even for a moment.

Many of the same issues that adults struggle with in regard to death are found in children. However, magical thinking is more prevalent in childhood. When children are very young, they believe that wishing for, or thinking about, something can make it happen. Children who have had hostile thoughts or death wishes toward the parent, as most children have at one time or another, need to be reassured that these thoughts did not cause the death to happen. Children may believe that it was the fighting with a sibling that caused a parent's death and that if they had ceased fighting it would have prevented the parent from dying. They need reassurance that the parent's or family member's death was not their fault, and that it was caused by an accident or illness. It is comforting to be told that they cannot control parents getting sick or having an accident or dying. This can be contrasted with things they can control, such as the games they plan, whether or not they play fairly, or whether or not they do their chores and homework.

There will be intense feelings of grief following the realization of the loss of loved ones. Grief is characterized by intense feelings of sadness, loneliness, and crying. Reactions observed in grieving individuals include denial and a sense of the world shattering around them. It should be understood that mourning has a purpose and that crying by both a child and an adult is helpful. Children experiencing grief will become confused, sometimes disoriented or agitated, and will cling to family members. Others will appear emotionally numbed, or at times in a state of denial and seemingly unaffected by the tragedy. A child needs to be aware that thoughts about the dead person are likely to come to mind over and over, that healing takes time, and that overt mourning helps integrate the loss more quickly.

The family that expresses anger and annoyance at a child who repeats his questions about death needs to understand that this is the child's way of trying to understand death and loss. If the parents are having difficulty handling the loss, the child may become more reactive. Depression may be expressed in many ways, such as sadness, withdrawal, uncontrolled and unprovoked crying, loss of appetite, and sleep disturbance. The loss of a parent is the most traumatic event a child is likely to experience. When this occurs within the context of the chaos wrought by a disaster, the clinician treating the child faces a complex task. Bereft children must be helped to work through both the trauma of the death and grief for the loss of a family member and how to deal with the disaster. The basic aim throughout this is to help the child to express his or her sadness and feelings of despair, and to acknowledge his or her feelings of anger at having been abandoned.

Adult survivors also will require support and understanding of their own grief, and should be offered advice that will help them understand their own and their children's reactions to death. The therapist knows that assisting the parents in coping with their own grief is important in facilitating their children's mourning process. Parents who are in mourning may find it difficult to help the child and to recognize the child's needs. One way to meet the child's needs will be to restore routines to children's lives that will reestablish a dependable world. These routines would include such tasks as returning to school or child care, and resuming normal play activities. When there are likely to be aftershocks and repeated threats of danger, parents may be hesitant to allow their children to be separated from them. A therapist is likely to see signs of separation anxiety and anxious attachment in both children and their parents.

Children who are bereft will be confronted with constant reminders of the absence of the parent or sibling during normal family routines, such as mealtimes and bedtime. The therapist can advise parents of the importance of providing emotional support and understanding during these times, when the child is likely to be most upset. If it becomes evident that the parents are unable to meet their children's emotional needs because of their own emotional state of heightened vulnerability, the clinician will seek a therapeutic alliance with the family that will provide either family therapy or individual therapy. The therapist also can recommend calling on friends and extended family for help.

Suicidal Ideation

Threats or attempts to injure or kill oneself are infrequent in latency-age and younger children. Adolescents seriously traumatized by personal, meaningful loss frequently are susceptible to self-destructive behaviors (Hawton, 1982; Sudak, Ford, & Rushford, 1984). A number of factors have been identified as relating to suicidal behavior; among them, loss of a family member, friend, or sweetheart in a major disaster. This loss and its contributing elements of stress may increase the risk of suicidal acting-out by youth. In some instances, the experience of disaster may exacerbate the reaction to a previous loss of a friend or a family member. Being dislocated from their home environment also contributes to the increased risk for the vulnerable adolescent.

A number of behaviors and feelings may signal the possibility of suicidal thoughts or tendencies:

- feelings of helplessness, hopelessness, and worthlessness, expressed verbally or nonverbally;
- behavioral signs, such as withdrawal, asocial behavior, loss of interest, agitation, and fighting;
- physical symptoms, such as sleep and appetite disturbance, psychosomatic symptoms;
- cognitive process changes, such as reasoning ability, poor judgment, loss of ability to attend and to concentrate, feelings of loss of future; and
- affective signs, such as depression, apathy, irritability, extreme mood swings, recurrent thoughts of inadequacy, repeated expressions of despair.

The following are questions to ask in the evaluation of suicidal risk in older children and adolescents (Pfeffer, 1986). Some of the questions apply before there has been any attempt at self-harm; others apply after an attempt has occurred.

- Suicidal fantasies or actions: Have you been having thoughts of hurting yourself? Have you ever thought of hurting yourself? Have you ever attempted to hurt yourself? Have you ever wished you were dead? Have you ever wished or tried to kill yourself? Have you ever threatened to commit suicide?
- Motivations for suicidal behavior: Why do you want to kill yourself? Why did you try to kill yourself? Did you feel rejected by someone? Were you feeling hopeless? Did you want to frighten someone? Were you angry at someone? Did you want to get even with someone? Did you wish someone would rescue you before you tried to hurt yourself? Did you hear voices telling you to kill yourself? Did you have very frightening thoughts? What else was a reason for your wish to kill yourself? Did you really want to die?
- Concepts of what would happen: What do you want to happen? What do you think would happen if you tried to hurt or kill yourself? Did you think you would die? Did you think you might have severe injuries?
- Circumstances at the time of the child's suicidal behavior: What was happening at the time you thought about killing yourself or tried to kill yourself? What was happening before you thought about killing yourself? Was anyone else with you or near you when you thought about suicide or tried to kill yourself?
- Previous experiences with suicidal behavior: Have you ever thought about killing yourself or tried to kill yourself before? Do you know of anyone who either thought about, attempted, or committed suicide? What did this person do? When did this occur? Why do you think that this person wanted to kill himself? What was happening at the time this person thought about suicide or tried to kill himself?

- Experiences and concepts of death: What happens when people die? Can they come back again? Do they go to a better place? Do you often think about people dying? Do you often think about your own death? Do you often dream about people or yourself dying? Do you know anyone who has died? What was the cause of this person's death? When did this person die? When do you think you will die? What will happen when you die?
- Depression and other affects: Do you ever feel sad, upset, angry, bad? Do you ever feel that no one cares about you? Do you ever feel that you are not a worthwhile person? Do you cry a lot? Do you get angry often? Do you often fight with other people? Do you have difficulty sleeping, eating, concentrating on school work? Do you have trouble getting along with friends? Do you prefer to stay by yourself? Do you often feel tired? Do you blame yourself for things that happen? Do you often feel guilty?
- Family and environmental situations: Do you have difficulty in school? Do you worry about doing well in school? Do you worry that your parents will punish you for doing poorly in school? Do you get teased by other children? Have you started a new school? Did you move to a new home? Did anyone leave home? Did anyone die? Was anyone sick in your family? Have you been separated from your parents? Are your parents separated or divorced? Do you think that your parents treat you harshly? Do your parents fight a lot? Does anyone get hurt? Is anyone in your family sad, depressed, very upset? Who? Did anyone in your family talk about suicide or try to kill himself?

Showing caring and concern are the most immediate, effective elements in responding to evidence of suicidal tendencies. These can be provided within the process of crisis counseling. Any indication of suicidal feelings must be taken seriously; persons with suicidal ideas, thoughts, feelings, or statements should be referred to professional help for evaluation. Avoid expressing or showing criticism or judgment.

Children with Special Needs

There are at least two groups of children with special needs, who require special attention in a disaster: exceptional children and those who have been injured or have become ill as a result of the disaster. *Exceptional children* are defined as those who have developmental disabilities or intellectual or physical limitations. This would include blindness, hearing impairment, orthopedic handicaps, developmental delay, mental retardation, and cerebral palsy. Parents of exceptional children have the burden of meeting the emotional and physical needs of their children on a day-to-day basis. With the emotional needs of exceptional children likely to be heightened by a disaster of any magnitude, disasters and their periods of disruption bring additional problems to the parents of exceptional children.

Most exceptional children live in their own homes, although they often require considerable assistance from community service agencies. The agencies, which are part of the network of mental health and other services in the community, need to be alert to the special needs of children in home settings when a disaster occurs. Hopefully, they will have been included in the preparation of the community disaster plan. Exceptional children find it more difficult to function when their usual home environment is disturbed or when they are moved to new or strange surroundings. Exceptional children depend to a greater extent than other children on the consistency and predictability of the people around them and their environment. Familiarity with their surroundings is particularly important for children who are mentally retarded because they tend to become confused and agitated by traumatic events. A common symptom is an increased level of clinging behavior.

Helping such children to understand what has occurred requires considerable patience and sensitivity. Generally, it would be desirable to have the professionals who normally are in contact with the children assist in providing help. The professionals previously involved with these children can help locate and identify the children in the community and determine what special services they need. When this resource is not available, parents of the children can function in this role, with the support of the crisis counselor. The parents need to understand that their children have a greater need for reassurance at this time, and that they need to be tolerant of the increased demands. The parents also would benefit from a group with other parents of exceptional children at this time.

Many school systems have children in special education settings or in special schools for children who have physical and emotional disabilities, learning disabilities, or serious behavior problems. The disaster mental health consultant can be particularly helpful in special education settings by providing understanding and support to the teacher, by doing active case-finding, and by arranging group support for these children and their parents. The children require a high level of attention from teachers on a daily basis. Following a disaster, these children are likely to be more upset and more troubled than children in regular classrooms. Special education teachers are a major source of support and assistance for the children and their families. Since the teachers are trusted by the families and the children, they can be very effective in assisting in the wake of a disaster. Parents sometimes become overprotective of these children after a disaster and may need to be encouraged to return their children to school as soon as the school returns to normal functioning.

In a consultation session for classroom teachers of children with physical disabilities, following a recent disaster training session, the teachers were advised that their first priority was to protect themselves, similar to the advice given to airline passengers to adjust their own oxygen mask before attending to setting one on their child. The teachers of these children are so accustomed to protecting their wards that self-protective behavior as the first step was difficult and seemed inappropriate to them.

The following are questions that can be asked of special education teachers:

- What behaviors have you observed in the children that are the result of the disaster?
- What were the reactions of the children's parents? Were they different than the reactions of parents of other children?
- Whom are you most concerned about? Why?
- Do you think it would be helpful to have some of the children meet in a group?
- What kind of help have you received and what more do you need?

Plans for the needs of children in residential settings should be made well in advance of a disaster. Treatment centers for children who are mentally ill, mentally retarded, or physically handicapped and day programs for such children should have high priority for special help from emergency services providers. These agencies should all have their own plans that include staff deployment, evacuation to alternate settings, and a way to keep families informed of the location of their children and of their well-being. Hospital disaster plans should include the needs of hospitalized children during a mass emergency. Unlike residential agencies, children in hospitals will not be as familiar with their caregivers or with the setting, and therefore will require more attention from the medical personnel providing their care.

Children who have been physically injured in a disaster or who have become ill and have been brought to the hospital will be less upset by the injury if the medical procedures that are about to occur are explained to them beforehand. In most up-to-date hospitals, this is now a part of the hospital routine. Every effort should be made to have a member of the immediate family remain with the child during hospital stays and to be present when the child receives medical care, since this is reassuring both to the family and to the child.

☐ Evaluating the Clinical Status of the Child

Assessments of the emotional status of children after a disaster are sought for two purposes: clinical intervention and research. Although the two objectives frequently overlap, it is helpful to differentiate between them. Information for clinical intervention is obtained for the express purpose of determining the current emotional state of the child. Such information may include the evaluation of symptoms of pathology or emotional distress, the current level of affective and cognitive functioning, the degree of impairment of coping and defensive mechanisms, the extent of developmental regression if any, and the changes in behavior and relationships. The objective of the assessment includes the recommendation of short- or long-term intervention aimed toward restoration of predisaster levels of functioning as early as possible.

In contrast, the purpose of research studies is to gather information using epidemiological and large-scale sampling techniques to measure disruption and adjustment of the mental health of the community and its subgroups, with implications for long-range planning for prevention, mitigation, and effective response. In many cases, clinical schedules, instruments and interviews will be the principal means of obtaining the information necessary both for clinical intervention and as survey instruments for evaluating the impact of the disaster on a variety of questions, such as educational needs, levels of emotional and physical health of the community, and the establishment of planning and policy procedures for the community. Research-oriented clinicians, who view the opportunity for inquiry into the puzzling questions of disaster mental health programs as compelling, should consult the National Institute of Mental Health (NIMH) for information on availability of funding and ongoing research programs that might be relevant to their own proposed investigations.

Mental health agencies considering applying for funding of postdisaster clinical interventions will need to arrive at some estimate of the extent of the need for services. The question arises as to which assessment instruments would be appropriate for the task. In most instances, the grant application will require approximations of damage to the community, personal injuries, displacement, social disruption, and the capacity of local mental health resources to meet community needs. These data, together with other sources of information, become the basis for an estimate of the extent and kinds of emotional distress likely to occur in the immediate phase and ensuing phases, and of the special needs of subgroups at greater risk within the local community. This will help the mental health agency justify its request for disaster mental health funding.

There have been restrictions on the use of FEMA funds to conduct assessments of disaster victims stemming from the conviction that every effort should be devoted toward providing immediate intervention and services to the largest number of people in the shortest time. This, at times, has hindered the clinician. NIMH uses the term *crisis counseling* as a description of the clinical services to be provided with the funds it provides. Some clinicians have tended to define the behaviors that emerge following a disaster as "problems of living" that result from community disruption to avoid stigmatizing help-seeking. Major longitudinal research has revealed ongoing emotional disturbances related to difficulties coping with disaster-induced distress. The studies have indicated that resource loss (that is, the disruption of personal, social, emotional, and financial resources provided by both individual and institutions) has resulted in continuing traumatic stress among survivors. Emotional reactions to these stressors emerge most often as individual psychopathology. It has been formally and appropriately classified as post-traumatic stress syndrome, and was initially recognized and codified in the *Diagnostic and Statistical Manual of Mental Disorders*, third edition *(DSM-III)* (American Psychiatric Association, 1980).

Generally few formal assessment tools are used in the period immediately following a disaster because of a sense of urgency to provide clinical help to the disaster population. Actually, it is desirable to obtain information about emotional status along with the details about problems of living, when possible. Assessment of emotional status can be carried out through observation, interview, and clinical evaluation. The depth and extent of information obtained from these methods will depend on the clinical skills of the therapist. Information will come from the child, the family, reports from emergency personnel, school personnel, and any others who might have contact with the child. Demographic and symptom survey findings will help in planning for clinical interventions. From the clinical observations in the wake of a disaster, inferences can be made of the diagnoses, the degree of specific affective disturbances, and the applicability of specific instruments. There are times when early clinical observations indicate that the stresses are likely to be transitory and that further assessment of clinical status is not necessary. There also are practical considerations involved in deciding whether to pursue further assessment. Such factors are the demand and availability of professional resources and skills which help establish priorities for the use of professional time after a disaster.

The original assessment will suggest the major types of emotional distress observed. Further assessment would be used to explore, in more depth, the problem areas identified with individual children. When further assessment is necessary, a number of individual clinical scales can be applied. For example, additional assessments might be desired in order to evaluate the degree and intensity of stress reactions and affective states, such as depression and anxiety, and to explore specific questions of social and family interactions. Age and developmental level of the child also will influence the choice of an assessment instrument, as well as the languages spoken in the family and other cultural concerns. Choice of various procedures also is dictated by the type and extent of a disaster, the severity or magnitude of the event, and the uses for the data. It is important that any assessment instrument used to evaluate victims should be easily administered and interpreted. A major consideration is brevity, particularly in the earlier phases of a disaster when the data are frequently collected in field locations. The rapidity of response is another critical factor, since the need for additional assessment tools depends on the information gained from the quicker procedure.

When the emergency phase has passed, and demand for immediate clinical care has been identified, a more in-depth clinical evaluation of the child who is traumatized may be carried out. At this point, clinicians may choose from a wide variety of clinical instruments. It may be advantageous to employ the same measures that have been used in previous disaster research. The following is a selected list of scales used in other studies to measure anxiety, fear, traumatic stress, and depression.

Measures of Anxiety in Children

Developed by Spielberger (1973), the State-Trait Anxiety Scale for Children consists of two 20-item subscales measuring how the child feels at the moment and how he or she usually feels, if there is a difference. The scale was used by Jones and Ribbe (1991) in their studies of a wildfire in southern California and by Mintz (1991) in Israel comparing reactions of children who were exposed to Scud missiles with those who were not exposed to the bombardment. Reynolds and Richmond (1978) developed the Child Manifest Anxiety Scale (CMAS), with 77 items. A revision of this scale—the Revised Child Manifest Anxiety Scale (RCMAS)—by Lonigan, Shannon, Finch, Daugherty, and Taylor (1991) reduced the number of items to 37 items, with subscales on worry, physiological reactions, and concentration; there also were two "lie" scales. It was used by Lonigan et al. (1991) to study 5,687 children in rural public schools in the 1989 Hurricane Hugo disaster. The RCMAS was used by Yule and Williams (1990) in the 1987 Herald of Enterprise ferry sinking, and again in the 1988 Jupiter ship sinking by Yule and Udwin (1991).

The Separation Anxiety Disorder Section of the Diagnostic Interview Schedule for Children and Adolescents (Herjanic & Reich, 1982) was used by Goenjian et al. (1995) in a study of the children who survived the Armenian earthquake in 1988. The separation anxiety (essentially, clinging behavior) seemed to follow the dose-of-exposure pattern, although there were indications that it may have been related to the higher rates of separation of family members in the more damaged areas.

The Children's Mental Health Checklist

A checklist was developed under the auspices of Project COPE, a FEMA-funded crisis counseling program activated in Santa Cruz, California, in response to the 1989 Loma Prieta earthquake, to determine the extent of psychological trauma, and whether or not professional mental health services are indicated.

1. Has the child had more than one major stress within a year BEFORE this disaster, such as a death in the family, a molestation, a major physical illness or divorce? If yes: +5
2. Does the child have a network of supportive, caring persons who continue to relate to him daily? If yes: −10
3. Has the child had to move out of his house because of the disaster? If yes: +5
4. Was there reliable housing within one week of the earthquake with resumption of the usual household members living together? If yes: −10
5. Is the child showing severe disobedience or delinquency? If yes: +5

    Is the child showing any of the following as NEW behaviors for more than three weeks after the disaster?

6. Nightly states of terror? +5
7. Waking from dreams confused or in a sweat? +5
8. Difficulty concentrating? +5
9. Extreme irritability? +5
10. Loss of previous achievements in toilet or speech? +5
11. Onset of stuttering or lisping? +5
12. Persistent severe anxiety or phobias? +5
13. Obstinacy? +5
14. New or exaggerated fears? +5
15. Rituals or compulsions? +5
16. Severe clinging to adults? +5
17. Inability to fall asleep or stay asleep? +5
18. Startling at any reminder of the disaster? +5
19. Loss of ambition for the future? +5
20. Loss of pleasure in usual activities? +5
21. Loss of curiosity? +5
22. Persistent sadness or crying? +5
23. Persistent headaches or stomach aches? +5
24. Hypochondria? +5
25. Has anyone in the child's immediate family been killed or severely injured in the disaster (including severe injury to the child)? +15

To score the checklist, sum the pluses and minuses for a final score. If the score is over 35, a mental health consultation is suggested. The following appears at the bottom of the checklist: "It is also recommended that any child who has been seriously injured or who has lost a parent, sibling, or caregiver by death, have a psychological evaluation and/or brief therapy."

Measures of Fear in Children

The Louisville Fear Survey for Children (1972) is a 104-item scale, with subscales on frequency and intensity, developed to measure fears of storm, death, dying, noises, sleep, bodily penetration, enclosed spaces, embarrassment, and specific fears about persons and animals. The instrument was used by Dollinger, O'Donnell, and Staley (1984) to study reactions to a lightning strike during a soccer game in a midwestern town, which had killed one child and injured many others. The study matched 29 children at the event for sex and age with a control group from another town, and found that mothers reported fewer fears than their children reported, and that children who had more emotional distress reported having the greatest number of fears.

Dollinger (1986) used the Sleep and Somatization scales of the Missouri Children's Behavior Checklist (MCBC) to assess the study population again 2 years after the event The study team asked mothers to report on their children's current status and found that adjustment had improved over time, but those children who had been most upset by the trauma still reported more sleep and somatic disorders.

A revision of the Louisville scale, renamed the Fear Survey Schedule for Children—Revised (FSSC-R) (Ollendick, 1983), reduced the original 104-item instrument to 80 items containing five factors; namely, fears of failure, the unknown, injury and small animals, danger and death, and medical problems. Yule and Udwin (1991) also used this instrument in their study of the 1988 Jupiter ship sinking.

Measures of Stress in Children

One of the most useful brief instruments developed to measure event-related stress in children is the Impact of Event Scale (IES) (Horowitz, Wilner, & Alvarez, 1979). The instrument was used by Yule and Williams (1990) in their study of the 1987 *Herald of Free Enterprise* ferry sinking in the English Channel. The IES reported significant disturbances in over half of the children.

The Reaction Index (RI) (Frederick, 1985) was originally developed from the criteria listed in *DSM-III* for PTSD to measure stress in adults, and was later modified for use with children. It has been used a number of times:

with children who witnessed the 49th Street School shooting (Pynoos et al., 1987); following the 1989 Loma Prieta earthquake in northern California (Bradburn, 1991); after Hurricane Hugo struck in Florida in 1989 (Belter, Dunn, & Jeney, 1991; Lonigan et al., 1991); by Martini, Ryan, Nakayama, and Ramenofsky (1990) in their study of the Pittsburgh regatta accident in which a boat went out of control and plowed into a crowd of adults and children; and by Schwartz and Kowalski (1991) in their study of a school shooting.

The children's version of the RI has been modified and revised further and was used extensively by Pynoos et al. (1993) and Goenjian et al. (1995) in their studies $1\frac{1}{2}$ years after the impact of an earthquake in Armenia. Two hundred thirty-one children, ranging in age from 8 to 16 (median age 12.8 years), from three cities of varying distances from the epicenter were studied. The Childrens' Post-Traumatic Stress Disorder-Reaction Index (CPTSD-RI), a Likert-form scale with ratings of the items ranging from 0 to 4, was found to have good correspondence with interviews for PTSD, using *DSM-III* guidelines, of randomly selected children. A step-wise discrimination function analysis indicated that five items together determined PTSD (77.7% variance): frequently troubled by traumatic reminders that arouse fear of recurrence, emotional constriction, hyperarousal, avoidance of reminders, and reported frequency of reminders. The investigators found the PTSD reactions to be pervasive, severe, and chronic, but they seemed to diminish gradually over the first year, even among the most exposed children. There was a strong correlation of the severity of the reaction to proximity to the epicenter. Girls had higher total mean CPTSD-RI scores, reporting more anticipatory fears, bad dreams, and subjective disorders when thinking about what happened.

There have been other efforts to measure childhood post-traumatic stress disorder. Wolfe et al. (1989), using diagnostic criteria from the *DSM-III*, drew 20 items from the Child Behavior Checklist (CBC) (Achenbach & Edelbrock, 1983) to study children who had been sexually abused. Their Children's Impact of Traumatic Events Scale (CITES) (Wolfe, Gentile, & Wolfe, 1989) contains 54 statements that provide 9 subscales, with 6 of the subscales related to reactions to impact and 3 related to measuring attributions. While originally designed to assess reactions to sexual abuse, the measure also may lend itself to disaster studies.

Blom (1986) developed a 42-item checklist of children's stress behaviors to measure obsession, phobic anxiety, somatic reactions, and depressive and regressive behaviors in children who either were under a pedestrian skywalk when it collapsed or who had witnessed the event from the playground.

Several measures were developed for evaluation of stress in Israeli children during the Persian Gulf War. Klingman (1992) constructed a stress reaction scale consisting of 14 items measuring cognitive impairment, emotional reactions, and physiological disturbance. Schwarzwald et al. (1991) measured stress reactions of school-age children, specifically on their response to bombardment by Scud missiles.

Saigh developed the Children's PTSD Inventory (1989) to measure trauma-related ideation, traumatization, general affect, and diverse symptoms.

In their study of children after maltreatment, Famularo, Kinscherf, and Fenton (1990) constructed a 33-item scale that differentiated between acute and chronic PTSD. The children with acute PTSD showed more nightmares, hypervigilence, startle reactions and agitation, and those with chronic PTSD reported more estrangement, restricted affect, depressed feelings, sadness, and unhappiness.

The Child Stress Reaction Survey, used by Cardena and Spiegel (1993) in a study of children in the Virgin Islands after Hurricane Marilyn, asked parents to rate the frequency of their children's behavior on 12 items describing pre- and postbehaviors: reflecting developmental regression (enuresis, not wanting to sleep alone), dissociative phenomena, anxiety and anger symptoms, and preoccupation with the traumatic event. The behaviors are rated on a 5-point Likert-type scale ranging from "never" to "very often." The survey, unpublished at this time, has high internal consistency (.89) and face validity. In the same study, Cardena and Spiegel measured parental stress with the Stanford Acute Stress Reaction Questionnaire, a 30-item self-report questionnaire measuring dissociative and anxiety symptoms, avoidance, impaired functioning, and traumatic reenactment. Internal consistency is high for anxiety (alpha = .91)

Measures of Depression in Children

The Depression Self-Rating Scale for Children (DSRSC) (Birleson, 1981), an 18-item scale, was used by Yule and Williams (1990) in their study of the *Herald of Free Enterprise* sinking. It also was used by Goenjian et al. (1995, 1997) in their studies of children and adolescents after the earthquake in Armenia in 1988. The study by Goenjian et al. (1995) of the same children found a high ratio of current comorbid PTSD and depressive disorder along with a lower rate of current separation anxiety disorder among the children with high levels of exposure. Extent of loss of family was positively correlated with severity of PTSD reactions. Being easily angered was the most frequently reported symptom in the children who were closer to the epicenter.

Milne used the 18-item depression Section (measuring affect, physical symptoms, biological reactions, self-negation, and essential despair) that is part of the 371-item Interview Schedule (described in detail in Warheit, Holzer, & Arey, 1975), along with his own Before and Now Disaster Checklist (BNDC), a 21-item scale (measuring maladaptation, addictiveness, psychosomatic disturbances, and family stress), to study survivors of Cyclone Tracy in Australia.

Projective Techniques

Draw-a-Person, Three Wishes, and storytelling techniques were used by Newman (1976) to investigate children's reactions to the Buffalo Creek flood in West Virginia.

Two pictures out of the Thematic Appreciation Test (TAT) series that showed lightning were used by Dollinger et al. (1984) in a study of the impact of a lightning strike in the Midwest. Projective techniques also were used with children who witnessed the 49th Street School shooting (Nader, Pynoos, Fairbanks, & Frederick, 1990; Pynoos et al., 1987). Zeidner, Klingman, and Itzkovitz (1992) used a projective test of images by significant others to get at the fears, anxieties, and attitudes to family as a source of support in their study of fourth- and fifth-grade students during the Persian Gulf War.

General and Miscellaneous Measures

The Diagnostic Interview for Children and Adolescents (DICA-R) measures current and past behaviors through both child (Reich, 1991a) and parent versions (Reich, 1991b). The DICA-R was used in a study of survivors of a 1982 flood in Missouri (Earls, Smith, Reich, & Jung, 1988) and in the 1990 southern California wildfires (Jones & Ribbe, 1991).

The Diagnostic Interview Schedule for Children (DISC) was developed by Edelbrock, Costello, Dulcan, Kalas, and Conover (1985) to provide a general picture of psychological status in terms of behaviors and diagnoses based on criteria in the *Diagnostic and Statistical Manual of Mental Disorders*, third edition, revised (*DSM-III-R*) (American Psychiatric Association, 1987). Robins and Smith (1984) developed a DISC Disaster Supplement.

The CBC (Achenbach & Edelbrock, 1983) was used by Sullivan et al. (1991) and Saylor, Swenson, and Powell (1992) in their studies of children after Hurricane Hugo struck in Florida in 1989, and by Guerin, Junn, and Rushbrook (1991) after the 1989 Loma Prieta earthquake in California.

The Nowicki-Strickland Locus of Control Scale (NSLCS) (Nowicki & Strickland, 1973) was used by Pietrowski and Dunham (1983), along with a semantic differential measure, in a study of Hurricane Eloise in Florida.

The Purdue Social Support Scale (PSSS) (Burge & Figley, 1987) assesses the resources of a family, such as emotional support, encouragement, advice, socializing, and helpfulness before and after a traumatic event.

The Family Adaptability and Cohesion Evaluation Scale (FACES) (Olson et al., 1983) measures the degree of adaptability and cohesion in a family and provides a profile of current functioning and a level of adaptation to the trauma.

The Social Adjustment Inventory for Children and Adults (SAICA) (John et al., 1987), a semistructured measure, evaluates functioning in school and spare time activities with siblings and parents, and looks into behavior problem areas.

The Hassles Scale (HS) (Kanner et al., 1981) probes into 117 issues related to work, health, family, friends, environment, practical considerations, and chance occurrences, and arrives at three summary scales of frequency, cumulative severity, and intensity.

The Uplift Scale (US) (Kanner et al., 1981) asks about 135 uplifting experiences, such as relaxing, spending time with friends, and using skills at work, to arrive at frequency and intensity scores.

The Checklist of Characteristics of Youth Who Have Caused School-Associated Violent Deaths (National School Safety Center, 1998) has been constructed to identify students who potentially might be dangerous to themselves and to others. The checklist is derived from tracking school-associated violent deaths in the United States from July 1992 to the present. It is used only as a starting point in efforts to address the needs of such students through meetings with parents, provision of school counseling, guidance and mentoring services, and possibly referrals to appropriate health care and social services. The checklist contains 20 items:

1. Has a history of tantrums and uncontrollable angry outbursts.
2. Characteristically resorts to name calling, cursing or abusive language.
3. Habitually makes violent threats when angry.
4. Has previously brought a weapon to school.
5. Has a background of serious disciplinary problems at school and in the community.
6. Has a background of drug, alcohol or other substance abuse or dependency.
7. Is on the fringe of his/her peer group with few or no close friends.
8. Is preoccupied with weapons, explosives or other incendiary devices.
9. Has previously been truant, suspended or expelled from school.
10. Displays cruelty to animals.
11. Has little or no supervision and support from parents or a caring adult.
12. Has witnessed or been a victim of abuse or neglect in the home.
13. Has been bullied and/or bullies or intimidates peers or younger children.
14. Tends to blame others for difficulties and problems s/he causes her/himself.
15. Consistently prefers TV shows, movies or music expressing violent themes or acts.
16. Prefers reading materials dealing with violent themes, rituals and abuse.

17. Reflects anger, frustration and the dark side of life in school essays or writing projects.
18. Is involved in a gang or an antisocial group on the fringe of peer acceptance.
19. Is often depressed and/or has significant mood shifts.
20. Has threatened or attempted suicide.

In establishing a diagnosis for the children he has worked with, the clinician will need to distinguish between psychopathological behavior and emotionally distressed behavior. Most of the time, the reactions to disaster will fall into the category of "behavior due to emotional distress." The diagnostic category within the *Diagnositc Statistical Manual of Mental Disorders,* fourth edition, *(DSM-IV)* (American Psychiatric Association, 1994) that has been found to fit most often has been adjustment disorder, which meets the criteria developed in *DSM-IV* of marked distress or significant impairment serially occurring within 3 months after the stressor and is not merely an exacerbation of a preexisting Axis I clinical disorders such as psychosis, mood disorder, and somatic disorder or Axis II personality disorders, such as antisocial personality, histrionic personality, and obsessive compulsive personality. Generally, the symptoms should subside within 6 months, but the diagnosis can be used with the addition of "chronic" when the stressor continues, as it would with repeated aftershocks after an earthquake, or with severe economic and occupational stress after a flood which has wiped out a whole town or school system. In all cases, the clinician should explore, in the assessment, the temporal aspects, the intensity of the precipitating event, and the actual reactions of the child to that event. The intensity of the event can be determined by exploring whether the child and the family indeed did have an "uncommon" stress experience and whether or not the child has developed an emotional condition that is severe enough to warrant a psychopathological diagnosis. In general, a hasty labeling of the symptoms as pathology should be avoided, especially among child disaster victims where, for example, a child's whining and clinging may verge on the borderline of being psychopathological, but more often have been found to be a temporary state of emotional distress resulting from the disruptive disaster experience (Rubonis & Bickman, 1991).

The temporal dimension (that is, the persistence of the response to the event over time) sometimes determines the degree or level of reaction. If the reaction occurs after 3 months, then it does not qualify as an adjustment disorder, and a post-traumatic stress disorder label should be considered. It seems that with the introduction of the PTSD classification, there has been an overreadiness to apply this diagnosis to disaster victims. According to *DSM III-R*, these particular requirements were developed specifically for diagnosing adults in terms of the onset of symptoms and their persistence over time. The structural framework of the PTSD category requires that essential elements must be present before assigning the diagnostic label; namely, there has been exposure to an extreme traumatic stressor that has involved death or injury to self or a loved; that the symptoms have involved persistent reexperiencing of the traumatic event, with numbing, intrusive memories; and there have been arousal symptoms reflecting persistent psychological distress. The condition may last for months or even years.

Disaster is an objective event or series of events that are measurable and observable, and commonly agreed on and recognized as a stressor, unlike "problems of living." However, reactions to a disaster may vary in intensity and duration. The relevance of these diagnostic categories to children and the kinds of events that may meet the criteria for PTSD varies with the severity of the event. The following questions are suggested to assist in the evaluation of the presence or absence of PTSD in children:

- The child's perception of the event: How does the child perceive the event? What enters into that perception? What happened, according to the child?
- The child's reaction to the event: What type of event occurred? How long did the actual event last? Where was the child when it occurred? Who was with the child?
- Exposure to the event: Was the child or a family member injured? Did the child witness injury, death, or physical damage?
- Aftermath of the event: What occurred during the period following the event? What was the extent of damage to the environment? Has the family been dislocated from the home and forced to relocate to a shelter or trailer camp? Are environmental and physical dangers still present? Is the family unit physically intact? Are reminders of the event still present?
- Disruption in the child's life: To what extent is the child's life disrupted? Has the child been separated from the family? Has there been a change in the child's physical or social surroundings, especially in the neighborhood and the school? What is the effect on the family?

The choice of a diagnostic or research instrument will depend on the goals and objectives of the clinician or researcher. The aforementioned instruments are available for examination, and a more in-depth literature search will reveal the considerable numbers of schedules and reports now available for study. It also is advisable to include assessment tools in the disaster planning protocols of mental health agencies and school districts.

☐ Summary

Working with children who are traumatized by disaster begins with the recognition that they essentially are normal functioning children who have been subjected to sudden unusual and great stress. The primary aim in crisis intervention is to identify, assess, and relieve stress as quickly as possible.

The usual steps are establishing rapport, identifying the immediate and most pressing problem, assessing resources, and developing a plan to resolve the problem quickly. Early case-finding may come from the personnel in the shelters or the emergency centers. Referral of the child and family also may come from the physician, teacher, or another family member. The first crisis interview may occur in an inconvenient place, with little physical comfort or privacy. The initial interview aims to evaluate the child's current status, the predisaster status and vulnerability, and the need for further assessment or referral. The child always is interviewed with the parent present. The goal of crisis intervention is to restore the family's sense of competence and to reestablish a sense of order in a personal world that has been disrupted. As the therapy proceeds, the emphasis shifts from its focus on the child and his or her problems to an exploration and assessment of the family dynamics. Preexisting problems may be revealed; these may account, at least in part, for some of the current problems. The treatment process may take a variety of approaches, with individual counseling, children's groups, and parent or family groups functioning at the same time.

The experience of the death of loved ones or the loss of cherished objects may be difficult for children who have had no previous encounter with such events. The level of understanding will vary with age and psychological development.

Much of the therapy may consist of grief work aimed at helping the child to understand the fact of death and to tolerate the frightening helplessness of irreparable loss. The therapist also will need to help the parents and other adult family members in the mourning and grief work so that they will be able to tend to the child's emotional needs. The mental health professional needs to be alert to possible suicidal feelings in response to such losses. Responding with caring, concern, and nonjudgmental compassion is the most immediate and effective factor in reducing the strength of any suicidal tendencies. Exceptional children with special needs require much patience and sensitivity. Special education teachers may have to learn that their first priority is to protect themselves before they can attend to the needs of their charges. Optimally, the needs of children in residential settings are prepared by exhaustive predisaster planning. An increasing number of assessment tools have become available to assist in conducting appropriate research and improving procedures for measuring specific areas, such as levels of anxiety, extent and kinds of fears, intensity of stress experiences, depth of depression, and personality structure.

7
CHAPTER

The Competent Community

A competent community is defined as one in which all the needs for human services are addressed (Cottrell, 1976; Iscoe, 1974). To accomplish this goal, mental health professionals have to become an integral part of the emergency services network. In some communities, they have played an active role in the planning process, supportive to the emergency response of the lead agencies of law enforcement, fire and safety, search and rescue, and so forth. In order to assure that the community will receive emergency mental health services, it is necessary to participate in predisaster planning efforts and to take an active role. By serving on committees and introducing mental health issues and concerns whenever the opportunity appears, the mental health professional will educate the other agencies and benefit the community in its task of predisaster planning and postdisaster recovery (Austin, 1992).

An early first step toward this collaboration would be for mental health professionals to develop a disaster mental health visibility within their own organizations. It would be characterized by the following elements:

- a standing committee chaired by an experienced mental health professional who is committed to disaster mental health;
- a plan that would include procedures to mobilize and to integrate the mental health professional community with established emergency services organizations; and
- a plan for coordination and collaboration with existing community-wide organizations, such as United Way and other nonprofit service organizations, schools, colleges, and churches. Liaison with other local-level or-

155

ganizations, such as Neighborhood Watch and homeowners associations, also will be crucial to implementing the objectives of a comprehensive mental health response for their community. These elements would be assembled through periodic meetings to develop, refine, and maintain an ongoing level of awareness and preparation. This form of organizational participation is necessary to achieve the goal of becoming a competent community.

It also will be necessary for the news media become an integral element in planning to assure that accurate facts and information about mental health services is disseminated.

☐ Disaster Mental Health: Planning and Policy Considerations

The perception of the emergent field of disaster mental health has changed considerably over the decades. In the past, it essentially consisted of a series of disaster events involving a few interested clinicians or researchers. From these beginnings has grown a major field that has become a part of government policy, with professional involvement and with community concern and integration into disaster agency planning. Expanding public awareness of the extent of the emotional consequences of a disaster promises continued growth of the field. Emergency services originally focused on specific needs for food, clothing, and shelter and neglected an essential human need—relief from emotional distress. Procedures for amelioration of emotional distress are constantly being developed and incorporated.

The need for the involvement of the mental health professional in the disaster response is now recognized. As evidence, federal funds are provided for public and nonprofit sector programs, the Red Cross has expanded its range of counseling services, and crisis response teams can now be found in almost every major school district throughout the country. Critical incident stress debriefing has become a commonly accepted technique in emergency services agencies and school systems, and a special interest division within mental health professional associations is being developed in recognition of this expanding field. An example of the latter is the establishment of the Disaster Relief Network (DRN) in 1992 by the American Psychological Association, which was preceded in 1991 by a Statement of Understanding with the American Red Cross to work collaboratively in providing free mental health services to disaster victims and relief workers. DRN has worked with the Federal Emergency Management Agency (FEMA), state emergency management teams, and other relief groups. The goals of DRN are to offer short-term crisis intervention services to survivors and to identify local resources for ongoing psychological assistance. A long-term goal of DRN is to train an entire network in a national crisis intervention course and to expand the network into areas where the needs exist, but are not being met.

The involvement of mental health professionals in the disaster response has highlighted the existence of the need of emergency services personnel for relief from the stress of their work and, once provided, it has enabled them to function more effectively. Emergency personnel soon recognized that their stress reactions, including burnout, could be relieved by debriefing, defusing, and mental health counseling. In many communities, mental health departments have arranged with emergency services agencies to provide stress counseling to their personnel. Through their experiences, emergency services personnel have become advocates of mental health intervention for adult and child survivors in disaster-impacted communities. As a result, mental health services increasingly have been included and involved in emergency preparedness plans in most communities.

Despite this amount of progress, there still are a number of areas where consultation and planning activities are needed. Technical assistance must be available for localities to help them ascertain the extent of need for mental health services in the immediate aftermath of a disaster and in the various phases of the postdisaster period. Help should be available for conducting a needs assessment to determine the risk potential of a community. Mental health professionals and social scientists can provide significant data to planners regarding the differing needs of the community and the multicultural populations in both urban and rural areas. There remains a need for ongoing community education and training to be provided by professional associations, activities that would require ongoing and consistent funding.

If mental health professionals are to assume greater influence in disaster policy, the thrust must come from the leaders of the professional mental health associations. All of these groups need to recognize the importance of their roles in developing a "policy voice" on a level with state departments of mental health and federal agencies, such as FEMA and the National Institute of Mental Health (NIMH).

Community-Based Planning

In recent years, publicly financed services have been seriously threatened with cutbacks in funding. This means that services previously depended on may no longer be available or that they have been compressed to a point where they provide only a small fraction of their former capability. It is urgent that a planning committee take into account this diminished capability and consider ways to restore the services' diminishing capabilities. It might be useful to invite administrators from the public and private sector agencies that have suffered the cutbacks to the planning committee meetings so that their information can be continually updated. Similarly, local elected officials or their field representatives should play an important role in this planning effort because they play a significant role in postdisaster reconstruction by their allocation of funds. Although local officials participate in the overall master planning for emergency services, they need to be aware of and support local efforts to develop mental health interventions following a disaster.

A strong tradition of voluntary social action has been developed as one means of resolving a variety of problems. In recent decades, coalitions on behalf of people who are mentally ill, children who are developmentally disabled, and families who are homeless have lobbied hard for the needs of these vulnerable populations. During an era of diminishing public spending for people who are disadvantaged and people with disabilities, the coalitions become important advocates on behalf of their constituencies. It may be difficult, at best, to refocus the single issue advocacy groups to a broader community concern; especially, one that may seem as remote as disaster. Nevertheless, a planning committee should be alert to the usefulness of enlisting the altruism and vision of the leadership of these organizations because their constituents are likely to be most affected when a disaster strikes a community.

It may be necessary to convey to these organizations that the disaster mental health planning efforts are not designed to be competitive with their ongoing programs, but are sensitive to the specific needs and problems of the community at large. It is important to include representatives of the specialized advocacy groups in the planning stage because, in the turmoil following a disaster, it will be more difficult to target and respond to the particular needs of the smaller population segments that they represent. Thus, these groups would be better able to provide for the specific needs of their constituencies within the context of the community disaster plan. Also, they would be able to function in the postdisaster environment more collaboratively; that is, within the network of emergency services and relief organizations.

Neighborhood involvement is crucial to the planning effort. The earliest interactions and activities following a disaster occur between families in the neighborhood. In areas where there are Neighborhood Watch and homeowners associations, these groups can be welcome channels for distributing information, including emergency mental health information. Parents can be given information to share with their children as part of a family emergency plan. This is especially important because such information assures children at an early point that their families and neighborhoods are concerned with their safety and well-being. Neighborhood associations that become educated and informed prior to a disaster also will be able to be much more sensitive to signs of emotional distress and be aware of where help might be found. Such proactive efforts will yield a greater sense of competence within families to meet their own needs and their concerns for the well-being of their neighbors. The purpose of this is to help develop a competent community that can be responsive, responsible, and reflective of the needs of the locality (Rubin, Saperstein, & Barbee, 1985).

The above community-based planning model parallels that of "community-based research" (Murphy, Scammell, & Sclove, 1997) involving the collaboration of lay community members and experts to produce new knowledge for social change. This research agenda carries on the seminal work of Warren (1971), Bennis, Benne, and Chin (1985), and other community development researchers who have been influential in creating the philosophical underpinnings for America's urban agenda since the late 1960s. This approach, which was fundamental to early federal model cities initiatives, is grounded in the problem-solving process. It values the involvement of community members in all aspects of need and data analysis so that, when action strategies are evolved, the people most impacted by their consequences will have a substantial investment in the action. It also promises some assurance that community members will continue to be participants over the long term.

Influencing Disaster Mental Health Policy

Funding for mental health services is undergoing major changes. Although it is impossible to predict the ways that funding will become available in the future, there seem to be two possibilities. The first is expansion of the funding currently distributed to the states for development of mental health services, including postdisaster counseling. This probably would involve expansion of the funding available for state and county mental health activities, as they are currently structured, with the major activities focused within the county mental health departments. Second, the growing influence of federal and private sector cooperative activities could result in an effort by localities to develop a "third sector;" that is, the private nonprofit organizations. Actually, localities could thus maximize their use of limited resources regardless of whether federal funds diminish, stabilize, or grow. The authors foresee the development of a community or constituency process in disaster-prone areas, with the centerpiece of this process taking the form of community advisory boards, similar to the ones already existing in United Way organizations nationwide. Neighborhood councils and faith-based organizations already are playing an increasing role in such activities (Anderson, Maton, & Ensor, 1991; Maton & Wells, 1995). Volunteerism, an essential element, is being emphasized and encouraged in the late 1990s by elected officials and other leaders.

Mental health practitioners affiliated with provider organizations would spearhead the increasing role of mental health in community-wide disaster planning. Those with training and experience in community organization would apply their skills to disaster planning efforts. Local mental health associations would advocate on behalf of increased services for children and families after disasters. The association's standing committee for disaster response, comprised of members who have experience and prior training in disaster mental health services would actively seek participation and collaboration with ongoing local emergency planning committees. Through participation in the planning process, mental health professionals can play an educational role to provide members of the committee with insights into the disaster-related trauma of families, children, and emergency service personnel.

The existing emergency services agencies have developed plans that include agreements for mutual assistance with similarly concerned agencies. The plans would require that public and private mental health agencies actively participate in and establish linkages in broader scale emergency planning and preparedness in their localities. Once these links are formed, public agencies would then approach the community emergency preparedness committee—representing both themselves and the private mental health sector—to develop their plan in liaison with the emergency plans of other departments. Although this process has occurred in some major urban centers, it has not yet become widespread.

Mental health professionals employed by company employee assistance plans (EAPs) also can play a significant role in furthering the direction of this initiative. EAPs have recognized the need to intervene with employees and their families after a catastrophic event. For example, an EAP-initiated "self-help" program at the Los Angeles Fire Department includes spouses, who have been trained in crisis intervention, as staff to provide peer counseling for stress-related problems of firefighters and their families.

☐ The Role of Schools

Schools frequently serve as hubs of community disaster response, and school personnel are particularly suited for immediate crisis counseling efforts on behalf of children and their families. After community-wide disasters, mental health staff in schools will be called on to provide crisis and ongoing mental health services. As a result, the school mental health staff may be overtaxed during and long after the federal programs for emergency care have lapsed. Recognition of the crucial function that schools play in a disaster emphasizes the need for inclusion of school administrators, school counselors, and teaching personnel in emergency planning activities. It is especially important that teachers be involved because they will be required, at least temporarily, to redefine their primary classroom function from an educational to a caretaking role. As the primary caretakers if a disaster strikes when the school is in session, they become responsible for the first-stage emotional support of the children in their care.

Because so much of the responsibility after a disaster falls on the schools, duties which may be burdensome after federal funds have been withdrawn, they need to be prepared for their role in community-wide efforts. As recognized centers of community interaction, schools are ideal locations for emergency preparedness, planning, and training sessions. Schools are especially prime settings for training other caregivers, such as child care providers, medical and nursing personnel, and even parents, on how to recognize and deal with childhood trauma.

School administrators currently play an active role in emergency planning. School psychologists, social workers, and counselors should emphasize the importance of the mental health aspects of the school's emergency planning at their school district's emergency preparedness planning meeting. Because school facilities often are used by the Red Cross as disaster centers, school mental health personnel should be encouraged to become familiar with local Red Cross disaster training. School districts should be prepared to mobilize their counseling resources immediately after a disaster by using predetermined methods. This points to the necessity for ongoing training in emergency procedures. Many school districts have created callout rosters to mobilize their crisis teams, which include mental health professionals who intervene in emergencies that occur on the school grounds before and after school hours.

Up to this point, major disasters have been emphasized. However, in recent years, the number of events of violence on school grounds, such as shootings, has increased dramatically. As a result, school crisis teams have been called on more frequently. Keeping the crisis teams enthusiastic and competent will require both ongoing training and support from administrators. It is important that emergency preparedness training for crisis teams and other school personnel includes detailed information about the emotional consequences likely to be found in children and the techniques for intervention. School personnel must be made aware that aftereffects of trauma can persist for weeks and months following an event, or may appear as symptoms many months after the event.

☐ The Competent Professional

Competent professionals are an integral part of community competence. To a large degree, competence requires recognition by the professional and his or her association of the major value of the professional to a highly integrated and adequately prepared community in a potential disaster. In order to attend effectively and efficiently to the needs of children following a disaster, the clinician needs to pursue disaster mental health training and to establish links with the professional association and with local governmental and nongovernmental agencies to determine where he or she can work most effectively in the event of an emergency. This will involve seeking out others with similar concerns.

For many mental health professionals, working with the community following a disaster is an exciting, relatively new, and challenging experience, as yet incompletely explored and eminently gratifying. For both researcher and clinician, activity in this area holds much reward. While the work may be stressful, there usually is great gratification that comes from the feeling of doing a necessary and important job. It takes the professional out of the confines of an office practice and into the chaos and confusion of a disaster scene. It requires the professional to work in conditions where he or she has never worked before, such as in a tent, a disaster assistance center (DAC), a school building, or a trailer park. It also brings the professional into close interaction with the emergency services personnel in the community. The mutual affiliation that develops through disaster work leads to an awareness and appreciation of community members that lends to the sense of a competent community.

In some instances, clinicians will be expected to work pro bono. In other circumstances, remuneration may be available. In all cases, the circumstances and arrangements should be clarified and thoroughly understood by all involved. In instances where clinicians work pro bono, they will need to clarify the policy for referral should further treatment be required, in order to avoid possibilities of conflict of interest.

The professional community should be aware that the effects of a disaster can continue long after the crisis has passed, and that therapists can expect increased demands for services by clients who are experiencing disaster-related problems. In the postdisaster period, a therapist will find it useful in interviewing new patients to probe for possible disaster experiences, even when the presenting complaint appears unrelated to the event. To deal effectively with disaster-related trauma, and problems associated with bereavement and loss, clinicians will need to reacquaint themselves with appropriate modes of treatment.

Child therapists are likely to hear complaints from parents about the persistence of postdisaster problem behaviors and symptoms. Children's fears frequently are linked to issues concerning separation and loss, issues which may be related to persistent fears that the parents may have had about their own disaster experiences. Parents can be alerted to the fact that their own fears often may be transferred to or reflected in the child. When the home is extensively damaged and there is long-term evidence of such damage, these constant reminders may continue to reinforce the fears of both parents and children. The therapist can expect that symptoms most often will fall into the category of childhood post-traumatic stress disorder and that the severity of the symptoms probably will be directly related to the child's proximity to the disaster or to the extent of residential displacement. The therapist will find it useful to instruct the parents in techniques that will enable them to develop closure about the precipitating event, both for themselves and for the child. This may involve using behavioral or cognitive techniques, or crisis counseling. Together with the parents, the aim is to quickly provide the most protection possible to the child. Evidence has shown that, with enough passage of time, most symptoms will disappear by themselves, but it always is desirable to facilitate their disappearance as soon as possible.

In communities where predisaster mental health planning and training has occurred, the professional likely will find useful sources of information. A planning committee may have developed a resource bank of training materials and brochures for the public, which contains information about frequently encountered problems, and an updated directory of mental health resources, including the lists of available trained and experienced mental health professionals in the community and in neighboring communities.

☐ Mental Health Professional Volunteer Cadres

In recent disasters, the number of trained mental health professionals who have volunteered their services has increased exponentially. Most of these volunteers have offered their services to established community organizations, such as the Red Cross, and to public mental health agencies. However, there are many other private and nonprofit counseling agencies within a community that will offer mental health services following a disaster. Professionals wishing to participate in a disaster mental health response will seek out volunteer opportunities where they feel their expertise will be most needed and useful. Generally, a local government agency, such as a county mental health department, will assume the responsibility of coordinating volunteer activities and will provide referral information about volunteer activities in the community.

Following a disaster, public and nonprofit agencies may find themselves burdened by the volume of individuals offering volunteer service. Community predisaster planning therefore should include procedures on how to accommodate and incorporate volunteers in the disaster response, as in instances where professional association disaster-trained cadres are available. There should be an organizational process whereby the expected proliferation of volunteers will be incorporated into the overall program. Depending on the nature and extent of the disaster, the organization will need to determine whether or not it will include the use of volunteers to supplement its already trained staff. If so, then the plan needs to include processes of screening, training, and supervision of the volunteer cadre when necessary. Screening would include a determination of acceptable professional capabilities. Training would include the presentation of established training in all aspects of disaster mental health intervention. Supervision would include provision for ongoing monitoring of the volunteers' activities and for the possibility of burnout.

The disaster plan also should take into account the possible need for insurance and license requirements. Some organizations may have the capacity to include volunteers in their own organization's liability insurance coverage. Organizations that include volunteers in their daily activities usually have already developed policies regarding the chain of responsibility for selection, use, and supervision of volunteers. Those that do not have these arrangements should keep in mind the possible need for volunteers and the consequent need to develop policies proactively. Some agencies will be reluctant to use volunteers, despite the heightened demands on the organization during a disaster. Demands for service may be increased to such a degree that the additional time needed to incorporate and supervise or monitor the volunteers is unwelcome and unpractical. In such cases, the agencies can refer individuals to other agencies that have opportunities for volunteer service.

After an emergency has passed, the question may arise about how to maintain the availability of professional volunteers. Once the crisis has abated and volunteers have dispersed, a national professional organization could maintain a registry of local professionals who could be mobilized rapidly in future disasters, as the American Psychological Association plans. To stimulate continuing professional interests in disaster mental health concerns, local chapters of national professional associations could distribute newsletters or offer regularly arranged seminars presenting updated information. The local initiatives also should coordinate with emergency services organizations, such as the Red Cross and the state office of emergency services for notice of further education and training. For example, the Los Angeles chapter of the American Red Cross offers meetings for mental health professionals who have attended disaster mental health training. The meetings serve the purpose of maintaining continued interest and involvement in disaster mental health activities.

Mental health professionals' interest can be maintained through newsletters providing new information and updated training opportunities. However, for many of the experienced professionals, continued interest in participation in the activity will be because of the multiple advantages that networking provides. These advantages include professional development, possible career opportunities, and availability of trained professionals for treating long-term postdisaster conditions. While it is hoped that local-level initiatives will evolve into regional and even national organizations among all the mental health professions, there has been relatively little involvement at this time. As part of their social responsibility, it would seem desirable for all national professional associations to become involved in the development of cadres of trained personnel available for future disasters. They might develop ongoing committees to encourage municipal and state governmental agencies to hold joint meetings with local practitioner associations and to coordinate with local Red Cross chapters in order to arrange such joint meetings.

☐ Organization and Management

There are any number of management tasks associated with providing disaster services, including taking advantage of funding opportunities and meeting requirements imposed by government contracts. These activities may be new to professionals who have not provided disaster services or who live in small communities without a centralized mental health system. However, this might be an opportunity to establish an organization which could be activated in times of disaster, especially if the community is in a disaster-prone area and one which would be eligible for funding. This type of organization would be needed most in smaller communities that have limited professional staff and facilities, and where the services that are needed following a disaster usually are brought in from outside of the local area.

Professionals with an interest and commitment to local-level approaches to disaster mental health can be proactive and organize a mental health response team. Once organized, the team would need to develop linkages with other members of the emergency services network, including the local Red Cross chapter, state and local mental health authorities, and social service agencies. The development of personal relationships with members of established organizations frequently provides the early framework for mutually advantageous professional activity. Networking with parent organizations, such as local school parent-teacher-student associations (PTSAs), may help to influence school administrators on behalf of the need for emergency preparedness and postdisaster counseling for children and youth.

Mental health professionals generally are familiar with the record keeping and documentation required by private and publicly funded programs. It is necessary to incorporate an evaluation design in any kind of funding process, a design that will incorporate both formative (process) and summative (outcome) styles of inquiry. Mental health professionals can plan a proactive role in developing an evaluation plan. When they are a part of the policy process, they already will be familiar with the emergency plan and the requisite mental health interventions, and thus will be able to focus on the expected outcomes. They also will be able to support methods of evaluating clinical transactions and to incorporate into the evaluation plan the risk characteristics that have been assumed in designing the intervention.

Planning and designing mental health programs suitable to a community are challenging to the mental health professional. Familiarity with the local community and its disaster proneness will enhance the efficacy of these efforts. Model programs and planning guidelines currently are available through state offices of human resources, mental health, and emergency services. Participating in a local response and in the widely available training programs will enhance a sense of competence in the professional, the professional association, and the community.

☐ Summary

A competent community must include the mental health services in the emergency services network. The mental health profession should participate in the preplanning procedures, along with the established emergency services organizations and existing nonprofit agencies, Neighborhood Watch, and homeowners associations regularly involved in disaster recovery. Originally ignored, mental health needs now have been more fully accepted by federal, state, and local governments. Federal funds have been provided for public and nonprofit sector programs, and the Red Cross has expanded its psychological services to children following a disaster. Predisaster training now is being provided to many agencies and organizations by mental health professionals. More needs to be done in such areas as assistance in needs assessment, special problems in rural areas and in multicultural communities, and expansion of ongoing training in communities and professional associations.

Planning committees need to take into account the threats of cutbacks in funding and to find ways to continually update information for their members. The special needs of children with mental illness and developmental disabilities, families who are homeless, and other populations who are vulnerable should not be ignored in the chaos following a disaster. Homeowners associations can play a crucial role in distributing information on possible mental health problems and their prevention, provided there is adequate proactive education and training. Because of major changes in federal funding for mental health services that are occurring, future funding may come through expansion of state and local mental health activities, and through greater involvement of private nonprofit organizations, including Neighborhood Watch and homeowners associations. Community advisory boards might be formed with involvement of mental health professionals who have experience in community organization and who could apply their skills to disaster planning and training efforts. EAPs established in community-based corporations may play a significant role in developing this initiative. Schools also would be very important in the development of community predisaster efforts. As recognized centers of the community, many of them with already established crisis response teams, schools are ideal locations for emergency preparedness, planning, and training activities.

Working with the community following a disaster is an exciting, challenging, and highly gratifying experience for the competent mental health professional. It takes the practitioner out of the office into the field to work in strange environments and unfamiliar surroundings, with the opportunity to see immediate positive results. It involves the practitioner with the community and provides numerous opportunities for pioneering research. Participating in the planning for disaster response in the community and assuring the provision of care and concern for the mental health of the community enhances the sense of competence in both the mental health professional and the community. While the contributions of mental health finally have been recognized as playing a critical role in improving the response and recovery from the distress experienced by a community and its members when struck by a disaster, its contributions seem destined to increase as research and clinical experience accumulates.

REFERENCES

Achenbach, T. M., & Edelbrock, C. S. (1983). *Manual for the Child Behavior Checklist and Revised Child Behavior Profile.* Burlington: University of Vermont, Department of Psychiatry.

Alameda County Mental Health Services. (1993). *East Bay Hills firestorm recovery program. Final report: FEMA-919-DR-CA:* October 1992–January, 1993. Oakland, CA: Author.

Allen, R. D., & Rosse, W. (1998). *Children's response to exposure to traumatic events* (Report No. 103). Boulder, CO: Natural Hazards Research and Applications Information Center.

American Psychiatric Association. (1980). *Diagnostic and statistical manual of mental disorders* (3rd ed.). Washington, DC: Author.

American Psychiatric Association. (1987). *Diagnostic and statistical manual of mental disorders* (3rd ed., rev.). Washington, DC: Author.

American Psychiatric Association. (1994). *Diagnostic and statistical manual of mental disorders* (4th ed.). Washington, DC: Author.

Anderson, R. W., Jr., Maton, K. I., & Ensor, B. E. (1991). Prevention theory and action from the religious perspective. *Prevention in Human Services, 10,* 9–27.

Antonovsky, A. (1979). *Health, stress and coping.* San Francisco: Jossey-Bass.

Antonovsky, A. (1987). *Unraveling the mystery of health.* San Francisco: Jossey-Bass.

Austin, L. S. (Ed.). (1992). *Responding to disaster: A guide for mental health professionals.* Washington, DC: American Psychiatric Press.

Avery, A., & Orner, R. (1998, Summer). First report of psychological debriefing abandoned—The end of an era? *Traumatic Stress Points: News for the International Society for Traumatic Stress Studies, 12,* 3–4.

Bandura, A., Reese, L., & Adams, N. E. (1982). Microanalysis of action and fear arousal as a function of differential levels of perceived self-efficacy. *Journal of Personality and Social Psychology, 43,* 5–21.

Belter, R. W., Dunn, S. E., & Jeney, P. (1991). The psychological impact of Hurricane Hugo on children: A needs assessment. *Advances in Behavior Research and Therapy 13*(3), 155–216.

Benight, C. C., Ironson, G., Wynings, C., Klebe, K., Burnett, K., Greenwood, D., Carver, C. S., Baum, A., & Schneiderman, N. (in press). Coping self-efficacy as a predictor of psychological distress following a natural disaster: A causal model analysis. *Journal of Consulting and Clinical Psychology.*

Benini, J. B. (1998). Government and community-based organizations: Models for working together. *Natural Hazards Observer 22*(6), 1–11.

Bennis, W. G., Benne, K. D., & Chin, R. (Eds.). (1985). *The planning of change* (4th ed.). New York.

Birleson, P. (1981). The validity of depressive disorder in childhood and the development of a self-rating scale: A research report. *Journal of Child Psychology and Psychiatry 21*, 83–88.

Blaufarb, H., & Levine, J. (1972). Crisis intervention in an earthquake. *Social Work 17*, 16–19.

Bloch, D. A., Silber, E., & Perry, S. E. (1956). Some factors in the emotional reactions of children to disaster. *American Journal of Psychiatry 133*, 416–422.

Blom, G. E. (1986). A school disaster—Intervention and research aspects. *Journal of the American Academy of Child Psychiatry 25*, 336–345.

Bolin, R. (1982). *Long term family recovery from disaster.* Boulder: University of Colorado, Institute of Behavioral Science.

Bolin, R. (1993). *Household and community recovery after earthquakes* (Program on Environment and Behavior Monograph No. 56). Boulder: University of Colorado, Institute of Behavioral Science.

Bowlby, J. (1973). *Attachment and loss II: Separation: Anxiety and anger.* New York: Basic Books.

Bowlby, J. (1980). *Attachment and loss III: Loss, sadness and depression.* New York: Basic Books.

Bowlby, J. (1982). *Attachment and loss I: Attachment.* (2nd ed.). New York: Basic Books.

Bowlby, J. (1988). *A secure base.* New York: Basic Books.

Bradburn, I. S. (1991). After the earth shook: Children's stress symptoms 6–8 months after a disaster. *Advances in Behavior Research and Therapy 13*, 173–179.

Bromet, E. J., Hough, L., & Connell, M. (1984). Mental health of children near the Three Mile Island reactor. *Journal of Preventive Psychiatry 2*, 276–301.

Bronfenbrenner, U. (1979). *The ecology of human development: experiments by nature and design.* Cambridge, MA: Harvard University Press.

Bronfenbrenner, U. (1989). Ecological systems theory. In: R. Vasta (Ed.), *Annals of child development, Vol. 6* (pp. 187–251). Greenwich, CT: JAI Press.

Brown, V. B. (1980). The community in crisis. *New Directions for Mental Health Services 6*, 45–56.

Burge, S. K., & Figley, C. R. (1987). The Social Support Scale: Development and initial estimates of reliability and validity. *Victimology 12*(1), 14–22.

Burke, J. D., Borus, J. F., Burns, B. J., Millstein, K. H., & Beasley, M. C. (1982). Changes in children's behavior after a natural disaster. *American Journal of Psychiatry 139*, 1010–1014.

California State Department of Education, Child Development Division. (1997). *Reducing exceptional stress and trauma—curriculum & intervention guidelines: Resources to help staff and children identify and work through trauma, stress, and grief.* Sacramento: Author.

California State Department of Education, Instructional Support Services Division. (1987). *Suicide prevention program for California public schools.* Sacramento: Author.

California State Department of Mental Health. (1994). *Final report: Los Angeles fires and civil unrest crisis counseling assistance and training program. FEMA 942-DR-CA. Regular services program. November 5, 1992–November 4, 1995.* Sacramento: Author.

California State Department of Mental Health. (1995). *Final report: January 17, 1994 Northridge earthquake crisis counseling assistance and training program. FEMA 1008-DR-CA. Regular Services Program. May 18, 1994–August 17, 1995.* Sacramento: Author.

California State Department of Mental Health. (1996b). *Final report: Late winter storms '95 crisis counseling assistance and training program. FEMA 1046-DR-CA. Regular services program. July 11, 1995–April 10, 1996.* Sacramento: Author.

Caplan, G. (1964). *Principles of preventive psychiatry.* New York: Basic Books.

Caplan, G. (1970). *Theory and practice of mental health consultation.* New York: Basic Books.

Caplan, G. (1980). An approach to preventive intervention in child psychiatry. *Canadian Journal of Psychiatry 25*, 671–682.

Cardena, E., & Spiegel, D. (1993). Dissociative reactions to the Bay Area earthquake. *American Journal of Psychiatry 150*, 474–478.

City of Berkeley Mental Health. (1993). *City of Berkeley crisis counseling program. Final report. Eastbay firestorm 1991. FEMA 919-DR-CA: March 1, 1992 to February 28, 1993.* Berkeley, CA: Author.

Cottrell, L. S. (1976). The competent community. In B. H. Kaplan, R. N. Wilson, & A. H. Leighton, (Eds.). *Further explorations in community psychiatry* (pp. 195–209). New York: Basic Books.

Craig, G. J., & Kermis, M. (1995). *Children today*. Englewood Cliffs, NJ: Prentice-Hall.

Dollinger, S. J. (1986). The measurement of children's sleep disturbances and somatic complaints following a disaster. *Child Psychiatry and Human Development 16*, 148–153.

Dollinger, S. J., O'Donnell, J. P., & Staley A. A. (1984). Lightening-strike disaster: Effects on children's fears and worries. *Journal of Consulting and Clinical Psychology 52*, 1028–1038.

Drabek, T. E. (1987). Emergent structures. In: R. R. Dynes, B. De Marchi, & C. Pelanda, (Eds.), *Sociology of disasters: Contribution of sociology to disaster research* (pp. 260–290). Milan, Italy: Franco Angeli.

Drabek, T. E., & Kay, W. H. (1976). The impact of disaster on primary group linkages. *Mass Emergencies 1*, 89–105.

Dynes, R. R. (1970). *Organizational behavior in disaster*. Lexington, MA: Heath.

Earls, F., Smith, E., Reich, W., & Jung, K. G. (1988). Investigating psychopathological consequences of a disaster in children: A pilot study incorporating a structured diagnostic interview. *Journal of the American Academy of Child and Adolescent Psychiatry 29*, 90–95.

Edelbrock, C., Costello, A. J., Dulcan, M., Kalas, R., & Conover, N. C. (1985). Age differences in the reliability of the psychiatric interview of the child. *Child Development 56*, 265–275.

Erikson, E. H. (1963). *Childhood and society* (2nd ed.). New York: Norton.

Erikson, K. T. (1976a). *Everything in its path*. New York: Simon & Schuster.

Erikson, K. T. (1976b). Loss of communality at Buffalo Creek. *American Journal of Psychiatry 133*, 302–305.

Erikson, K. T. (1994). *A new species of trouble: The human experience of modern disasters*. New York: Norton.

Eth, S. (1992). Clinical response to traumatized children. In L. S. Austin (Ed.), *Responding to disaster: A guide for mental health professionals* (pp. 101–123). Washington, DC: American Psychiatric Press.

Eyerman, R., & Jamison, A. (1991). *Social movements: A cognitive approach*. University Park: Pennsylvania State University Press.

Famularo, R., Kinscherf, R., & Fenton, T. (1990). Symptom differences in acute and chronic presentation of childhood posttraumatic stress disorder. *Child Abuse & Neglect 14*, 439–444.

Farberow, N. L., & Frederick, C. J. (1978). *Human problems in disasters: A pamphlet for government emergency disaster services personnel*. Rockville, MD: U.S. Department of Health and Human Services.

Farberow, N. L., & Gordon, N. S. (1981). *Manual for child health workers in major disasters*. Rockville, MD: U.S. Department of Health and Human Services.

Festinger, L. (1957). *A theory of cognitive dissonance*. Stanford, CA: Stanford University Press.

Figley, C. R. (1989a). *Helping traumatized families*. San Francisco: Jossey-Bass.

Figley, C. R. (Ed.). (1989b). *Treating stress in families*. New York: Brunner/Mazel.

Frederick, C. J. (1985). Children traumatized by catastrophic situations, In S. Eth & R. Pynoos (Eds.), *Post-traumatic stress disorder in children* (pp. 73–99). Washington, DC.: American Psychiatric Press.

Freedy, J. R., Shaw, D. L., Jarrell, M. P., & Masters, C. R. (1992). Towards an understanding of the psychological impact of natural disasters: An application of the Conservation of Resources Stress Model. *Journal of Traumatic Stress 5*, 441–455.

Freud, A., & Burlingham, D. T. (1944). *War and children*. New York: International Universities Press.

Fried, M. (1963). Grieving for a lost home. In L. J. Duhl (Ed.), *The urban condition: People and policy in the metropolis* (p. 156). New York: Basic Books.

Fritz, C. E. (1957). Disasters compared in six communities. *Human Organization 16*, 6–9.

Garmezy, N. (1991). Resiliency and vulnerability to adverse developmental outcomes associated with poverty. *American Behavioral Scientist 34*, 416–430.

Garmezy, N., & Masten, A. S. (1994). Chronic adversities. In M. Rutter, L. Herzov, & E. Taylor, (Eds.), *Child and adolescent psychiatry* (pp. 213–233). Oxford: Blackwell Scientific.

Garmezy, N., Masten, A., Nordstrom, L., & Ferrarese, M. (1979). The nature of competence in normal and deviant children. In M. W. Kent & J. E. Rolf, (Eds.), *Social competence in children* (pp. 23–43). Hanover, NH: University Press of New England.

Goenjian, A. K., Karayan, I., Pynoos, R. S., Minassian, D., Najarian, L. M., Steinberg, A. M., & Fairbanks, L. A. (1997). Outcome of psychotherapy among early adolescents after trauma. *American Journal of Psychiatry 154*, 536–542.

Goenjian, A. K., Pynoos, R. S., Steinberg, A. M., Najarian, L. M., Asarnow, J. R., Karayan, I., Ghurabi, M., & Fairbanks, L. A. (1995). Psychiatry comorbidity in children after the 1988 earthquake in Armenia. *Journal of the American Academy of Child and Adolescent Psychiatry 34*, 1174–1184.

Goltz, J. D., Russell, L. A., & Bourque, L. B. (1992). Initial behavioral response to a rapid onset disaster: A case study of the October 1, 1987 Whittier Narrows earthquake. *International Journal of Mass Emergencies and Disasters 10*, 43–69.

Gordon, N. S., & Maida, C. A. (1989). *Post-disaster adaptive patterns: Parent-child reactions to the 1987 Los Angeles area/Whittier Narrows earthquake* (Report No. QR 29). Boulder, CO: Natural Hazards Research and Applications Information Center.

Gordon, N. S., Maida, C. A., & Farberow, N. L. (1992). *The immediate community response to disaster: The 1991 East Bay Hills fire* (Report No. QR51). Boulder, CO: Natural Hazards Research and Applications Information Center.

Gordon, N. S., Maida, C. A., Farberow, N. L., & Fidell, L. (1995). *Residential loss and displacement among survivors of the 1993 Altadena fire* (Report No. QR 73). Boulder, CO: Natural Hazards Research and Applications Information Center.

Gordon, N. S., Maida, C. A., Steinberg, A. M., & Gordon, G. (1986). *The psychosocial impact of the Baldwin Hills fire* (Report No. QR 08). Boulder, CO: Natural Hazards Research and Applications Information Center.

Green, B., Lindy, J. D., Grace, M. C., Gleser, G. C., Leonard, A. C., Korol, M., & Winget, C. (1990). Buffalo Creek survivors in the second decade: Stability of stress symptoms. *American Journal Orthopsychiatry 60*(1), 43–54.

Guerin, D. W., Junn, E., & Rushbrook, S. (1991). Preschoolers' reactions to the 1989 Bay Area earthquake as assessed by parent report on the Child Behavior Checklist. In J. M. Vogel, (Chair), *Children's responses to disasters: The aftermath of Hurricane Hugo and the 1989 Bay Area earthquake*. Symposium conducted at the biennial meeting of the Society for Research in Child Development, Seattle.

Handford, H. A., Mayes, S. D., Mattison, R. E., Humphrey, F. J., Bagnato, S., Bixler, E. O., & Kales, J. D. (1986). Child and parent reaction to the Three Mile Island nuclear accident. *Journal of the American Academy of Child Psychiatry 25*, 346–356.

Harwood, R. L., Miller, J. G., & Irizarry, N. L. (1995). *Culture and attachment: Perceptions of the child in context.* New York: Guilford.

Hawton, K. (1982). Attempted suicide in children and adolescents. *Journal of Child Psychology and Psychiatry 23*, 497–503.

Heft, L. (1993). Helping traumatized children: A protocol for running post-disaster parents groups. *Journal of Social Behavior and Personality 8*(5), 149–154.

Herjanic, B., & Reich, W. (1982). Development of a structured psychiatric interview for children: Agreement between child and parent on individual symptoms. *Journal of Abnormal Child Psychology 10*, 307–324.

Hobfell, S. E. (1989). Conservation of resources: A new attempt at conceptualizing stress. *American Psychologist 44*, 513–524.

Horowitz, M., Wilner, N., & Alvarez, W. (1979). Impact of event scale: A measure of subjective stress. *Psychosomatic Medicine 41*, 209–218.

Howard, S. J. (1980). Children and the San Fernando earthquake. *Earthquake Information Bulletin 12*(5), 190–192.

Howard, S. J., & Gordon, N. S. (1972). *Final progress report: Mental health intervention in a major disaster* (NIMH Small Research Grant MH21649-01). Van Nuys, CA: San Fernando Valley Child Guidance Clinic.

Iscoe, I. (1974). Community psychology and the competent community. *American Psychologist 29*, 607–613.

Iscoe, I. (1982). Towards a viable community health psychology: Caveats from the experience of the community mental health movement. *American Psychologist 37*, 961–965.

John, K., Gammon, G. D., Prusoff, B. A., & Warner, V. (1987). The social adjustment inventory for children and adolescents (SAICA): Testing of a new semistructured interview. *Journal of the American Academy of Child and Adolescent Psychiatry 26*(6), 898–911.

Jones, R. T., & Ribbe, D. P. (1991). Child, adolescent and adult victims of residential fire: Psychosocial consequences. *Behavior Modification 15*, 560–580.

Kachur, S. P., Stennies, G. M., Powell, K. E., Modzeleski, W., Stephens, R., Murphy, R., Kresnow, M., Sleet, D., & Lowry, P. (1996). School-associated violent deaths in the United States, 1992 to 1994. *Journal of the American Medical Association 275*, 1729–1733.

Kanner, A. D., Coyne, J. C., Schaefer, C., & Lazarus, R. S. (1981). Comparisons of two modes of stress management. Daily hassles & uplifts versus major life events. *Journal of Behavioral Medicine 4*(1), 1–39.

Ketterer, R. F. (1981). *Consultation and education in mental health: Problems and prospects.* Newbury Park, CA: Sage.

Klingman, A. (1992). Stress reactions of Israeli youth during the Gulf War: A quantitative study. *Professional Psychology: Research and Practice 23*, 521–527.

Kreps, G. A. (1989). Disaster and the social order. In G. A. Kreps (Ed.). *Social structure and disaster* (pp. 31–51). Newark: University of Delaware Press.

Larson, D. B., Hohmann, A. A., Kessler, L. G., Meador, K. G., Boyd, J. H., & McSherry, E. (1988). The couch and the cloth: The need for linkage. *Hospital and Community Psychiatry 10*, 1064–1069.

Lave, T. R., & Lave, L. B. (1991). Public perceptions of the risks of floods: Implications for communication. *Risk Analysis 11*, 255–268.

Lewin, K. (1935). *A dynamic theory of personality.* New York: McGraw-Hill.

Lewin, K. (1951). *Field theory in social science.* New York: Harper & Row.

Lindemann, E. (1944). Symptomatology and management of acute grief. *American Journal of Psychiatry 101*, 141–148.

Lindy, J. D. (1985). The trauma membrane and other clinical concepts derived from psychotherapeutic work with survivors of natural disasters. *Psychiatric Annals 15*, 153–160.

Lindy, J. D., Grace, M. C., & Green, B. L. (1981). Survivors: Outreach to a reluctant population. *American Journal of Orthopsychiatry 51*, 468–478.

Lonigan, C. J., Shannon, M. P., Finch, A. J., Daugherty, T. K., & Taylor, C. M. (1991). Children's reactions to a natural disaster: Symptom severity and degree of exposure. *Advances in Behavior Research and Therapy 13*, 135–154.

Los Angeles County Department of Mental Health. (1993). *Final report. Crisis counseling program grant. FEMA FT-1008-CA: Northridge earthquake.* Los Angeles, CA: Author.

Los Angeles County Department of Mental Health. (1995). *Final report. Crisis counseling program: Los Angeles fires and civil unrest. FEMA 942-DR-CA: November 5, 1992–November 4, 1993.* Los Angeles, CA: Author.

Lystad, M. L. (Ed.). (1985). *Innovations in mental health services to disaster victims.* Rockville, MD: U.S. Department of Health and Human Services.

Maida, C. A., Gordon, N. S., Steinberg, A., & Gordon, G. (1989). Psychosocial impact of disasters: Victims of the Baldwin Hills fire. *Journal of Traumatic Stress 2*, 37–41.

Maida, C. A., Gordon, N. S., & Strauss, G. (1993). Child and parent reactions to the Los Angeles Area Whittier Narrows earthquake. *Journal of Social Behavior and Personality 8*, 421–436.

Malony, H. N. (1992). Religious diagnosis in evaluations of mental health. In J. F. Schumaker (Ed.), *Religion and mental health* (pp. 245–256). New York: Oxford University Press.

Marris, P. (1974). *Loss and change*. London: Routledge & Kegan Paul.

Martini, D. R., Ryan, C., Nakayama, D., & Ramenofsky, M. (1990). Psychiatric sequelae after traumatic injury: The Pittsburgh regatta accident. *Journal of the American Academy of Child and Adolescent Psychiatry 29*, 70–75.

Masten, A. S., & Coatsworth, J. D. (1998). The development of competence in favorable and unfavorable environments: Lessons from research on successful children. *American Psychologist 53*, 205–220.

Maton, K. I., & Wells, E. A. (1995). Religion as a community resource for well-being: Prevention, healing and empowerment pathways. *Journal of Social Issues 51*(2), 177–193.

McFarlane, A. C., Policansky, S., & Irwin, C. P. (1987). A longitudinal study of the psychological morbidity in children due to a natural disaster. *Psychological Medicine 17*, 727–738.

Mega, L. T., & McCammon, S. L. (1992). Tornado in eastern North Carolina: Outreach to school and community. In: L. S. Austin (Ed.), *Responding to disaster: A guide for mental health professionals* (pp. 211–230). Washington, DC: American Psychiatric Press.

Michael S., Lurie, E., Russell, N., & Unger, L. (1985). Rapid response mutual aid groups: A new response to social crises and natural disasters. *Social Work 30*, 245–252.

Milne, G. (1977). Cyclone Tracy: 2. The effects on Darwin children. *Australian Psychologist 12*(1), 55–62.

Mintz, M. (1991). A comparison between children in two areas following the Gulf War. Unpublished manuscript, Department of Psychology, Tel Aviv University.

Mitchell, J. T. (1985). Healing the helper. In National Institute of Mental Health, *Role stressors and supports for emergency workers*. DHHS Publication No. (ADM) 85-1408. Rockville, MD: U.S. Department of Health and Human Services.

Mitchell, J. T., & Everly, G. S. Jr. (1995). *Critical incident stress debriefing: An operations manual for the prevention of traumatic stress among emergency services and disaster workers* (2nd ed., pp. 101–114). Elliott City, MD: Chevron.

Murphy, L., Pynoos, R. S., & James, C. B. (1997). The trauma/grief-focused group psychotherapy module of an elementary school-based violence prevention/intervention program. In: J. D. Osofsky (Ed.), *Children in a violent society*. (pp. 223–255). New York: Guilford Press.

Murphy, D., Scammell, M., & Sclove, R. (1997). *Doing community based research: A reader*. Amherst, MA: Loka Institute.

Nader, K., Pynoos, R. S., Fairbanks, L., & Frederick, C. (1990). Children's PTSD reactions one year after a sniper attack at their school. *American Journal of Psychiatry 147*, 1526–1530.

National Research Council. (1989). *Improving risk communication*. Washington, DC: National Academy Press.

National School Safety Center. (1998). *Checklist of characteristics of youth who have caused school-associated violent deaths*. Westlake Village, CA: Author.

Newman, C. J. (1976). Children of disaster: Clinical observations at Buffalo Creek. *American Journal of Psychiatry 133*, 306–312.

Nowicki, S., & Strickland, B. R. (1973). A locus of control scale for children. *Journal of Consulting and Clinical Psychology 40*, 148–154.

Ollendick, T. H. (1983). Reliability and validity of the Revised Fear Survey Schedule for Children (FSSC-R). *Behavior Research and Therapy 21*, 685–692.

Olson, D. H., McCubbin, H. I., Barnes, H., Larsen, A., Muxen, M., & Wilson, M. (1983). *Families: What makes them work*. Newbury Park, CA: Sage.

O'Neill, J. (1989). *The communicative body*. Evanston, IL: Northwestern University Press.

Ordway, J. E. (1984). A home burns: Stress in the family. *The Psychiatric Journal of the University of Ottawa 9*, 127–131.

Pargament, K. I., Ensing, D. S., Falgout, E., Olsen, J., Reilly, B., Van Haitsma, K., & Warren, R. (1990). God help me: I. Religious coping efforts as predictors of the outcomes to significant negative life events. *American Journal of Community Psychology 18*, 793–824.

Parkes, C. M., & Stevenson-Hinde, J. (Eds.). (1982). *The place of attachment in human behavior.* New York: Basic Books.

Pfeffer, C. R. (1986). *The suicidal child.* New York: The Guilford Press.

Piotrowski, C., & Dunham, F. Y. (1983). Locus of control orientation and perception of "Hurricane" in fifth graders. *Journal of General Psychology 109*, 119–127.

Price, R. H, Ketterer, R. F., Bader, B. C., & Monahan, J. (Eds.). (1980). *Prevention in mental health: Research, policy and practice.* Beverly Hills, CA: Sage.

Propst, L. R., Ostrom, R., Watkins, P., Dean, T., & Mashburn, D. (1992). Comparative efficacy of religious and non-religious cognitive behavioral therapy for treatment of clinical depression in religious individuals. *Journal of Consulting and Clinical Psychology 60*, 94–103.

Pynoos, R. S., Frederick, C. J., Nader, K., Arroyo, W., Steinberg, A., Eth, S., Nunez, F., & Fairbanks, L. (1987). Life-threatening and post-traumatic stress in school age children. *Archives of General Psychiatry 44*, 1057–1063.

Pynoos, R. S., Goenjian, A., & Steinberg, A. M. (1995). Strategies of disaster intervention for children and adolescents. In S. E. Hobfell & M. W. de Vries (Eds.), *Extreme stress in communties: Impact and intervention* (pp. 445–471). The Netherlands: Kluwer.

Pynoos, R. S., Goenjian, A., Tashjian, M., Karakashian, M., Manjikian, R., Manoukian, G., Steinberg, A. M., & Fairbanks, L. A. (1993). Post-traumatic stress reactions in children after the 1988 Armenian earthquake. *British Journal of Psychiatry 163*, 239–247.

Pynoos, R. S., Nader, K., & March, J. (1991). Childhood post-traumatic stress. In J. Weiner (Ed.), *The textbook of child and adolescent psychiatry.* Washington, DC: American Psychiatric Press.

Pynoos, R. S., Sorenson, S. B., & Steinberg, A. M. (1993). Interpersonal violence and traumatic stress reactions. In L. Goldberger & S. Breznitz (Eds.), *Handbook of stress: Theoretical and clinical approaches.* (2nd ed, pp. 573–590). New York: Free Press.

Pynoos, R. S., Steinberg, A. M., & Wraith, R. (1995). A developmental model of childhood traumatic stress. In D. Cicchetti & D. Cohen (Eds.), *Manual of developmental psychopathology: Vol. 2. Risk, disorder, and adaptation.* (pp. 72–95). New York: Wiley.

Quarantelli, E. L. (1970). Emergent accommodation groups: Beyond current collective behavior typologies. In T. Shibutani (Ed.), *Human nature and collective behavior* (pp. 111–123). Englewood Cliffs, NJ: Prentice-Hall.

Quarantelli, E. L. (1984). *Emergent behavior at the emergency time periods of disasters. Final report.* Columbus, OH: Ohio State University, Disaster Research Center.

Raphael, B. (1983). *The anatomy of bereavement.* New York: Basic Books.

Raphael, B. (1986). *When disaster strikes: How individuals and communities cope with catastrophe.* New York: Basic Books.

Reich, W. (1991a). *Diagnostic interview for children and adolescents—Child version.* Unpublished manuscript, Washington University School of Medicine.

Reich, W. (1991b). *Diagnostic interview for children and adolescents—parent version.* Unpublished manuscript, Washington University School of Medicine.

Reynolds, C. R., & Richmond, B. O. (1978). "What I think and feel": A revised measure of the children's manifest anxiety scale. *Journal of Abnormal Child Psychology 6*, 271–280.

Rice, R. E., & Atkin, C. K. (Eds.). (1989). *Public communication campaigns* (2nd ed.). Thousand Oaks, CA: Sage.

Richard, W. C. (1974). Crisis intervention services following natural disaster: The Pennsylvania recovery project. *Journal of Community Psychology 2*, 211–218.

Richards, M. P. M. (Ed.). (1974). *The integration of a child into a social world*. Cambridge: Cambridge University Press.

Robins, L. N., & Smith, E. M. (1984). *Diagnostic interview schedule/disaster supplement*. St. Louis: Washington University, Department of Psychology.

Rogers, E., & Storey, J. (1987). Communication campaigns. In S. Chaffee & C. Berger (Eds.), *Handbook of communication science*. Thousand Oaks, CA: Sage.

Ruben, H. L. (1992). Interacting with the media after trauma in the community. In L. S. Austin (Ed.). (1992). *Responding to disaster: A guide for mental health professionals* (pp. 125–136). Washington, DC: American Psychiatric Press.

Rubin, C. B., Saperstein, M. D., & Barbee, D. G. (1985). *Community recovery from a major natural disaster* (Program on Environment and Behavior Monograph No. 41). Boulder, CO: University of Colorado, Institute of Behavioral Science.

Rubonis, A. V., & Bickman, L. (1991). Psychological impairment in the wake of disaster: The disaster-psychopathological relationship. *Psychological Bulletin 109*, 384–399.

Rutter, M. (1979). Protective factors in children's response to stress and disadvantage. In M. W. Kent & J. E. Rolf (Eds.), *Social competence in children*. Hanover, NH: University Press of New England.

Sable, P. (1995). Attachment theory and post-traumatic stress disorder. *Journal of Analytic Social Work 2*(4), 89–109.

Saigh, P. A. (1989). The development and validation of the children's posttraumatic stress disorder inventory. *International Journal of Special Education 4*, 75–84.

San Bernardino County Department of Mental Health. (1993). *Landers/Big Bear earthquakes recovery program. Regular services program. Final report. FEMA-947-DR-CA: November 5, 1992–November 4, 1993*. San Bernardino, CA: Author.

Saylor, C. F. (Ed.). (1993). *Children and disasters*. New York: Plenum Press.

Saylor, C. F., Swenson, C. C., & Powell, P. (1992). Hurrican Hugo blow down the broccoli: Preschoolers' post-disaster play and adjustment. *Child Psychiatry and Human Development 22*, 139–149.

Schein, E. H. (1969). *Process Consultation*. Reading, MA: Addison-Wesley.

Schein, E. H. (1987). *The clinical perspective in fieldwork*. Newbury Park, CA: Sage.

Schwartz, E. D., & Kowalski, J. M. (1991). Malignant memories: Posttraumatic stress disorder in children following a school shooting. *Journal of the American Academy of Child and Adolescent Psychiatry 30*(6), pp. 936–944.

Schwarzwald, J., Weisenberg, M., Waysman, M., Solomon, Z., & Klingman, A. (1991). *Stress reaction of school-age children to the bombardment by Scud missiles*. Unpublished manuscript, Department of Mental Health, Medical Corps, Israel Defense Forces.

Seamon, D., & Mugerauer, R. (Eds.). (1989). *Dwelling, place and environment*. New York: Columbia University Press.

Speilberger, C. D. (1973). *Preliminary manual for the State-Trait Anxiety Inventory for Children*. Palo Alto, CA: Consulting Psychologists Press.

Stallings, R. A. (1978). The structural patterns of four types of organizations in disaster. In E. L. Quarantelli (Ed.), *Disasters: Theory and research* (pp. 87–104). Beverly Hills, CA: Sage.

Sudak, H. S., Ford, A. B., & Rushford, N. B. (1984). Adolescent suicide: An overview. *American Journal of Psychotherapy 38*, 350–363.

Sullivan, M. A., Saylor, C. F., & Foster, K. Y. (1991). Posthurricane adjustment of preschoolers and their families. *Advances in Behavioral Research and Theory: Vol. 13* (pp. 163–172).

Sutter-Yuba Mental Health Services. (1998). *1996/97 Winter storms. Project CARE crisis counseling assistance and training regular program. Final report. FEMA 155-DR-CA, May 5, 1997–February 5, 1998*. Yuba City, CA: Author.

Terr, L. C. (1981). Psychic trauma in children: Observations following the Chowchilla school bus kidnapping. *American Journal of Psychiatry 138*, 14–19.

Tuan, Y.-F. (1977). *Space and place*. Minneapolis: University of Minnesota Press.

Turner, B. S. (1984). *The body and society*. Oxford: Basil Blackwell.

Tyhurst, J. S. (1957). The role of transition states—including disaster—in mental illness. In National Research Council (Ed.), *Walter Reed Symposium on Preventive and Social Psychiatry*. (pp. 1–21). Washington, DC: U.S. Government Printing Office.

Underwood, M. M., & Dunne-Maxim, K. (1997). *Managing sudden traumatic loss in the schools*. Piscataway, NJ: University of Medicine and Dentistry of New Jersey, University Behavioral HealthCare.

U.S. Department of Education. (1997). *Principal/school disciplinarian survey on school violence* (Fast Response Survey System, FRSS 63). National Center for Educational Statistics.

van der Kolk, B. A. (1988). The trauma spectrum: The interaction of biological and social events in the genesis of the trauma response. *Journal of Traumatic Stress 1*, 273–290.

Ventura County Department of Mental Health. (1995). *Project COPE crisis counseling program. Final report, FEMA 1008-DR-CA: May 18, 1994 to July 28, 1995*. Ventura, CA: Author.

Wainrib, B. R., & Bloch, E. L. (1998). *Crisis intervention and trauma response: Theory and practice*. New York: Springer.

Wallace, A. F. C. (1957). Mazeway disintegration: The individual's perception of socio-cultural disorganization. *Human Organization 16*, 23–27.

Wallrich, B. (1986). The evolving role of community-based organizations in disaster recovery. *Natural Hazards Observer 21*(2), 12–13.

Warheit, C. J., Holzer, C. E., & Arey, S. A. (1975). Race and mental illness: An epidemiologic update. *Journal of Health and Social Behavior, 16*(3), 243–256.

Warren, R. L. (1971). The sociology of knowledge and the problems of the inner cities. *Social Science Quarterly 52*, 468–485.

Waters, E., Vaughn, B. E., Posada, G., & Kondo-Ikemura, K. (Eds.). (1995). *Caregiving, cultural, and cognitive perspectives on secure-base behavior and working models: New growing points on attachment theory and research*. Chicago: University of Chicago Press.

Winnicott, D. W. (1971). *Playing and reality*. New York: Tavistock.

Wolfe V. V., Gentile, C., & Wolfe, D. A. (1989). The impact of sexual abuse on children: A PTSD formulation. *Behavior Therapy 20*, 215–228.

Worden, J. W. (1996). *Children and grief*. New York: Guilford Press.

Wright, K. M., Ursano, R. J., Bartone, P. T., & Ingraham, L. H. (1990). The shared experience of catastrophe: An expanded classification of the disaster community. *American Journal of Orthopsychiatry 60*, 35–42.

Wright, M. O., Masten, A. S., Northwood, A., & Hubbard, J. J. (1998). Long-term effects of massive trauma: Developmental and psychobiological perspectives. In D. Cicchetti & S. L. Toth (Eds.). *Rochester Symposium: Vol. 8. Developmental perspectives on trauma: Theory, research, intervention*. Rochester, NY: University of Rochester Press.

Young, M., & Willmott, P. (1957). *Family and kinship in East London*. London: Routledge & Kegan Paul.

Yule, W., & Udwin, O. (1991). Screening child survivors for post-traumatic stress disorders: Experience from the "Jupiter" sinking. *British Journal of Clinical Psychology 30*, 131–138.

Yule, W., & Williams, R. M. (1990). Post-traumatic stress reactions in children. *Journal of Traumatic Stress 3*, 279–295.

Zeidner, M., Klingman, A., & Itzkovitz, R. (1993). Children's affective reactions and coping under missile attack: A semi-projective assessment procedure. *Journal of Personality Assessment 60*(3), 435–457.

Zimmerman, M. A., & Arunkumar, R. (1994). Resiliency research: Implications for school and policy. *Social Policy Report: Society for Child Development 8*(4), 1–17.

APPENDIX:
SELECTED RESOURCES

☐ Manuals and Training Materials

Coping with Children's Reactions to Earthquakes and Other Disasters.
(FEMA Publication 48, July 1986) Federal Emergency Management
Agency. This pamphlet has been prepared to help parents deal with
children's fears and anxieties following a disaster. (Order from Federal
Emergency Management Agency, P.O. Box 70274, Washington, DC 20024;
phone: 800-480-2520; Website: http://www.fema.gov)

Field Manual for Human Service Workers in Major Disasters.
(DHHS Publication No. ADM 90-537, 1990) U.S. Department of Health
and Human Services, National Institute of Mental Health. (Order from
National Mental Health Services Knowledge Exchange Network, P.O. Box
42490, Washington, DC 20015; phone: 800-789-2647; Website:
http://www.mentalhealth.org)

How to Help Children After a Disaster: A Guidebook for Teachers.
(FEMA Publication 219, November 1991) Federal Emergency Management
Agency. This guide is meant to be a resource for the classroom teacher in
helping children recover from the effects of a disaster. (Order from Federal
Emergency Management Agency, P.O. Box 70274, Washington, DC 20024;
phone: 800-480-2520; Website: http://www.fema.gov)

Managing Sudden Traumatic Loss in the Schools. Maureen M. Underwood,
LCSW and Karen Dunne-Maxim, MS, RN. University of Medicine and
Dentistry of New Jersey, University Behavioral HealthCare, 1997. (Order

from the University of Medicine and Dentistry of New Jersey, University Behavioral HealthCare, Office of Prevention Services, P.O. Box 1392, Piscataway, NJ 08855-1392; phone: 908-235-4109)

Manual for Child Health Workers in Major Disasters. (DHHS Publication No. ADM 86-1070, 1986) U.S. Department of Health and Human Services, National Institute of Mental Health. (Order from National Mental Health Services Knowledge Exchange Network, P.O. Box 42490, Washington, DC 20015; phone: 800-789-2647; Website: http://www.mentalhealth.org)

Psychosocial Issues for Children and Families in Disaster: A Guide for the Primary Care Physician. (DHHS Publication No. SMA 95-3022, May 1995) U.S. Department of Health and Human Services, Public Health Service, Substance Abuse and Mental Health Services Administration, Center for Mental Health Services. Provides physicians with information to explore a variety of roles in disaster response and recovery as well as tools to better assess and treat the needs of their patients. (Order from National Mental Health Services Knowledge Exchange Network, P.O. Box 42490, Washington, DC 20015; phone: 800-789-2647; Website: http://www.mentalhealth.org)

Reducing Exceptional Stress and Trauma: Curriculum and Intervention Guidelines. Resources to Help Staff and Children Identify and Work Through Trauma, Stress and Grief. California Department of Education, Child Development Division, Sacramento, 1997. ISBN 0-8011-1356-6 (Order from the Bureau of Publications, Sales Unit, California Department of Education, Box 271, Sacramento, California, 95812-0271; phone: 916-445-1260; FAX: 916-323-0823)

☐ Video

Children and Trauma: The School's Response. Directed by Eric Thiermann and Mark Schwartz. A program for mental health professionals, school administrators, and teachers about trauma's impact on children and schools, normal and prolonged stress responses, assessment considerations, and intervention models. Funded by the Federal Emergency Management Agency through the National Institute of Mental Health and administered by the California State Department of Mental Health.(Copies available from Impact Productions, 1725 B Seabright Avenue, Santa Cruz, CA 95062)

☐ Agencies

American Red Cross
Consult your telephone directory for the address and phone number
of your local chapter.

Center for Mental Health Services (CMHS)
Emergency Services and Disaster Relief Branch
U.S. Department of Health and Human Services
Public Health Service
Website: http://www.samhsa.gov/cmhs/cmhs.htm

Federal Emergency Management Agency (FEMA)
FEMA Helps
500 C Street
Washington, DC 20472
Website: http://www.fema.gov

☐ Professional Organizations

American Academy of Child and Adolescent Psychiatry
Public Information
Box 96106
Washington, DC 20090
Website: http://www.psych.org

American Psychological Association
Disaster Response Network
750 First St.
Washington, DC 20002
Website: http://www.apa.org

AUTHOR INDEX

SUBJECT INDEX

187